Living in France

A practical guide to your new life in France

by

Patricia Mansfield-Devine

D0910889

Boca Raton Public Library, Boca Raton, FL

HARRIMAN HOUSE LTD

3A Penns Road
Petersfield
Hampshire
GU32 2EW
GREAT BRITAIN

Tel: +44 (0)1730 233870
Fax: +44 (0)1730 233880
Email: enquiries@harriman-house.com
Website: www.harriman-house.com

First published in Great Britain in 2008

Copyright © Harriman House Ltd

The right of Patricia Mansfield-Devine to be identified as the author has been asserted in accordance with the Copyright, Design and Patents Act 1988.

ISBN: 1-8975-9792-4
ISBN 13: 978-1-897597-92-7

British Library Cataloguing in Publication Data
A CIP catalogue record for this book can be obtained from the British Library.

All rights reserved; no part of this publication may be reproduced, stored in a retrieval system, or transmitted in any form or by any means, electronic, mechanical, photocopying, recording, or otherwise without the prior written permission of the Publisher. This book may not be lent, resold, hired out or otherwise disposed of by way of trade in any form of binding or cover other than that in which it is published without the prior written consent of the Publisher.

Printed and bound by the CPI Group, Antony Rowe, Chippenham.

No responsibility for loss occasioned to any person or corporate body acting or refraining to act as a result of reading material in this book can be accepted by the Publisher, by the Author, or by the employer of the Author.

Contents

About the author

Patricia Mansfield-Devine is a writer and journalist. She and her husband Steve, a writer and photographer, live in Normandy with a menagerie of animals.

Acknowledgements

I would like to thank first and foremost my husband, Steve Mansfield-Devine, whose help and encouragement, not to mention proof-reading skills, have been invaluable in the year in which I have been writing this book. I also owe a debt to the many interviewees I spoke with, especially those in the case studies. They were forthcoming, and often surprising, about their own individual experiences in France and I am very grateful for their help.

Preface

What the book covers

When asked to write a book about France, the idea is initially daunting. Then it becomes terrifying. Apart from the size of the task and worrying where you'll find the information, the principal issue is what do you leave out? The truth is that information about France is as long as a piece of string – it could go on almost forever – and I could have spent the rest of my life writing this book, as I learn something new every day. Rather than covering all the bases, therefore, this book contains simply what I wish I had known when I moved here, in the hope that other Britons won't make the same mistakes. I apologise for anything that I have left out, and refer the reader to the vast array of publications available, each of which will give a different viewpoint.

Who the book is for

I have also, necessarily, made some assumptions about the reader. I have taken you to be someone who is buying in France rather than visiting as a student, and buying for lifestyle reasons rather than for investment. I also take it that you have most likely bought a rural property. I have not assumed any particular level of income, nor any age range, but this book is generally aimed at those of average means, rather than those of high net worth, who scarcely need my advice on how to make their dead septic tank come back to life.

Supporting websites

Throughout the text, I have included useful weblinks wherever possible. However, the web is in a state of flux and URLs (web addresses) have a habit of becoming out of date. To minimise this problem, I have used general links to the site (rather than to a specific page or document) wherever the information being discussed is easy to find on the site – via the site's search facility, for example.

In some cases, however, the information is buried deep within the site and here I have given more specific URLs. These were all correct at the time of writing, but if you have a problem with one of these specific links, try deleting the section after the domain name and searching from there. For example, if the link to a specific page is something like:

www.example.com/documents/id/ref/info.html

try using www.example.com instead.

All of the links in this book are also available on my website at www.webvivant.com. This list of links will be checked and updated regularly.

Foreword

A dream of France

It began, as most ideas do, very insidiously. I was wearied by the endless commuting from our grim neighbourhood in north London to a caffeine-fuelled 12-hour workday in Soho, while Steve was becoming increasingly exhausted by long days alone in his 'office' overlooking our neighbour's yard. Weekends we celebrated with a takeaway pizza on Friday night before coming down with a cold for two days. Life needed to change, and soon.

We had talked for some time about moving to the country, and Cornwall had seemed a likely choice – we had even gone so far as to get property details. But separately, each of us – unbeknown to the other – had also had a small seed growing in the heart. Two years before, we had spent a couple of holidays at my brother's house in Normandy. It was a ramshackle, half-renovated medieval pile near Putanges, on the Orne river, and although the facilities were a tad primitive, there was something about it that we couldn't quite forget.

Whether it's the smell of coffee in the *Gard du Nord*, seeing *Dubonnet* adverts in the Métro tunnels, savouring the moment when you unwrap the cakes, nestling in their pyramid box tied with pink ribbon, listening to the neighbour's cock crowing, or enjoying the needlessly elegant suit of the woman at the *chocolaterie*. Or the deep feather beds at the small hotel, with the bidet in the bathroom and strangely-latched windows that open inwards. Or the view from the window across a dozen *potagers*, with their neat rows of leeks and beans to the plume of smoke rising from the wood-burning bakery. Whatever it is, France has a multitude of ways of seducing the visitor, and for us, as for many British, the pull proved irresistible.

After our initial excitement at the idea came the feasibility study. How much would it cost? Could we undertake the same kind of work? Could we live on less? Would we miss England, or our friends and families? What about getting back for business meetings? Should we try self-sufficiency? Would I be able to stand the heat of the south? I didn't fly, which might prove a problem, so we decided to look in the north. In Normandy, in fact, in the Orne, where at least we would be close to my brother's holiday home.

The Internet was in its infancy in the mid-1990s, and if you wanted a house, you looked in 'French Property News', then sent off for written details of suitable properties. And there one day, among the piles of junk, we found a mill for sale. In the usual manner of French house ads, there was almost no information other than its location (the Orne), a couple of photos and the floor area in square metres.

We viewed on May bank holiday, in the wettest, coldest spring since time began, and everything looked uninhabitable and dismal. Bleary-eyed with lack of sleep and food, we scrambled and poked around in the mill (which we dismissed straight away); we then went on to a horrible modern house that had looked picturesque in the photos but which had pebble dash on the inside and no living room; and then a beautiful, enormous, perfect house but which was situated on a hideous windswept plateau. After a brief sleep in the car we met another estate agent in the Mayenne market town of Gorron, a chic Parisienne who listened carefully to our budget and our needs and then took us for a drive.

Thus, it was at the very end of the day, after climbing over a fallen cherry tree that blocked the driveway, that we had our first sight of what would be our French home. A strange tea-cosy-shaped house perched on a steep hillside, looking as if no-one had lived there since the Crusades. It was twice the price we had intended, and larger than we needed, but before we crossed the threshold we knew it was ours. In buying it, we made almost every mistake it was possible to make.

That was eleven years ago, and after four years of part-time living and seven years of full-time living in France, we now think of this country as home. We are used to the utter blackness of evening, after the *tabac*s close at 8.00pm; we jump if we hear a car engine, as no-one comes up this driveway but ourselves. We know that *normalement* means the tradesman will NEVER turn up until you've phoned for the ninth time, and we've learned to do much of our own plumbing and DIY.

France has a multitude of irritations, including the tax system and the difficulty of making ends meet, but wild horses can hardly drag us back to the UK, where we find the pace of life incredibly wearing. The traffic, the pollution, the stress; no wonder the British are moving to France in droves in search of a more tranquil life.

They do not all succeed in remaining, however, and that is where this book comes in. It is brief, but I hope will help you to avoid the pitfalls and enjoy the many wonderful benefits that living in France has to offer.

Patricia Mansfield-Devine, Normandie, January 2008

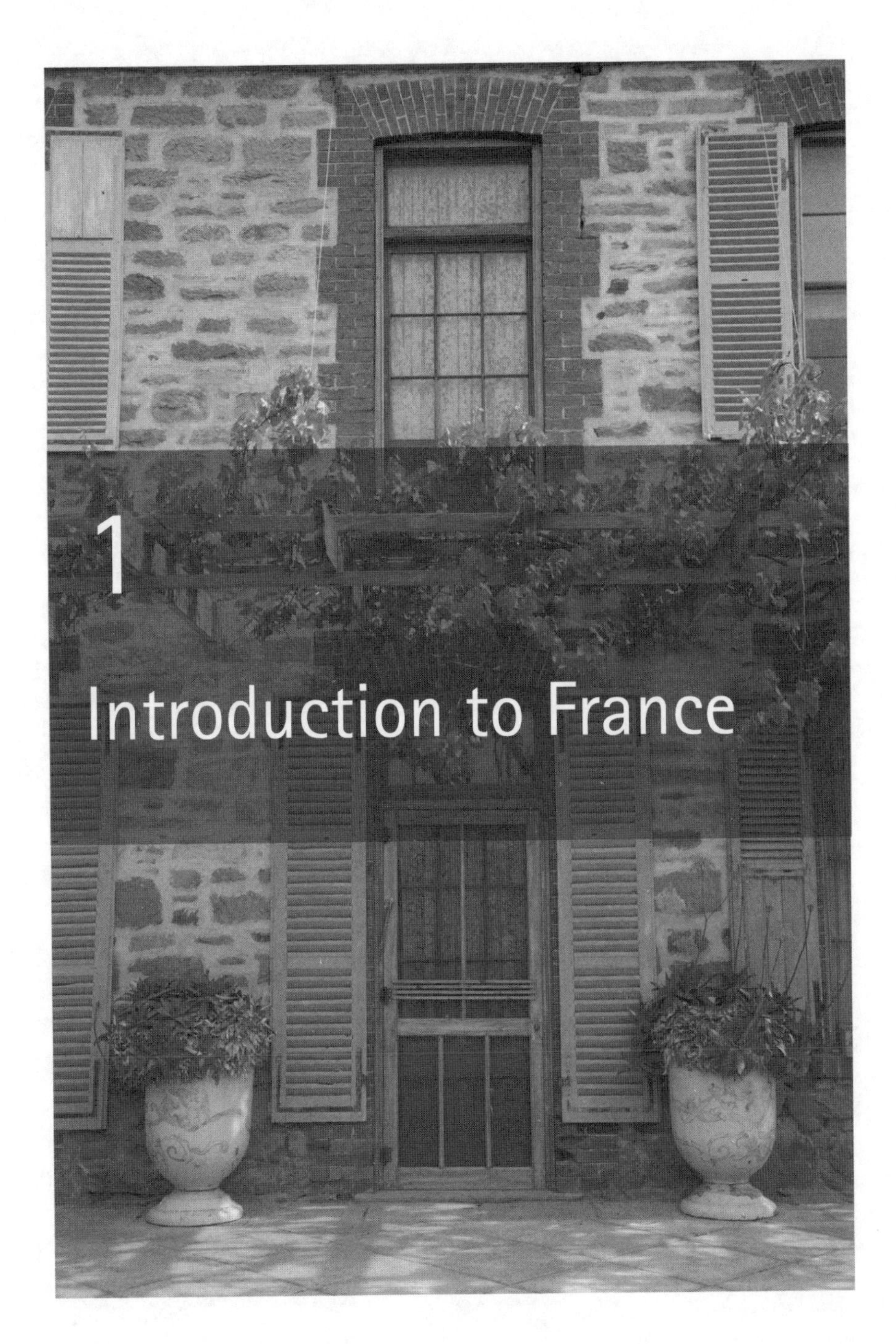

1 Introduction to France

France may be close to the UK, but it's a surprisingly different country.

It covers roughly twice the land mass, with a surface area of 550,000 km^2, although its population is about 60 million – roughly the same as the UK. Around two-thirds of the country consists of plains and hills that provide good agricultural land – one reason that France still remains a more agricultural country than Britain.

Population density is considerably lower than in the UK, partly because of that greater land mass, but also because France has more cities with a population of over 500,000 (though few as large as Britain's major cities such as Birmingham). The French began to move to the cities in the 1930s, a trend which accelerated from the 1960s onwards and has left the countryside relatively depopulated. Many areas have been declared *desert*, with houses and sometimes entire villages being abandoned.

This is a strikingly different situation from overcrowded Britain. England in particular is one of the most densely populated areas of Europe, with about 377 people per square kilometre – even higher in the crowded south-east. In contrast, France has 109 people per square kilometre – even less in rural areas.

This lack of population density affects every level of French life, from the negative impacts such as lack of railway network provision, to positive ones (for the British at least) such as the low cost of housing. But with country areas depopulated as young people move to the cities to work, it's not unusual for Britons moving to the French countryside to find that they are surrounded largely by a population of retirement age. This can prove something of a shock if you're not expecting it.

It is quite possible in France to live near a city and still maintain a rural way of life. French towns and villages tend to remain small and although there is often new housing on the outskirts, they do not yet suffer from the endless suburban creep seen in the UK. "Sleepy" is a word Britons often use to describe them – good news if you're seeking a more tranquil way of life on the Continent. Towns are also often quite well-appointed, and even a small town of a two thousand people might have one or two bakeries, a *charcuterie*, a *chocolatier*, and various bars and restaurants in addition to one or two representatives of the proliferating supermarket chains. There might be a library and a swimming pool, a few clothes shops, a shoe shop, an optician and a pharmacy or two. You would probably have pretty much everything you needed within walking distance (though there might not be much choice and prices tend to be high).

Your local café/bar

French bars and cafés can be the stuff that dreams are made of, but it's also true that many villages in France would be none the worse for an old-fashioned British pub with comfy sofas and a log fire.

French bars vary a great deal in style. Some, in the poor part of town, or in some villages, are forlornly cold in atmosphere, with formica tables, lino floors and fluorescent lighting over a few sickly pool tables. On the other hand, you may strike lucky and find an old-fashioned zinc-topped bar and wooden tables and chairs. At a *Bar Jeux*, there will be games available to play, such as table football (babyfoot) or pool, while in a *Bar des Sports*, the television will be on all day, tuned to the football, cycling or racing. It's not uncommon for a bar to also act as a *tabac*, restaurant, café, or even a shop or bread-delivery station. If the sign over the door says *tabac* rather than bar, you may find that drinks are also served, but if it's a bar, it still may not have a tobacco licence.

In rural France, the bars and cafés are often family-run businesses with little or nothing in the way of hired staff. This means they tend to close on Sunday afternoon, all day Monday, plus Wednesday if the hosts have children of school age (children are off school on Wednesday afternoons, and all day Wednesday every fourth week). Rural hostelries also tend to close at around 8pm if they're not serving food, as they usually open at 8am or 9am.

In towns, hours are often longer as staff are more freely available and there are more clientele, and, as in the UK, you will also have a wider range of atmospheres to choose from. Bar drinks tend to be expensive compared to drinking at home.

However, it is also likely to be very quiet, with the library and pool only open a few days a week, no nightlife at all, most shops (family-run) closing at lunchtime and 5pm, and the bars and *tabacs* often closing at 8pm. The entire rural landscape can plunge into darkness at 11pm, as the French close their shutters and the village lights are extinguished. Many Britons who have been seduced by the tranquillity of the French countryside admit that in retrospect they wish they had been closer to a large town or city – having to commute 30km for a litre of fresh milk can prove something of an irritation once the initial glow has worn off!

France is divided into 100 *départements*, which are roughly the equivalent of the UK's counties. With the exception of the Paris/Ile de France area, they are numbered in rough alphabetical order, with Ain, in the Rhône Alpes region at number one. Most French know these numbers off by heart, and you will also see them on local car number plates (immediately telling you if someone is an out-of-towner). Each *département* has a capital (like a county town), which is the administrative centre of the *département*, and this is generally the town you will have to visit for official business such as renewing a driving licence, etc.

Chez the hairdresser

It took me six years to pluck up the courage to have my hair cut in France. This wasn't from a reluctance to speak French in any way, it was one look at local women's haircuts that did it. Butch wasn't the word. Short, spiky, and dyed red – no matter what your age, this was the local look, and it tended to make everyone appear strangely alike. My British friends also had horror stories – short short short, they said. No matter where they had gone, their hair had ended up much shorter than they wanted it.

So if you're heading for the hairdresser, take along some pictures to show her what you want. Don't rely on there being magazines at the salon – there are, of course, but they're French magazines, with French styles, on French women. British women look different, and we have different haircuts – it's one of the reasons most locals know you're British before you even open your mouth.

My hair's in a bob. It's been long, short, black, blonde and even pink, razored or cut scissor over comb, graduated or one-length, but always a bob of some sort, for the past 40 years. This type of haircut hasn't got a name in France, so don't believe anyone who tells you it's a *Coupe Jeanne D'Arc* – ask for that and you'll get a pudding basin in the front and the back clipped so high that you won't want to go out for a month. To minimise risk I chose a salon in a 'posh' local spa town, and took along three photographs, explaining that I wanted the fringe from this one, the length from that one and streaks like these, please.

I got EXACTLY what I asked for, and the quality was superb. From start to finish, I knew I was in the hands of a real professional, of the standard you'd expect from a high-class salon in London (where I used to get my hair cut at Vidal Sassoon). This is the advantage of the French training system – a career as a hairdresser is taken very seriously in France, as is that of beautician or nail technician. Students are properly apprenticed and spend a long time training; they learn all about bleach and dye, about conditioning, and also about service. I walked away feeling lighter than air, and with my pockets nearly as heavy as when I went in – haircuts and treatments cost so little in France that some French women even have their hair washed in the morning before work rather than doing it themselves.

Climate

France is such a big country that it offers far more climates and terrains than the UK. It has mountains and flatlands, marshes and ski slopes, a wild Atlantic coast, and the packed beaches of the Mediterranean. The different temperatures, topography and ways of life in France can leave an English person rather spoilt for choice, and when deciding to live in France, there is really no substitute for travelling around and deciding what kind of area suits you best.

The country has four major climates. The oceanic climate, which runs from Brittany to Flanders, is characterised by cool summers and warm, wet winters (hence, perhaps, the French saying that it's the area that the greatest number of French want to visit, but the least number of French want to live in). The continental-type climate runs from the Paris basin to Alsace and offers more extreme temperatures – cold, dry winters with quite hot summers, and a large temperature difference between night and day, particularly in autumn.

The third climate zone – Mediterranean – is found all around the Mediterranean cornice, characterised by mild winters and very hot, humid summers with a lot of sunshine, and often quite stormy and extreme weather.

The fourth climate is mountainous, found in the Alpine region and areas such as the Jura or Auverge – here you can expect a short, hot summer and a long, snow-bound winter. However, there are also numerous sub-climates in France, such as that found in the Charente (the sunniest area of France outside the Med) and parts of the Aquitaine. In many areas it is altitude that is the most significant factor, and temperatures and winter snowfall can vary widely across a single region.

If you decide to live in France, there is no substitute for living in an area for at least a year to decide whether you can take extremes of heat, cold, wind and rain to which many Britons are simply not accustomed. Holidaying in an area is one thing, but working and possibly earning a living are quite another.

Landscape

Because France was for so long primarily an agricultural country, the different methods of agriculture have affected housing provision. Champagne country (areas of open fields, which are found in northern and north-eastern France) usually has large villages, while the Bocage (hedged fields, typical of western and north-western France) tends to be characterised more by scattered hamlets and isolated farms. The Mediterranean landscape has closely-built villages, while in Aquitaine (something of a zone apart, with its fields sheltered by hedges that act as windbreaks) there are villages in the plains and scattered hamlets in the hills.

In general, although it is a cultivated country with no wild areas, France has a grandeur that is lacking in most areas of the UK. Depending on where you settle, you can find yourself surrounded by soaring cliffs, proper mountains, lakes, forests and magnificent rivers.

Temperament

It's hardly rocket science to say that the French are temperamentally rather different from the British. Speaking as someone who's lived here for some years, I would say the French are more argumentative, and less diffident about complaining in shops or about disagreeing with you in conversation.

The French love nothing so much as a political argument, and if you invite your neighbours for dinner and you want to see sparks fly, try mentioning a subject such as the Royal Family and whether Britain should have a president instead!

Another tradition that most French guard diligently is the two-hour lunch, beginning at either 12 noon or 12.30pm and going on till 2pm or 2.30pm. Most French people still eat their main meal at this time, rather than in the evening, and even workmen in their *bleu de travail* will often change into something smarter and go to a restaurant to eat lunch.

Body language

The structure of the French language, with its formal *vous* form, sometimes replaces formality in other areas, and allows the French to be quite relaxed in their body language and general demeanour – for instance, businessmen often dress more casually than their English equivalents, even at quite a senior level.

As most British are well aware, the French greet one another more formally than the British – entering a room and waving and saying "hi" is considered impolite. The general rule is handshakes all around at a first meeting and on formal occasions. On non-formal occasions, men always shake hands with one another and do not kiss, no matter how well acquainted they are, but in subsequent meetings with women, they will usually kiss on both cheeks. Women shake hands at a first meeting and then kiss acquaintances thereafter, whether they are greeting men or women. Two kisses is the norm, but local customs vary – where I live, working class people kiss four times but middle-class people kiss only twice (and obviously if it's something formal, like meeting your doctor or insurance agent, you always shake hands). Children are kissed once.

If you have to shake hands with someone whose hands are dirty, they will usually proffer their wrist or sleeve instead. If you need to give someone change at a bar, supermarket, etc., you're expected to put it in the tray provided rather than directly into the server's hand.

In my region, it would be very impolite to enter a room, shop or restaurant without greeting firstly the host, and then everyone else with a general: "*Bonjour messieurs dames.*"

Dinner at the neighbours

At some point after your purchase in France, you're bound to be invited to dine at the neighbours. Depending on how good your French is and how used you are to dinner parties, this can either be a relaxing or a nerve-wracking experience. Years ago I was told it was bad form to bring wine, as this is an insult to your host's cellar. In fact, I've found that most hosts are more than glad for you to bring wine, though they'd infinitely prefer a drop of the hard stuff. However, I would still not take wine the first time I'm invited, but would choose very good chocolates from a local *chocolatier*. If you decide on flowers instead, watch out for a classic *faux ami* in October and don't buy a pot of chrysanthemums – these are grave flowers, laid on memorials for *Toussaints* (All Hallow's Eve) – and fill every florist shop in late autumn.

It's quite common in France to never get further than the kitchen or dining room in someone's house – indeed, in rural areas, your hosts may either not have a living room or never use it except for family get-togethers. So expect to sit at the table all evening. During one dinner party, our hosts watched the Eurovision Song Contest on television throughout the meal.

You may also not be invited for a full dinner the first time – French people sometimes prefer to invite strangers for dessert as a way of breaking the ice. If you're invited for dessert, expect there to be sweet wine served with it.

A full dinner, on the other hand, usually starts with an aperitif, followed by at least three courses. In my experience, most hosts are pretty lavish with the wine, providing reds and whites with the entrée and main course, a *moelleux* with dessert, a *liquoreux* afterwards and finishing up with something like Agen prunes in brandy, which has a kick like a mule. Watch out for this if you're driving. Sometimes the only way to stop your glass being endlessly refilled is not to empty it in the first place – your protestations about not drinking and driving, or only wanting 'one' glass, or being on 'really powerful medication' can fall on deaf ears.

> If you are a vegetarian or have some other (from the French point of view) 'faddy' eating habit, explain this in advance, and wait for the blank look. You need to be clear about what you will and won't eat – fish are vegetables to most French, and some think that applies to chicken too. If you're a meat-eater, your hesitation to down pig-snout pâté, chitterling sausage or steak tartar made with horse may not be understood, but my advice here is to grit your teeth and tuck in – most of it is actually delicious.

The French are also rather more family-oriented than the British, and many Britons would say that this makes the nation more child-friendly. Children are generally welcome at events such as *moules frites* night at the village hall, where they will stay up until the small hours – and they are commonly seen in restaurants eating with their families from a very young age. This leaves most Britons with the indelible impression that French children are better behaved than British children, and even if this is not true, they certainly do know which knives and forks to use.

The French are also keen on their 'rights' and will readily take to the streets in defence of them, opposing the government, protesting wage cuts, taking part in demonstrations and going out on strike. For the most part, they are proud to live in a republic, and have learned the lessons they were taught at school that they are citizens, all equal, with rights that must be respected and upheld. Conversely, it tends to make them somewhat intolerant of difference, and you can encounter French people who are openly racist, for instance, in a way that startles the more silent, but perhaps no less prejudiced, British.

Assimilation and acceptance

There are thought to be about 300,000 Britons living in France on a permanent basis, with another 200,000 owning holiday homes, and they assimilate to varying degrees. While most wish to assimilate, there is no actual need to do so unless you want to work. To work, not only will you need to understand your new culture and environment, you will also need both the language and relevant qualifications as required by your profession (see section on working in France).

The truth is that many Britons living in France settle for feeling accepted rather than assimilated in their new country, partly due to the language barrier and partly due to cultural differences. For starters, if you do not learn to speak the language well, you will dramatically limit your opportunities to interact with French people who, although they may have learned English at school, are often too shy to use it. Using French media such as television, radio and newspapers is also important if you want to understand your new environment and the kinds of cultural references French people routinely make in conversation.

If you wish to get involved with the life of your French community, having young children is by far the best entrance qualification. With children, you have a ready-made opportunity to chat to other parents at the school gates, join the various out-of-school clubs and *kermesse* fund-raising events, and sit on the parent/teacher committee. Without children, and in the absence of a customer-facing job, your best bets are to join local clubs and societies, volunteer your services at the *mairie* (the mayor's office, which may be in the town hall), or walk your dog around the place and chat to whoever stops you. Whatever you choose, it pays to remain polite and learn at least enough French to say please and thank you properly – something which, sadly, seems beyond the ability of some British ex-pats.

Some Britons come to France in search of a quiet life, and are quite happy keeping to themselves, remaining on cordial terms with their neighbours, attending village events, but staying outside local politics, etc., and having largely English friends, or French friends who speak English relatively well. The French are very rarely rude and disagreeable to the British in their areas, unless it is filling up with Britons who may be blamed for pushing up property prices and buying up local businesses, in which case, bad feelings sometimes arise.

For those Britons keen to join village life, however, it can come as a shock that their suggestions for change at the local *comité des fêtes* are sometimes met with a stonewall. In a rural community this is usually due more to 'country ways' than to anything specifically French. When you move into a village, it pays to remember that you can't force your presence on people. Everyone there knows everyone else, they probably all went to school together, and quite a few may be related by marriage.

The village fête

French villages typically hold at least one fête a year in midsummer, for something like the Sainte Jeanne, though different villages also hold fêtes for local specialities or production – such as the olive festival, sheep fair or rose fête. Neighbouring villages tend to co-operate and stagger their festivals, which means that throughout the summer months in rural France, there is usually something happening somewhere on every weekend from May to the end of September.

'France' magazine produces a listing of festivals every year, including those held in cities, such as the Bordeaux Wine Festival, open-air rock concerts, etc. However, the best place to look for events in your area is usually the local paper. This, or these if there are several, is often found at the supermarket checkout as well as in the local *presse* (newsagent), and they are published on different days of the week, so you'll have to get to know your local papers to know which days to buy. Upcoming events are published under *événements*. Posters will also be displayed at the supermarket and in the windows of local businesses.

If a village fête is well attended, expect to have to park off-road in a nearby farmer's field, and that access through the village will be blocked for the day. You might also have to pay to get in. It's also quite likely that there will be cycle races held on that day, as the French are very fond of attaching these to any local event, so watch out for diversions on neighbouring roads, even if you're not attending the fête itself.

Attractions at one of my local fêtes, the *Flories d'Antan*, held on 15 August each year, include exhibitions of fancy chickens, blacksmithing techniques, country dances, vintage tractors, a concours of vintage cars, refreshment tents, and stalls selling sheep's cheese, bread baked in a wood-fired oven, arts and crafts and wooden games.

A close-knit community of this kind is hard to truly penetrate other than by marrying into it, and since outside the cities the French tend to socialise within the family rather than with friends, the average Briton often finds himself falling back either on other Britons, or on the odd, lonely French city-dweller who's moved to the countryside (where they are generally even less accepted than the British). After three years of to-ing and fro-ing and eight years living full-time in our village, we can still only count the number of our French friends on one hand.

You can remain on good terms with your neighbours by keeping your dogs quiet and your boundaries clean. In a rural area it's a requirement to kill off plants such as dock, for instance, while everywhere your hedges and fences must be kept in good order. Invite your neighbours over as soon as you can, as they will probably expect you, as the newcomer, to make the first move, but they will doubtless be curious to see who you are and what you're up to.

When you move to France, it's a very good idea to introduce yourself to your local mayor. Not only is it polite, mayors wield a lot of power in France, and it's wise to be on cordial terms with the person in charge of your future planning permission.

In a small village, you'll find the mayor at the *mairie*, probably for something like two half-days per week, and he or she is likely to be a local luminary such as a retired teacher. In a larger town, the *mairie* might be in the *hotel de ville* (town hall) and the mayor's job is more likely to be a full-time position.

Chez the mayor

Visiting the mayor is one of the first things you should do when you are considering buying, or have bought, your property. Mayors wield a lot of power locally and this person will be responsible for deciding whether you get permission to build a conservatory, install a Velux window or park a caravan in your garden, so it pays to get to know him or her.

Mayors in small villages typically hold a surgery at the *mairie* twice a week, once in the morning, once in the afternoon, and may work alone or with an assistant. Don't expect the mayor to speak English or to be efficient in any way – it's quite possible that he's only got the job because no one else wants it. On the other hand, he may be a model of efficiency, interested in you and your business ideas and keen to welcome newcomers to the neighbourhood. When he's available for consultation, there is usually a flag flying outside the *mairie*. Here, you will also find legal announcements and bans posted, such as your neighbour's project to construct chicken sheds right on your doorstep.

In a town or city, the mayorship will be a full-time position and the mayor will work out of the town hall (*hotel de ville*), with a small or large staff depending on the population for which he's responsible. In this case he's quite likely to speak English, but it's still best to make your request, or announcement, etc., in French.

Most mayors, like most French businessmen, are quite informal in their dress and comportment and don't usually stand on ceremony. Their friendliness and helpfulness have often surprised British people, and although the French reputation for red tape is certainly deserved, your mayor is one of the people whose job is to help you through it.

Top tips

- France is much less crowded than Britain and moving to rural France is often more like Scotland or Wales in terms of population density.
- You can live near a French town or city and still have a rural way of life.
- French rural towns are well appointed but many businesses close on Sundays, Mondays, Wednesday afternoons, lunchtimes and quite early – many restaurants will not seat guests after 8.00pm without a booking.
- France offers very different climate and terrain from the UK and it pays to live in an area for a year before buying so that you can experience all four seasons.
- French methods of agriculture have affected the density and type of vernacular housing that is available.
- The French differ from the British in temperament and sometimes mistake the British reserve for coldness.
- The British usually perceive the French as more child- and family-oriented.
- You can live in France without assimilating, but if you wish to do so, there are many ways of going about it.
- Rural communities are generally polite to strangers, but not appreciative if you, as an outsider, try to change things.
- Try to remain on good terms with your neighbours by respecting their boundaries.

Glossary

Desert – Uninhabited/unpopulated

Charcuterie – Delicatessen

Chocolaterie – Chocolate shop

Bar des Sports – A bar in which the television will be on all day and tuned to the football, cycling, racing, etc.

Bar Jeux – A bar in which there will be games available to play, such as table football (babyfoot) or pool

Tabac – Tobacconist – often a cafe and/or bar, too. These also sell newspapers, lottery tickets, phone cards etc.

Département – Geographical area similar to a county. France is divided geographically into 100 *départements*

Bleu de travail – Blue overalls worn for work

Vous – You (plural, or formal singular)

Chocolatier – Chocolate maker

Toussaints – All Saints' Day/All Hallows

Moelleux – Soft/smooth. Often used when referring to wine

Liquoreux – Syrupy, rich and sweet. Generally used when referring to dessert wine

Moules frites – Mussels and chips

Kermesse – Bazaar

Mairie – Mayor's office

Comité des fêtes – Entertainments committee

Presse – Newsagent

Événements – Events

Concours – Competition/combination

Hotel de ville – Town hall

2

Moving to France

Permits

The permits you need to stay in France depend on your nationality and what you intend to do there.

If you're an EU citizen, life is made easier by the EU's automatic right of entry. As you will see if you visit the EU website www.europa.eu: "All Union citizens have the right to enter another member state by virtue of having an identity card or valid passport." Technically, you don't need an entry or exit visa and it's illegal for you to be required to produce one.

If any member of your family isn't an EU citizen, however, they don't have the same rights as you – this can occur when, for instance, a British person marries a non-EU national. In this case, your family member enjoys the same rights "as the citizen who they have accompanied", but they may be subject to a short-stay visa requirement under Regulation (EC) No 539/2001. Residence permits are deemed equivalent to short-stay visas.

For stays of less than three months, the only requirement of EU citizens is that they possess a valid identity document or passport. The host member state may require the persons concerned to register their presence in the country "within a reasonable and non-discriminatory period of time".

In other words, entry is one thing and residency is another. You're not technically permitted to remain in France for more than a few months if you can't prove that you're:

- working (employed or self-employed), or
- are not a burden on the state (i.e. have savings and/or health insurance), or
- are a student, or
- are a family member of someone in one of the above three categories.

Carte de Séjour

There is no longer an EU requirement for you to obtain a residency permit (*Carte de Séjour*, or *Titre de Séjour*) if you're an EU citizen, but try telling that to the French. French law is perfectly clear in this regard (see www.service-public.fr for details) – you must still obtain a *Carte*, and you will need it for every kind of official business.

In the usual manner of French bureaucracy, the old *Carte de Séjour* has now been replaced by several different *Cartes*.

- *The Carte de Séjour Temporaire* allows you to stay for one year.
- *The Carte de Séjour Compétences et Talents* is valid for three years and is renewable.
- *The Carte de Résident* is valid for ten years and is renewable.
- *The Carte de Séjour Retraité*, for retirees is valid for ten years and is renewable.

For details on who is qualified to apply for what, visit www.service-public.fr and click on *Plan du Site*, then *Etrangers en France*, under the heading *Vos droits et démarches par thème.*

Despite the changes in legislation, however, most French officials still call the residency permit the *Carte de Séjour*. Contact your local *mairie* or town hall and ask which pieces of documentation you'll need to produce in order to obtain your *Carte*, but expect it to include the following:

- A valid passport.
- Three black & white passport photos.
- Birth certificate.
- Marriage certificate – if applicable.
- Birth certificates of your children – if applicable.
- Two stamped self-addressed envelopes.
- Proof of a permanent address in France (electricity bill, deed of sale, rental agreement, etc.)

- Proof of means of income/solvency, such as your work contract if you're employed, your *Siret* number if you're a registered business, proof of your student status (if applicable) or simply French bank statements showing that you're solvent or have regular monthly transfers.
- Proof of health insurance (whether private, under a work contract or receipt of disability benefit, etc.)
- Family details including your mother's maiden name.
- Translations, if required, of your birth and marriage certificates.

Another reason it's still useful to obtain a residency permit is that you are quite likely at some point to be asked to produce some form of ID, which may be needed for all manner of transactions, including signing cheques. French citizens have ID cards, and a residency permit takes up less wallet space than a passport and the consequences are less drastic if you should lose it. A French driving licence will suffice also, as it has both your address and a photograph.

Again, if any of your family members is not an EU citizen, different residency rules apply, and they are legally required to obtain a residency permit, which lasts for five years. Ask at the *mairie* for details, and at the relevant country's embassy in France (preferably before you make a move). There is a list of foreign embassies in France on the www.embassyworld.com website.

Permanent residency

If you live legally in France for an uninterrupted period of five years (holidays abroad don't count against you), you're then entitled to an automatic right of residency, and so are all your family members, even if they're not EU citizens. This right of permanent residence is lost only if you spend more than two successive years outside France. If you're working, however, including as a self-employed person, you can claim permanent residency earlier, subject to certain conditions – ask at your town hall or *mairie*.

It should be pointed out that the French are perfectly entitled to kick you out of the country if you misbehave (working on the black, criminal activity, etc.) or if you can't support yourself and your family. You must not become a 'charge on the state'.

Removals

Moving all your belongings to France can be a stressful experience and there are several ways of going about it.

Firstly, decide if you really do need ALL your belongings. Removal companies are expensive, and your British furniture may not even fit or look right in your new home, so decide if it's actually worth paying someone else to pack your belongings and take them across the Channel. Now might be the perfect opportunity to declutter, and if you auction or sell the majority of your household goods, you can always use the money to buy new, more appropriate ones at the French end.

Secondly, you can't just pop back across the Channel willy-nilly whenever you've forgotten something, so make sure you've got long lists of everything you think you'll need and check them thoroughly (see 'At the UK end' below).

Certain goods are subject to import restrictions, with the list of restricted items including certain animal products, plants, wild fauna and flora and products derived from them, live animals (see below), medicines (see below), medical products, firearms and ammunition, certain goods and technologies with a dual civilian/military purpose, and works of art. For an up-to-date list, check with French Customs at www.douane.gouv.fr.

Fedex also maintains a list of items prohibited from import into France at: www.fedex.com – current items include bush meat, melatonin and Atlantic red tuna.

At the UK end

Make sure you've got a six-month supply of your favourite foods packed. Although French supermarkets do stock some English goods, there are plenty of things that aren't available, and those that are might be expensive, so make sure you've got enough to tide you over until you find French products that can replace them. Such items might include foodstuffs like baked beans, Marmite, crystallised ginger, McVitie's Digestive biscuits and pickled onions – I usually ask friends to bring these over when they visit, or sometimes you can order them online.

The same applies to toiletries and make-up – bring six month's supply with you until you find replacement products. For instance, talcum powder is in short supply in France, with virtually none of the major toiletry ranges offering talc to go alongside their eau de colognes and soaps. Almost the only brand you will find is Cadum baby powder, which comes in a vertical cardboard box, in the baby section of the supermarket. The French have also generally preferred deodorants to anti-perspirants, so these are quite hard to find. Many brand names readily available in Britain, such as Boots, Yardley, Rimmel, Elizabeth Arden, Revlon and Shiseido, are in short supply in France (though the larger cosmetics stores offer major make-up ranges such as YSL, Chanel and Lancôme). Nor are brands with familiar names, such as Nivea, exactly the same in France as in the UK – often the product breakdown is different.

You may also want to bring a supply of trade white vinyl paint. Although the DIY market in France is improving, many British ex-pats find French paint is almost their biggest bugbear, and a good supply of paint will tide you over for a year or two if you are renovating. French DIY stores offer many types of paint pigment and universal stainer for you to mix your own colours.

You will also need plug converters for your UK appliances – assuming, of course that your French house has French sockets (ours didn't, as it had been renovated by Britons). And you should bring some spare consumables such as printer cartridges, vacuum cleaner bags, etc. You'll need these until you find a replacement supplier in France, and bear in mind that it's possible you won't – even if the same make is available in France, the model numbers may be different.

Finally, write down the names, addresses, phone numbers and birthdays of all your family members and friends, and, as with any move, make sure the electricity, gas and other utilities are transferred to the new owner of your UK property so that you can surrender the keys in good faith.

At the French end

Before you move, make sure the electricity, gas, water bills, etc. have been transferred to your name, or (if you're renovating) have been connected to the property. Your estate agent should be able to help you here. If you are aiming to live in a mobile home while renovating, make sure you have permission from the local *mairie* or town hall to park the vehicle on your land.

Removals firms

It's entirely up to you whether you choose a professional removals company to haul your belongings across the Channel or do it yourself. However, there are sound reasons for hiring a removals company:

- The removals firm provides some muscle, so you split the workload.
- The firm will provide proper packing cases.
- The removals men are trained in packing and loading contents into a vehicle.
- They are also trained in lifting and manoeuvring heavy furniture.
- Your goods are insured in transit and you are entitled to compensation if anything gets broken.
- The removals company understands the paperwork and will ensure that any relevant documentation is completed.
- Insurance for breakables is usually only covered if they are packed by a removals firm.

Get three quotes from removals firms and choose only those which are members of the International Federation of Furniture Removers (FIDI) or the Overseas Moving Network International (OMNI, www.omnimoving.com), and have experience in France. Quotes vary widely, and there have been cases of one proprietor of a standard British three-bedroom semi being quoted between £3,000 and £9,000 for removals (2006 figures).

Make a photographic record of all your valuables, in case anything gets lost or damaged, and provide the removals firm with a floor plan of your new property. Annotate the pallets to match the floor plan, and then your removers will know what goes where – this way they can pack and unpack in the correct order. Colour-coding your packing crates per room is often useful.

Ensure your belongings with a reputable third-party insurance company rather than the removals firm itself. Premiums are usually 1-2 per cent of the declared value of the goods, depending on what level of cover you choose.

Expect the removal to take 2-3 days, unless you agree a part-load discount, in which case you may have to wait for longer, as the lorry will have to travel to several different destinations.

Give the removal team detailed instructions about how to find your French property, and make sure that access to the property is unrestricted for the van, as you will be charged extra if the removers have to carry your goods further than they expected. It is not unknown for people to have to hire a second, smaller, self-drive van to ferry goods up a steep or narrow driveway – friends of ours recently took almost a day simply to move their goods from the removal van to the house because the driveway proved impassable for the larger vehicle.

Pets

If you're taking your pets to France, either on a temporary or a permanent basis, you'll need to make sure you comply with current legislation. The body that oversees pet export from the UK is DEFRA (Department for Environment, Food and Rural Affairs), and domestic animals come under the regulations for 'non-commercial pet animals'. See: www.defra.gov.uk for details, and also the website of the French Embassy in the UK, www.ambafrance-uk.org.

Current legislation for dogs, cats and ferrets (domestic carnivores)

The legislation was tightened up as at October 2004 (EU Regulation EC 998/2003), and now means that your animals must be both permanently identified (by means of a tattoo or microchip) and certified rabies-free by a Local Veterinary Inspector (LVI) before they can be imported into France – your veterinarian should be able to put you in touch with the nearest LVI. Pets must also have a Pet Passport validating that they have been inoculated against rabies. Treatments for tapeworms and ticks are not compulsory but are advisable.

The rules on dogs, cats and ferrets are set out quite clearly in the EU legislation, but DEFRA is still awaiting clarification from Brussels on certain other categories of animals, such as rabbits, birds and invertebrates. For animals other than dogs, cats and ferrets, it is wise to check with your LVI, as extra rules may apply (see below).

Previously, pets under three months old and unvaccinated were allowed into France under certain conditions, but this rule no longer applies. Since 28 May 2004, pets that are under three months old and not vaccinated against rabies are not allowed to enter France. If in doubt, consult the French Ministry of Agriculture's website at: www.agriculture.gouv.fr

Dangerous dogs

There are certain dog breeds that are considered dangerous in France, but not in the UK. These include Staffordshire terriers, Pitbulls, Rottweilers and mastiff types, including the Tosa. Regulations are strict, and also apply to dogs bearing the recognisable physical characteristics of these types of dogs. This means your pet could be denied entry. You may, however, be able to bring in the dog if it is a pedigree animal and you have the documentation to prove it. For details, see the French Ministry of Agriculture's website at: www.agriculture.gouv.fr

If you import a dog of any breed type considered to be dangerous, you must be:

- Over 18 years of age.
- Not be under guardianship.
- Not be convicted of an offence or in custody.
- Not have already been forbidden to possess a dog.

And you must:

- Register the dog with your town council.
- Keep it muzzled and on a lead in any public place.
- Obtain third-party insurance in case it injures someone.

Going back

If there is any possibility that you will not remain permanently in France, make sure to keep your animals up-to-date for import back into Britain, especially with their rabies vaccinations. It takes six months and two blood tests for rabies cover to become valid and many a Briton returning to the UK has been forced to leave their animals in France in the interim.

Regulations on import into the UK are tighter than for export into France, and your dog, cat or ferret must:

- Be identifiable by means of a microchip – British authorities do not accept identification by tattoo.
- Have a valid vaccination (both first vaccination and boosters) against rabies.
- Have a blood test, performed by an EU-approved laboratory, showing that the animal is clear of rabies (not required for ferrets).
- Have an EU Pet Passport (replaces the PETS certificate).
- Have been treated against parasites such as fleas, ticks and tapeworm between 24 and 48 hours before the animal is checked in on its journey into the UK. The details of the treatment must be recorded on an official document (usually in the Pet Passport).

Your animal must also enter the UK via an approved transport company and route (i.e. not on your boat or light aircraft, for instance). Information regarding routes and transport companies that may be used can be found on the DEFRA website. All these requirements also apply to guide dogs for the blind, and hearing dogs.

Pets other than dogs, cats and ferrets

To import pets such as birds, rodents and invertebrates into France, you will need a certificate in both French and English from an LVI, stating that the animal is in good general health and is free from disease, particularly any disease specific to its species (such as myxomatosis in rabbits). This must be issued within 5 days of embarking on the journey across the Channel.

You must also declare that you are the animal's owner and that you are not going to sell it on. It is up to you to check that your pet is not on the endangered species list. Consult www.cites.org and www.unep-wcmc.org for details and an index.

Travelling with animals

Most vets do not recommend tranquillisers for cats, as they suffer more from the fear of being out of control than from the journey itself, though they may be useful for dogs that are traumatised by travelling. Have your documentation to hand at the British end of the journey so that you can show it to Customs if required. You will have to leave your animals in your vehicle during a ferry crossing, but the ferry companies may allow you to visit them mid-way if you make arrangements in advance. Once you arrive in France, chances are, you will be waved through, but keep your documentation handy just in case.

Veterinary medicine

If your pet is having medical treatment and you need to bring its drugs into France with you, you will need the prescription written by the vet and proof that you have bought the treatment legally (pharmacy receipt).

Useful addresses:

Department for Environment, Food and Rural Affairs

✉ 1A Page Street, London, England SW1 4PQ
☎ Tel: +44 (0) 207 904 6222
Fax +44 (0) 207 904 6834
@ quarantine@ahvg.maff.gsi.gov.uk
💻 www.defra.gov.uk

For further information, you can also contact the UK Embassy in France:

Ambassade de Grande-Bretagne

✉ 32 bd du Faubourg Saint-Honoré, 75 383 Paris Cedex 08
☎ 00 33 1 44 51 32 56
Fax 00 33 1 44 51 33 11
💻 www.amb-grandebretagne.fr

The French Ministry of Agriculture

✉ Ministère de l'agriculture et de la Pêche, Bureau de l'identification et du contrôle des mouvements des animaux, 251 rue de Vaugirard, 75 015 PARIS
☎ 0033 1 49 55 84 72
Fax 0033 1 49 55 81 97
💻 www.agriculture.gouv.fr

Health and retirement issues

It's sensible to have a health check before you leave the UK, including an eye examination, so that you know your general state of health before you leave the country. Ask your doctor to let you know the generic names of any medicines that you take regularly, as brand names differ in France (Doliprane, for instance, is the most common French brand of paracetamol). You are entitled to bring medicines with you to France provided they're on prescription, subject to any anti-terrorism measures that may be applicable at the time you travel.

Make sure that you have your EHIC card (this replaced the E111), as this will provide you with emergency cover until you obtain your *Carte Vitale* French healthcard. You can obtain an EHIC application form from the Post Office.

If you're retiring to France, you should contact the Department for Work and Pensions several weeks before departure and explain your situation, as the procedure can be complicated, depending upon your age, health and dependants. More information can be found at: www.thepensionservice.gov.uk

The journey

Above all, leave yourself plenty of time for holdups and snags. During the journey, take every opportunity you can to eat, rest and use the bathroom, and pack some snack foods, mineral water, tea bags and a bottle of milk in the cool box – you're bound to want a cuppa when you arrive at your new house, exhausted but satisfied.

CASE STUDY: Removals

Steve Bodman and Nicola Newsome moved to the Limousin from Warwickshire in 2000 with a full load – themselves, the family dog Oscar, Leo the cat, two horses and the contents of a five-bedroom house.

"We priced up removals firms," says Steve, "but they were all too expensive. The average quote was about £2,000, whereas self-drive worked out at less than £500."

Steve hired a 7.5-ton truck for three days and the couple packed all their belongings into it themselves. Steve then drove it to the Limousin (without insuring the contents in transit), dumped the belongings and came back to collect Nicky and the house animals, while the horses were dealt with by a specialist transporter, John Parker International.

"We knew we needed an experienced transporter for the horses, especially as one of them was very old," says Nicky. "I found John Parker in 'Horse and Hound', and although I also got estimates from another carrier, I liked Parker's system, so we went with them. It was well worth the money – they handled all the paperwork, Customs, etc., and took the horses door-to-door without a hitch."

Meanwhile, Steve, Nicky, Leo and Oscar boarded Eurostar in their Volvo, an option the couple chose so that they would not have to be separated from the animals. In particular, Leo was 13 at the time and they didn't want to leave him alone on the ferry for hours. As for paperwork, says Nicky: "It was a complete waste of time. We'd gone through all the business with DEFRA, and we'd done all the right things, but no-one, even once, looked at the animals – we could have had anything in the car."

Steve and Nicky had chosen to rent in the Limousin while they looked for a house, but although the region had looked perfect on paper, in the end the couple decided it was not the right environment for their horses. Six months later, they bought a property in Normandy, which entailed moving again. "This time, we asked our blacksmith for a recommendation," says Nicky, "and that's how we found our horse transporter and we had contacts at the other end to help him find the house. We also hired two men and a van – other ex-pats – to move our stuff, which was mostly still in boxes because we'd never unpacked it, and we ourselves once again piled into the Volvo."

On this occasion, they gave Leo a cat tranquilliser which knocked him out for two days, but he had been traumatised by his previous long journey and they felt it was the better option.

Although their method of getting to France was rather haphazard, they don't wish they'd done it differently. "It all worked out in the end," says Steve, "and that's what I'd say to other Brits – try as you might, you'll never remember everything, so just do it."

Top tips

- Introduce yourself to your mayor once you have arrived in France.
- You have the right, as an EU citizen, to remain in France for three months without a permit.
- Consider obtaining a *Carte de Séjour*, although one is no longer required.
- Consider selling some of your belongings before moving over – the money saved on removals costs can often pay for new furniture in France.
- If your move is permanent, bring six months' supply of your favourite toiletries and foodstuffs, and plenty of white trade paint.
- There are sound reasons for using a bona fide removals company, including insurance.
- If you are exporting pets to France, contact DEFRA at www.defra.gov.uk for details.
- The French have different definitions for dangerous dogs – check that the breed of your dog is considered safe in France.
- Some items cannot be imported into France, such as firearms and certain plants – check with British Customs for details.
- Have a health check and eye examination before leaving the UK and check that you have good supplies of your prescription medicines.

Glossary

Carte/Titre de Séjour – Residency permit

Carte de Séjour Temporaire – Residency permit which allows you to stay for one year

Carte de Séjour Compétences et Talents – Residency permit which is valid for three years and is renewable

Carte de Résident – Residency permit which is valid for ten years and is renewable

Carte de Séjour Retraité – Residency permit for retirees which is valid for ten years and is renewable

Mairie – Mayor's office

Siret – A company registration number

Carte Vitale – The French healthcard, which contains all your social security details, including your insurance cover

3

Language

At some point in your sojourn in France, you're going to come up against the thorny issue of speaking French, because the truth is that the only way to become truly assimilated in your new home is to learn the language.

There are many ways of learning and which approach is best depends on you as an individual. Some people work well in a classroom environment, while to others this is anathema. Some people prefer to pick up the language as they go along while others find they require the structure of a course. You can learn French before you move over, after you've moved over, or by taking full-time courses of varying lengths, where you immerse yourself in the language. Many people end up doing a mixture of all three.

Whatever method(s) you decide, ANY French that you acquire will be useful, even if it is only basic.

Getting by

Many Britons in France, particularly those who only buy holiday homes, don't speak very much French. This is less of a problem in cities, but in rural areas, where people may be less educated, you are quite unlikely to find English speakers. Even French people who speak English are reluctant to use it in front of native English speakers (probably because they can hear how terrible our French is...), and you can know someone for years without ever realising that they understand your native tongue.

I've also noticed that with many British couples, it is the women who speak French and the men who don't. This does not always hold true, of course, but women are generally more gregarious and have a greater need for personal relationships in which they talk (as opposed to DOING things like playing squash), so their need for language is perhaps greater. This means that many couples are dependent on each other in a way that they are not in the UK, and cannot make trips to the dentist or the supermarket without each other.

A smile will get you a long way, but it is not difficult to learn French to at least the level of 'please' and 'thank you'. Arm yourself with a dictionary and a phrasebook, which will help with pronunciation, and don't be rude enough to address French people only in English. Listen to how French people speak to you and to one another – for instance, if you enter a shop and the shopkeeper says: "bonjour monsieur", don't answer by pointing at a croissant and saying "I want..." in English. At least be polite enough to say "bonjour monsieur" in return, before switching out of his native tongue into your own.

Basic vocabulary you really can't manage without includes numbers 1-10, the days of the week, 'please' and 'thank you', 'hello' and 'goodbye', and 'yes' and 'no'. You can listen to examples of this kind of basic French on the BBC's Learning French homepage.

Before you move over

Classroom learning

If you live in a university town, you may be able to attend college lectures in French, though this is not a cheap option.

There may also be part-time classes at a local adult education centre. Courses are structured, which can be an advantage, but they may be held during the daytime, which may be inconvenient. You might also find they are not available in the summer months, when the college is in recess, though equally, this is precisely the time when some local authorities encourage outside learning, in order to make more use of their buildings.

If you live in London you can choose from the huge range of French courses offered under the Floodlight scheme (visit www.floodlight.co.uk). Courses normally begin in term times (autumn, spring and summer) and there are hundreds of different types available, including day classes, evening classes and weekend workshops. As well as language, you can take courses focusing on French culture and literature.

The Institut Français, founded in 1910, is the official French government centre of language and culture in London and offers a wide variety of French courses for all levels. You can choose from once-a-week general courses, fast-track courses, business French, and courses that cover French cultural and social issues. Visit the Institut site at: www.institut-francais.org.uk for details.

The Alliance Française, which is dedicated to fostering Franco-British relations, has its main UK office in London but offers French courses in nearly 60 UK locations. Courses cover any level of French, and can be via workshops, evening classes, for those who need professional qualifications, or customised courses including private tuition. Visit the Alliance Française website at: www.alliance-fr.org

Private tuition

If you don't thrive in a classroom but prefer the idea of private tuition, bear in mind that rates will vary depending on the age and experience of your tutor, and whether the classes are held at your home (more expensive) or the tutor's home (cheaper). Tuition might be on a one-to-one basis (more expensive), or in small groups (cheaper). The main advantages of private tuition are that you can attend classes at a time that suits you, and to a certain extent you can dictate the course as the tutor will be able to respond more exactly to your needs – this means you will neither be held back by slower learners, nor left behind by fast ones.

To find a private tutor, contact the Alliance Française as above, look in the Yellow Pages or Thomson Directory under tutoring or language courses, or search online. If you live near a university town, you could also consider taking tuition from a graduate or postgraduate French student or a lecturer. Visit the central student library and post a notice to see if anyone's interested. You can also find tutors via agencies such as www.personal-tutors.co.uk. Prices quoted usually include agency commission.

Whether you prefer a French speaker or an English speaker as your tutor depends upon you as an individual, but if you choose a native French speaker, make sure they're qualified as a language teacher so that they understand how to explain French grammar to you in English – many French people, like English people, don't have a full grasp of the grammar of their own language.

Courses for the committed

You can take a BA in French as an external student at the University of London (see the website at: www.londonexternal.ac.uk). Royal Holloway College is the host college and you can complete the course over a period of eight years if you study part-time, though it can be done in as little as three if you study full-time (and this option works out cheaper). At the end, you have a Bachelor of Arts degree from the external programme of the University of London, which has the same standing as a normal student degree. To qualify for the course you need to have the same sorts of grades as would be required of an ordinary student (see the website for details). The college notes that you must provide your own course books.

The Open University (www.open.ac.uk) offers a wide variety of French courses for everyone from complete beginners (who need no entry requirements) to advanced students, with the more advanced courses leading to recognised qualifications such as certificates and diplomas. Face-to-face tuition is offered in groups and online group tuition is also available, along with access to discussion rooms where you can talk to fellow students. All the courses provide books and audio and video materials for private study.

The beginners course, *Bon Départ*, brings you up to GCSE level over the course of one year and you don't need to have any previous knowledge of French. The next course up, *Ouverture*, requires that you already have French equivalent to GCSE level or above and leads to the Certificate in French. *Nouvelles Mises au Point*, the most advanced course, leads to a Diploma in French. The OU also offers residential courses in France, and combined French/business studies degrees. More details, including student reviews of all the above courses can be seen on the OU website.

For a flexible approach to distance learning, the tuition agency 'Anysubject' offers online tuition at a frequency, date and time of your choosing. You can also choose your medium – emails, written conversation, or voice and picture (for which you need a webcam). You can arrange tuition individually, or in small groups. Visit www.anysubject.com for details.

You can also study at home for GCSE or A Level French via the National Extension College. Fees include readers, a grammar summary and audio material, and you receive individual tuition. Contact www.nec.ac.uk for details.

Self-study

If you want to teach yourself French at home, there is a wide range of books, CDs, CD-Roms and DVDs available. Many of these offer a complete course and assume you're at one of three levels: beginner, intermediate or advanced. They generally allow you to listen and understand spoken French alongside written French, though some do not have a written component.

Just a few of the many available include: *The French Experience* by Mike Garnier and Jeanine Picard; *Breakthrough French* by Stephanie Rybak;

French with Michel Thomas Complete Course CD; *Teach Yourself: Improve Your French*; and Rosetta Stone (the choice of NASA no less), which also now offers its courses online at: www.rosettastone.co.uk.

Other online French courses include those offered by Linguaphone (www.linguaphone.co.uk) and Eurotalk (www.eurotalk.co.uk), which tend to be costly but comprehensive, and others that are free of charge, such as About.com (http://french.about.com) and the BBC (www.bbc.co.uk). The BBC site enables you to download files to your MP3 player, or watch interactive videos (for which you'll need broadband and Flash Player). There are more self-help courses coming on stream all the time, so it is worth browsing the web.

After you move over

Once you have moved to France, you will quickly find that you would like to improve your level of French – at least spoken French. Many people start out by saying that they'll be happy 'just to get by', then soon find they change their goals to speaking French 'adequately' or even 'well'.

The best way, bar none, to learn French is to work in a French workplace. Here, you are simply forced to pick up the language or die. However, it's also true that many Britons in France do not work alongside French people – many run their own business, work from home, are retired, or have downshifted. If you're in this category, however, there are plenty of other options.

Classroom learning: Residential

If you like the idea of learning French in a structured manner and a classroom setting, there are residential French language schools where you can immerse yourself in the language. When searching for a course, look for teachers who are FLE qualified (French as a Foreign Language) and schools that are recognised by the Ministry of Education as *Établissement d'Enseignement Supérieur Privé* and *Centre de Formation Continue*. A range of residency options is usually available, from lodging at the school or college, to staying with a host family, to half-board at a local hotel. You can find residential schools online or in the French property press.

Classroom learning: Non-residential

You may also be able to find language schools locally, especially if you live in a university town. The Alliance Française offers courses in over 30 locations in France and you can choose from workshops, evening courses, professional courses and customised courses, including private tuition (see the Alliance Française website for details).

If you prefer a more informal approach, you could visit your local *lycée* and ask if any of the teachers – or even *bac*-level pupils – would be interested in teaching you French. This is often a good way to get to know your environment and pick up local patois, as well as to meet people. You can also advertise in local newspapers or on the supermarket noticeboard, and there are also teachers who advertise in the ex-pat press or on ex-pat websites such as Angloinfo, which has a number of regional sites.

In any area where there is an influx of British, or where there is a twinning committee (you can tell if a French town is twinned with a UK one as it will be on the town boundary signs), it is worth asking at the town hall or *mairie* if there are any lessons held locally. Also, other Britons in an area often know of someone who will teach you. Often it's a retired language teacher: my first French teacher in France was a Frenchwoman who had taught French in the UK for 20 years.

Learning as you go along

If you really can't bear to learn French in a structured way, watch French films on DVD with English subtitles (you'll usually need to order these from the UK). As well as teaching you the language, this will also tell you something about French culture.

Also consider watching French television, especially a French satellite package, which will give you access to more varied programming. Programmes such as documentaries where the voiceover is in French are often useful, as voiceover speech is slightly slower than normal speech. Also useful are programmes where words appear on screen, such as shopping channels, or where there are interviews with English-speakers which are subtitled. Adventure movies with strong, easy to follow plots can be surprisingly helpful, though many French films are small budget talkies, where you may get lost. And newsreaders, as in the UK, usually speak French very well and without a strong accent, which can make it easier to pick up. However, one of the most useful programmes I came across in France was a very tacky show called 'Hollywood Stories' – the mixture of French voiceover and English-language interviews with French subtitles introduced me to phrases such as *faire un tabac* (make a killing) which I had never heard in general speech.

French magazines such as 'Paris Match' are a good way to learn the language, or children's books and product catalogues (anything where there are pictures as well as text – the captions alone will teach you French such as 'above', 'below' and 'facing'). Avoid the tougher publications such as 'Nouvel Observateur' if you don't have a wide vocabulary, but if you have a hobby or interest, buying French magazines on the subject can improve your language skills fairly painlessly, especially with regard to vocabulary.

Finally, having French friends to whom you wish to express ideas is a great incentive to learning, particularly if you don't mind them correcting you! Joining an association or club for a hobby or other activity kills two birds with one stone, and most French towns of any decent size have a whole raft of activities taking place both during the day and during the evening. Dance classes, sewing, horticulture, painting, canoeing, rock-climbing: whatever your interest, there will be something going on.

Reference books

A few good reference books are handy, whatever your level of French.

For an English/French dictionary the 'Collins-Robert French Dictionary' is one of the best, and comes in various sizes. The Complete and Unabridged version covers everything you should need, including how to write letters, etc. Even the smaller versions are weighty tomes, however, so it's also worth investing in a pocket (Gem) version to keep in the car.

A French-only dictionary is also crucial because it shows you how French is actually used in everyday conversation. The standard publisher here is Robert. 'Le Petit Robert: Dictionnaire de la Langue Française', is very well thought of, and the publisher also produces smaller dictionaries covering specific areas such as business language, medical terminology, proverbs, Internet use and so on.

A French food and drink dictionary is often surprisingly useful – small enough to carry around but covering terminology that properly belongs in a much larger lexicon. It's easy in a restaurant to think you know where you are with vocabulary, such as *ris-de-veau*, and then get a surprise on your plate (it's sweetbreads, not rice). Try something like the 'French Menu Reader' by Maggie Plunkett.

A verb table is also useful and here, the 'Collins Pocket French Verb Tables' is very good. The 'Bescherelle Complete Guide to Conjugating 12,000 Verbs' is sometimes cited as the definitive publication, and includes a French to English section at the back of the book.

All the above publications are available from www.amazon.co.uk, some are available from www.amazon.fr, and they should also be available from the language section of a good bookshop such as Borders. It is well worth browsing for others as there are many publications covering more esoteric uses of French, including idiom, slang, swearing, medical terms, business French, and even texting and 'Internet French'.

CASE STUDY: Language

Richard Frei learned French to O-level standard in the UK, but when he moved to France in 1996, he realised that it wasn't making himself understood that was difficult – it was the realisation that he was a different person when speaking French. "I like to think I'm reasonably bright and well-educated," he says, "but I'm sure some of the French people I meet regard me as a bit dim-witted."

This was never more true than when Richard, who holds a private pilot's licence, joined the local flying club. "In some ways they regarded me as a good catch, and they adopted me as a kind of pet project," he says.

"I was able to help them with their English, which is important in aviation, and I even brought business to the club by arranging fly-ins by UK pilots. They also appointed me as a member of the club committee – but that was where I was of least use and felt most stupid.

"The monthly committee meetings were always an occasion for furious debate," says Richard.

"The French love to argue and are passionate about their pastimes. This left me sitting bemused in the corner of the room while the discussion – couched in rapid patois and cut-off sentences – raged well above my level of comprehension.

"Then suddenly it would all stop, everyone would turn to look at me and they'd ask, 'Richard, what do you think?' At that point, what little French I knew immediately deserted me and I'd fumble for something to say. Then they'd give up waiting and resume the argument, no doubt thinking, 'poor sod. Nice chap but a bit slow'."

Only by learning the language well can you be yourself and express your true personality. Richard still hasn't quite got there but he found that practising his hobby and participating in club events helped enormously.

"Contrary to popular opinion, English is not used universally in flying," he says.

"In France, much of the radio traffic takes place in French. If you fly to the smaller airfields, you have to be able to make, and understand, all the radio calls in French. This isn't just a matter of convenience – it has very important safety implications. And when you're on the ground, you have to be able to cope with things like buying fuel, checking weather forecasts and so on. So I HAD to learn. Building my technical vocabulary and grammar helped my general level of comprehension and made me more confident in using the language."

Joining a local association

Joining a local association is one of the best ways to meet people in France and wherever you go, you are bound to have lots to choose from. If you're not sure where to find a course or association, ask at the local *mairies*. Associations have to have a licence, so they will be on the books, while local education centres are usually the location for evening courses. The local ex-pat community is usually helpful with finding English-speaking or English-friendly associations.

In most areas you can choose from a range of activities to suit your temperament, including: social dancing (about which the French are fanatics); indoor sports such as tennis, yoga and judo; outdoor sports such as kayaking, cycling and walking; and cultural and craft pastimes such as painting, horticulture and sewing. Many French women are skilled in crafts, and I have found American quilt-making to be their most popular pastime – for this, strangely, they often use English-language course books.

If you try one evening course or association and things don't work out, don't be discouraged – look around for something more suitable, with a different age group or more relaxed attitude. I attended one quilt-making course but found the woman who ran it quite terrifying and didactic, and no one seemed to be having a good time. But another association just a few kilometres away is friendly and welcoming, even to those like myself who live in another *département* and dare to cross a departmental boundary to take an evening class.

Top tips

- The extent to which you assimilate into French life depends on how well you speak the language.
- It is quite common in France for only one half of a British couple (usually the woman) to speak French well.
- Middle-class French people in towns and cities are the most likely to speak English. If you are in a rural area or an area of low education, you may well be surrounded by monoglot French speakers.
- There are many different ways to learn French, from Linguaphone tapes to intensive residential courses, to evening classes to private tuition.
- Most UK universities offer language courses, and are also good places to look for tutors.
- If you really cannot face French classes, consider watching French television programmes and films.
- Joining a local club or society is a good way to improve your language skills.

Glossary

Lycée – Sixth form

Mairie – Mayor's office

Département – Geographical area similar to a county. France is dividedgeographically into 100 *départements*

Phrases you can't do without

Bonjour – Hello

Au revoir – Goodbye

S'il vous plaît – Please

Merci – Thank you

Oui – Yes

Non – No

Un – One
Deux – Two
Trois – Three
Quatre – Four
Cinq – Five
Six – Six
Sept – Seven
Huit – Eight
Neuf – Nine
Dix – Ten

Lundi – Monday
Mardi – Tuesday
Mercredi – Wednesday
Jeudi – Thursday
Vendredi – Friday
Samedi – Saturday
Dimanche – Sunday

4

Daily life in France

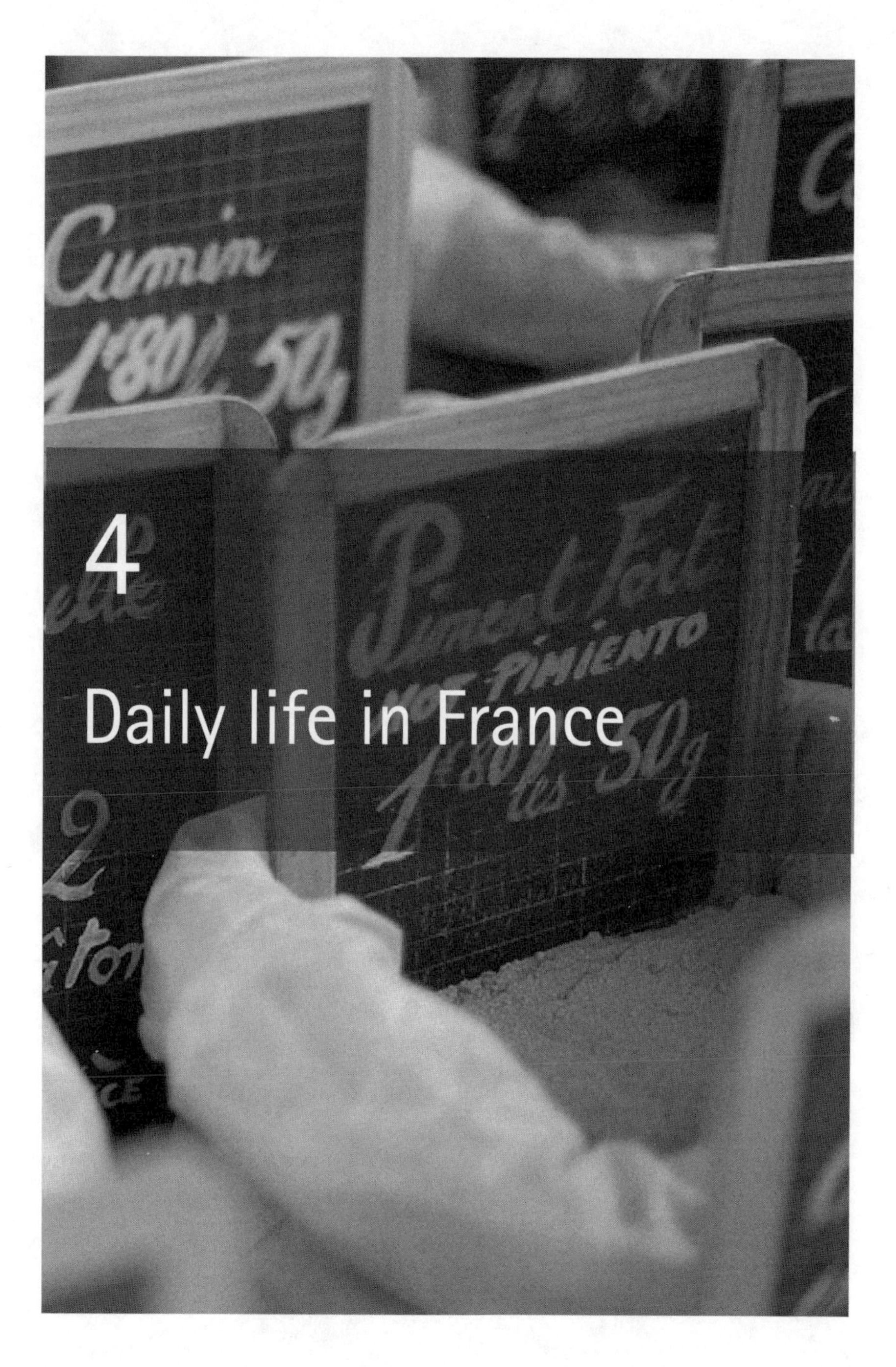

Shopping

The French have traditionally shopped at small shops – the *charcuterie*, *boulangerie* and *patisserie* – rather than the supermarket, and had their furniture made to order by local artisans rather than buying flat-packs.

However, this traditional way of life is changing. Any Briton moving to France can now expect even a small French town to boast one or two supermarkets, one or two DIY stores and a furniture store from a national chain, in addition to the local *charcutiers*, *boulangeries* and *chocolatiers* that traditionally lined the high street.

Low earnings and high social charges have taken their toll and it is sad but true that in many towns there is row after row of shuttered, closed-down shops. Unlike in run-down areas of the UK, however, this does not mean that wall-to-wall charity shops take their place, as this is not the traditional outlet for French second-hand goods (see 'Bargains, page 55').

Internet shopping

The French are surprisingly Internet-savvy and are among the nationalities most happy to buy online. However, this may mean that much of the business is going abroad: the French retail model often doesn't allow French companies to sell direct online but restricts goods to retail outlets only, so many sites from French companies only offer a shop window for their retail outlets (see chapter 8).

Markets

Most French towns of any size have at least one market day per week, and the day is staggered from town to town, with the result that almost any day of the week there is a market within a 50km radius. Goods are generally mainly seasonal produce, with a great deal of fruit, vegetables, cheese, fish, etc., with perhaps other stalls selling goods such as hats, bags, kitchenware or fabric.

Markets are a good place to obtain local items such as farm butter and cheeses that aren't available in the supermarket. In rural areas there are no 'farmers' markets' as such because the markets have always been farmer's markets selling produce straight from local farms.

Market day begins early and is often over by noon, and prices are sometimes – though not always – cheaper than in the supermarkets, particularly if there is a glut of one particular product.

French markets

Although every French and English person will tell you that French markets are not 'what they were', there are still many thousands of them held across France on pretty much any day of the week. Most towns with a population of two thousand or more will hold a weekly market, consisting of fruit and vegetable stalls, a cheese stall, perhaps fresh fish, charcuterie and odds and ends such as fabric, mirrors and hats. There's often a *crèpe* van in attendance, the equivalent of the British chip van, doling out hot *galettes au beurre* or sausages in a baguette.

Larger towns have larger markets and often include livestock. Here, you may have to queue to get into town and even have difficulty parking. It used to be the case that if you had something to sell, such as a surplus of fruit (very common in areas that produce gluts of tree fruit), you could hire a stall relatively easily by speaking to the local mayor. However, food production is now tightly regulated in France, and there have been crackdowns on unregulated sellers.

Market food has a reputation for being more expensive than supermarket food, but I have not found this reputation deserved. What you may find, however, is varieties that are not available in the supermarkets. Take along a stout shopping basket or two, or a trolley on wheels.

My biggest local market is held on Wednesdays, though there are other good ones on Mondays and Saturdays. Out of season, they are all a pleasant stroll around, but in season and full of livestock, it can take an hour to get in and get out of town. Attractions include cattle, rabbits, kittens and other pets, flowers, fruit and vegetables, cheeses, bread, seafood and *charcuterie*. And in whatever town, on whatever day, you need to get there by 9am as by 12pm it's all over.

Bargains

The French prefer quality goods and this is something that becomes evident to a British shopper very quickly. Although a thriving French high street might have its share of boutiques, lingerie shops, electronic goods shops, etc., prices tend to be high compared with the UK. France has fewer of the cut-price clothing chains seen in the UK, such as Primark and Matalan, though they are now beginning to appear in the commercial zones on the outskirts of town.

Sales are also few and far between. Shops in France cannot hold sales whenever they please – they are controlled by law and each shop is only allowed two per year, within a very tight timeframe. Therefore, you often find that all the shops in town are selling low-priced goods at the same time, then all the sales are over as suddenly as they began.

Low-price promotions are another matter. Typical 'promos' seen in French supermarkets are the *foire des vins* for wines, the *foire de faïence* for ceramic goods, and the *rentrée* sales of everything from rucksacks to pencils that occur in September when the children go back to school (*la rentrée* is a big deal in France and all French children are assumed to need an entire new wardrobe and lots of treats for the new school year). These promos, however, may consist of new goods specifically brought in, rather than existing stock at reduced prices. They are very handy for picking up bargains, so keep your eyes peeled for the free literature that is dropped through every local postbox when a promo is due. If you see something you want, buy it straightaway – don't expect it to be there next week. Also, a *liquidation totale* is a clearance sale – it does not necessarily mean the shop is closing down.

Anywhere in France, it is worth shopping around for discounts as the price of goods varies greatly from shop to shop. This is partly because even the supermarkets and DIY shops are often run as franchises. There is also a supermarket hierarchy similar to that of the Waitrose/Sainsbury's/KwikSave type seen in the UK, and every customer has his or her particular favourite. Supermarkets at the higher end of the market include SuperU, Intermarché and Leclerc, while those offering cut-price goods include Lidl, Netto (a subsidiary of Intermarché) and the unfortunately named Le Mutant.

Any town of reasonable size may well have some form of discount store on its outskirts, where you can pick up end-of-line goods, closeouts and sometimes seasonal items that are no longer wanted (Christmas items at New Year, for instance). Noz is one example.

Second-hand goods

Outside the cities, the French do not generally give their old clothes to charity shops. Instead, they get rid of them in a number of other ways. Local supermarkets often have a clothing recycling bin for used clothing in good condition – you simply bag it up and slide it through the slot.

There may also be a branch of Emmaus, which was originally set up to provide furniture to people on low incomes who could not otherwise furnish their properties. But from the basis of furniture, it has expanded to include all manner of goods, from carpets to white goods to clothing. Bargain hunters at Emmaus are as ruthless as jumble-sale officionados in the UK, and competition for items is fierce.

The third place where used clothing can be found is the *bourse aux vêtements*. These clothing 'swaps' have no equivalent in the UK: a *bourse* takes place over a number of days, starting with the drop-off date, when people can deposit any used clothing they want to get rid of. This is followed, generally a week later, by the sale of the items. Clothing is not actually swapped but sold, and as well as the organisers, anyone who wants to get rid of a lot of goods can book a stall and sell for profit. Prices at a *bourse* are often higher than Britons might expect from a UK charity shop – think consignment store rather than jumble sale.

Buying at small shops

Although there are many small artisanal shops in France, such as butchers, bakers and *chocolatiers*, most incoming British tend to shop in the supermarket because this is the retail model with which they are more familiar. This isn't necessarily a bad way to start, but it does mean you miss out on the more individual aspects of French life. Armed with a dictionary and a thick skin, it's well worth negotiating the local shops, as they desperately need trade to stay alive.

When it comes to food, there is really no substitute for trying something if you're uncertain. Each rural butcher, for instance, might well make his own sausages, or the *charcuterie* might stock local delicacies such as *museau de porc*, *gesiers* or *fromage de tête* (yes, those were pig-snout paté, chicken gizzards and brawn).

Supermarkets and 'grandes surfaces'

The first supermarket opened in France in the late 1950s. Carrefour, still a national chain, followed in 1963, and supermarkets continued to expand throughout the 1960s, along with chains of white goods, electronic goods, etc., such as Darty and Castorama.

Towards the end of the 1990s, the original chain stores came under threat from the superstores. These are generally found outside the town centre, in a sprawling *zone industriel* of sporting goods shops, furniture outlets, car sellers, white goods retailers and even the odd McDonalds or Formule 1 hotel. Shopping in these zones is more akin to the US than the UK, and you have to drive from outlet to outlet, parking up at each one individually.

The *grandes surfaces* include stores such as Conforama, the largest retailer in Europe. But even these giants, blamed by many for the decline in small businesses, have in turn been assailed by the cut-price stores such as Lidl and Leader Price, which are forcing the *grandes surfaces* to increasingly compete on price.

Supermarkets may offer services such as dry cleaning, photocopying, passport photographs and free wrapping. Many of the supermarkets and DIY chains also offer loyalty cards (*cartes de fidelité*) which give you points that you can cash in for goods. Ask at the kiosk or counter for details – as they may not be offered otherwise.

French supermarkets have a very good reputation worldwide, and it's mostly deserved. Even a small one may have a cheese counter, a *charcuterie* counter, live shellfish in a tank and a pretty good range of clothing. But it is only when you stand, faint-hearted, searching desperately for a bottle of dishwasher liquid that you realise how dependent you have become on British branding.

Here are a few tips

- Pledge furniture polish in France is called Pliz and looks exactly the same as the UK variety.
- Washing-up liquid (*lave-vaisselle*) tends to have names like Maison Verte or Paic, and comes in clear, flattish bottles, usually with a picture of a sparkling glass on the front. Fairy Liquid is not available.

- Although you may find Persil and Ariel wash powders and liquids, they are often not stocked by the same supermarket, and there will also be other brands such as Le Chat.
- K2R is a stain-remover similar to Vanish.
- Fabric softener goes under names such as Cajolaine or Soupline, and often has a picture of a baby on it.
- The French make use of *Savon de Marseilles* (white soap) in liquid, solid and flake forms for clothes and floor washing, as well as hand soap.
- The French do not generally use mops and mop-buckets, but prefer to wash floors with a cloth wrapped around the head of a stiff broom known as a *balai brosse*. You wring out the floorcloth into the bucket. Therefore, if you see a mop and mop-bucket for sale, you may want to snap it up straightaway, along with a spare mophead.
- Concentrated disinfectants that you add to water, such as Dettol or Zoflora, seem to be almost unknown – the French tend to use anti-bacterial floorwash instead.
- Because of their fondness for hard floors, the French have a wide variety of specialist floor cleaners to choose from. These include washes for terracotta (containing linseed to render the tile less absorbent), varnished parquet (usually containing beeswax) and fragile old floors such as reclaimed marble.
- The French use cleaning alcohol – *alcohol à brûler* – to clean items such as white goods. This comes in five-litre plastic bottles, or one-litre bottles with added scents, such as vanilla or lemon, and is very useful for cleaning coffee machines, the inside of the fridge, etc.
- *Alcohol à brûler*, very heavily scented, is also used in special lamps to purify the air, just like a scented candle.
- The French still use washing soda, which may go under the name *cristal de soude*, or the brand St Marc, which has added pine essence. Use it for degreasing and cleaning cooker tops, sinks, floors, etc., but do not flush the pine essence into the septic tank.
- For maintaining septic tanks, the French use enzyme powders that you flush down on a weekly basis. Eparcyl is one brand. Should the worst

occur, you can also buy special cleaner and restarter which is available at DIY shops rather than the supermarket.

- The French have not traditionally used antiperspirant, but rather deodorant, and there are not many types available. Brands such as Right Guard are unknown, but you can find familiar names such as Dove and Vaseline Intensive Care, along with French brands such as Rexona. Read the label carefully for the words *anti-transpirant* if you specifically want an antiperspirant.
- L'Oréal is a supermarket brand in France.
- The French name for Maybelline is Gemay.
- The French term for bleach is *eau javel*, which comes in tablet as well as liquid form.
- Products safe for use with a septic tank have: *sans danger pour fosses septiques* written on the reverse. These include toilet rolls and loo-blues as well as cleaners such as Toilet Duck.
- Sale goods are usually positioned at the ends of the aisles, and the cheaper the brand, the lower it is on the shelf. Most supermarkets have a range of own-brands, including a budget level, usually named something like *bien vue*.

Fair Trade in France

France lags behind the UK in providing fair trade (*commerce equitable*) goods, but they are now available in specialist shops and many of the major supermarkets, although the range may be limited.

Free trade goods usually display the international Free Trade symbol (a yin-yang symbol in blue and green), but Lidl has its own fair trade label, Fairglobe, which is the same blue and green coloration as the Fair Trade symbol, but a slightly different design. Personally, I haven't seen any other symbols, such as Tradefair or the International Fair Trade Association (IFAT) label.

Items you're likely to find fairly easily in the supermarket include tea, coffee, cocoa and chocolate, but items such as dates, rice, spices and clothing are harder to track down. Well-known brands include Lobodis (coffee) and Banania (drinking chocolate). In supermarkets, the goods are usually positioned in among similar, non-free trade items but also in a separate section with eco-friendly goods, diabetic foods and vitamin supplements.

The main body encouraging the uptake of free trade in France is non-profit-making firm Max Havelaar (www.maxhavelaarfrance.org). Goods that it designates as suitable have the words Max Havelaar printed on the label or packet, along with the Free Trade symbol.

The Max Havelaar website is a good place to start if you want to track down products, and it's worth becoming familiar with the different brands because many are available only from small, independently-owned outlets such as health food shops. Go to Max Havelaar and click on *Les produits*, then *Toute la gamme*. Here, over 2,000 products are listed in a number of different categories, including fresh foods, dried goods, clothing and cosmetics.

Many suppliers do not supply to retail outlets at all, so if you want to extend your options by buying online, again on the Max Havelaar site click on *Les produits*, then *Les points du vente*, then *Voir les sites* under *La vente a distance*. This takes you through directly to the supplier websites, who sell the usual items but also things like free trade jams and desserts, crockery and free trade teapots in which to enjoy your free trade cuppa.

At the website www.lemarchecitoyen.net you can find details of fair trade suppliers in some regions of France, including Brittany, the Ile de France, the Pas de Calais and the Rhône Alps.

Specialist shops supplying free trade goods include Boutique Alter Mundi, Artisans du Monde, Bioco-op, La Vie Claire, Naturalia and Satoriz.

Supermarkets and supplying free trade include Monoprix, Atac, Auchan, Carrefour, Champion, Co-op Alsace, Géant, Hyper/Super U, Ecomarché, Intermarché, Leclerc, Proxi, Supermarché Match, Petit Casino and Lidl. La Redoute also produces some clothing under the Max Havelaar designation.

You may find it's just as easy to buy your free trade goods internationally – just Google for suppliers, and check out eBay.co.uk and eBay.com.

Pharmacies – a source for toiletries

French pharmacies are individually owned and it is well worth visiting all the branches in any given town to see what make-up and toiletries are stocked, as these vary widely. They often include local products, too, if there is something like a spa town nearby. Brands stocked include names like Avène, Aderma and Kerastase. Pharmacies also stock herbal remedies, essential oils, flea and tick treatments for pets, orthopaedic products and baby products, in addition to medical items. See 'Chapter 14' section for more on pharmacies.

DIY shops

The DIY market in France lags behind that in the UK, partly because of the *métier* system – traditionally, if you wanted something done, you hired an artisan rather than doing it yourself. However, it's a growing and improving market.

It is well worth shopping around for DIY goods, as prices vary enormously from brand to brand and town to town. Most outlets are franchised, and pricing is set by the franchise owner, not head office, so even within a few miles you may find radically differing price structures. Outlets are usually on the edge of town.

The average DIY store stocks:

- Paint (mostly poor quality and very expensive compared with British paint).
- Brushes (mostly high quality).
- Woodburners, offering very serious heat output compared with those found in the UK.
- A very wide range of internal hard floorings but almost nothing in the way of carpet.
- External flooring such as concrete slabs, wooden decking and brick.
- Paint pigments such as those by Libéron, universal stainers, etc.
- Wall tiles.
- Animal feed, kennels, animal beds and accessories.
- Fly screens, windbreak fabric and fencing.

- Specialist cleaning materials for quarry tile, terracotta and so on.
- Lighting.
- Lawnmowers, paraffin stoves, chimney surrounds and bottle-gas cookers.
- Toilets, hand basins and other bathroom fittings.
- Plumbing equipment.
- Doors and windows.
- Wood for shelving, etc.

Heavier items such as plywood, gravel and exterior fencing can be found either here or in the builder's merchant.

Every Briton has his pet bugbear with what is and is not available in France. Outside the cities, if an item isn't in stock, you may not be able to find the second half of a matching pair, and may be met with infuriating intransigence if you attempt to order one. Seasonal goods such as garden furniture may only be stocked for a short period of time, so if you see something you want, buy it straightaway – don't go back for it.

Electrical goods

Many French shops that are branches of a large company, such as electrical goods chain Gitem, do not keep many items in stock. Instead, you are expected to order from the catalogue. So do not panic if you enter a shop and it seems to have nothing much on display. Unless you really want to have the item demonstrated to you, it is not worth travelling to a bigger outlet of the same chain, as the goods will be identical, and probably ordered from the same wholesaler. Electrical goods include all the leading Japanese makes such as Sony, and German and Italian brands such as Bosch and Zanussi, but also include French makes such as Thomson and Fagor (well thought of) and Arthur Martin (the French name for Electrolux).

Catalogue shopping

Perhaps because of its dispersed and once predominantly rural populace, catalogue shopping is very popular in France. You can find a range of catalogues in the *presse* (newsagent) or the *presse* section of the supermarket, and names include Blanches Portes, Trois Suisses and Quelle. All focus largely on women's clothing.

One of the best-known is La Redoute, which has a website at www.laredoute.fr, but may also be familiar to British shoppers via its .co.uk site. La Redoute sells well-made clothing in a range of prices from bargain to really quite expensive (and one flick of its pages makes a reader instantly aware of how the average French shop assistant manages to look so chic on so little money). It also sells men's clothing, children's clothing and layettes, household goods such as bedding and furniture, and some electrical goods, though not white goods. From the La Redoute main catalogue you can also order supplementary catalogues for specific clothing brands such as outsize makes. La Redoute doesn't sell much jewellery or maternity wear – for these, Quelle is probably a better option.

Many catalogue firms deliver to either a local drop-off point (free of charge) or to your house, and offer a range of delivery speeds, each with its own tariff. You can pay for your goods online, by credit card via the phone, by filling in the form in the catalogue and sending a cheque or credit card number, by loyalty card (such as *carte kangourou*), or finally, by cash on delivery (for which there is an extra charge). If the goods are not what you want, you have a reasonable timeframe to return them to a designated pick-up point. Strange as it may seem to a Briton, this is often at the local florist.

There are also catalogues available from companies such as JPG (office supplies, usually with next-day delivery to your door), Inmac (IT and technology), Conrad (electronic, IT, household and gardening items), and L'Homme Moderne (gadgets, men's fashion, IT and technology).

Antiques and collectibles

When it comes to 'antiquing', France is a very rich treasure trove, though what actually constitutes a good buy varies from area to area.

Broadly speaking, collectibles can be picked up in three main permanent locations: *antiquités* shops, which are very high end, *brocantes*, which are medium-priced, and *dépôts ventes*, where the real bargains are to be found. All three cross over to a certain extent, and many of them also cross over with architectural salvage – you may find the salvage outside in the yard, a *dépôt vente* section at one side of the building and finer furniture in the *brocante* proper. *Brocantes* in the countryside usually have better bargains than those in towns.

Antiquités shops are best avoided if you're looking for anything affordable. This is the place for the excellent quality Louis XV and XVI furniture, gilt, *Boulle* and ormolu that have made France the sina qua ultra of design.

Those of more modest means should head straight for the *brocantes* instead. The best are those tucked into some old hangar in an out-of-the-way village, which can still be found chock full of solid country furniture – nineteenth century oak armoires and cabinets, art deco three-piece suites and marble-topped 1930s kitchen units. Local furniture in *brocantes* is quite likely to have been made locally and from indigenous woods, so it should fit into your property and look correct. Pine furniture, incidentally, is rare outside the Alpine regions, as the French generally prefer hardwood – oak is often as cheap as pine and more plentiful, and other woods such as fruitwoods, chestnut and elm are also common.

Brocantes also tend to carry plenty of pressed glassware and earthenware, but an even better source for these is the *dépôt vente*, which are used by French people to get rid of their old belongings – everything from furniture to carpets to electrical goods. The *dépôt vente* owner sells on commission, agreeing a price with the vendor, which tends to make prices rather cheaper than you find in *brocantes*. *Dépôt ventes* also take in a lot of shop clearances, which can turn up lovely items such as apothecaries display cabinets, or ghastly items such as fake leopardskin boudoir sets complete with gilded claw feet.

Best bargains in antiques

Religious paraphernalia: plaster saints, Virgin *Maries*, straw-seated kneeling chairs, even confessional boxes. Plaster and wooden corbels and *boiseries* from stripped-out churches.

Buffets: the French equivalent of a kitchen dresser. The best bargains are twentieth century items and they are often extremely solid and heavy pieces of furniture. The lower doors are usually 1cm-thick oak, sometimes elm, with carved doors, either curved or flat. The top section may have either solid or mirror-backed glass doors, for food items you want to hide, or glassware you want to display. Many have marble tops, which must always be carried on their side when unsupported, otherwise they're liable to crack.

Stoneware: traditional pottery of the region. Depending on where you find yourself this might include Normandy or Breton earthenware, with its thick brown external glaze and greenish internal glaze, or Provençal pottery with its rich yellow and green glazes. Forget bargains in the highly decorative Quimper pottery of Brittany, however, as this is highly sought after. Pâté pots and *rillettes* jars (potted meat) are often abundantly available, along with *saloirs* (very deep pots for salting meat) or *vinaigriers* (vinegar makers), which are fat, lidded pots with a short spout (I use mine as a potato crock). You might, if lucky, even find a *beurrière* – a traditional dish with a water reservoir for keeping butter cool in summer.

Glassware: the pressed variety, especially the smaller glasses designed for drinking local beverages such as calvados or marc. They're equally useful for liqueurs or whisky. This comes in every colour under the sun and is often ex-restaurant ware.

Convent sheeting: often handmade on a narrow loom, so there's a seam up the middle. These might be linen, or a linen-cotton mix, or occasionally hemp. French sheets are usually rather narrow and long for English beds, but their robust quality makes them useful as curtains or loose covers.

Hiring tradesmen

Many Britons buying in France are planning to do some restoration, and the heavier or more specialised tasks will probably have to be outsourced to local artisans.

Building is a *métier* – a trade or craft – in France, which means there are very few general builders: nearly everyone trains in a specific skill, such as masonry or roofwork. This has both pros and cons – it means most French builders are very skilful, but that you won't be able to ask your stonemason to turn his hand to the odd bit of carpentry that crops up.

When it comes to finding a French builder no method is foolproof, but asking at the town hall is probably the safest option, and using local builders can be a good idea for a number of reasons. You're contributing to your local community (the British have a terrible reputation for bringing in outsiders) and local builders are also experienced in regional styles of architecture and construction – important if you want features such as an *oeil-de-boeuf* limestone window or a *torchis* wall. Their quotations are binding, their prices are usually quite reasonable, and their craftsmanship is usually excellent. All builders are bonded in France and their work is guaranteed, usually for 10 years. However, there can also be drawbacks – you may find that a local builder has only succeeded in staying out of court for so long because he's related to several families in the area. To be on the safe side, follow the same procedure as you would in the UK: ask three builders to quote on your job and make sure you get references from previous satisfied customers.

If, incidentally, you ask a builder to quote and he doesn't, it probably means he's not interested. Often, if a job is too small, a builder will convey this lack of interest by simply not getting back to you, a habit which has been known to drive Britons crazy.

Many British people who want to hire French builders are concerned that they won't be able to communicate their ideas, but the main difficulty isn't usually the language – it's getting hold of them in the first place. They are often booked up six months to a year in advance and can be quite reluctant to take on more work. In fact, so much is this the case, that it would be wise to be somewhat suspicious of anyone who CAN fit you in for a large project at short notice.

French builders have a reputation among the British for being lazy, but it is important to remember that life is more relaxed and slower in France, often to a level that drives the British to impotent fury. Be realistic and patient in your demands – usually the quality of the work is worth the wait.

There are some advantages to using British artisans, including the language, and their familiarity with some techniques that the French do not use, such as roofing felt and damp coursing. However, your British builder's qualifications MUST be valid in France. Crossover qualifications include membership of the Institution of Surveyors, Institute of Architecture or Chartered Institute of Building. Bear in mind also that many French people will not purchase a property where the work on it has not been bonded.

All French-registered tradesmen have a *Siret* number, including any Britons who are legally registered in France. It cannot be stressed enough that you MUST NOT hire anyone claiming to be registered in France who cannot provide you with a *Siret* number. This is your guarantee that the business is legal, is paying its taxes, and that its ten-year bond on the work will be valid. It is not, of course, any guarantee that the work will be any good.

If you are tempted to hire someone on the black, remember that the drawbacks are manifold: the worker is uninsured and can sue you if he has an accident; any quotes he gives are not legally binding; you cannot write the cost of the work off against CGT if you resell; you won't be eligible for a grant; and the work won't be guaranteed. Finally, you're liable to prosecution for tax evasion and although you may think yourself unlikely to be spotted, it can and does happen. Do you really want to find yourself facing a fine, jail or deportation?

There is nothing to stop you asking friends for help with renovating your property, but if you do this, their participation must be on a strictly voluntary basis. No actual cash must change hands.

Plumbers and electricians

Plumbers and electricians in France may be multi-tasking. Again, their rates are often much lower than in the UK but they can be reluctant to take on small jobs. If you are renovating a property you may find yourself becoming more familiar with plumbing techniques, such as installing bathroom suites, than you ever thought you would.

Cleaners and domestic help – Chèque emploi-service

If you want a cleaner, the place to find one is the notice board in the local supermarkets. Here, you can place a free advertisement or find others posted by people looking for work. In rural France, it's a seller's market and you may find it difficult to find a cleaner who doesn't refuse to do certain jobs, such as windows or ceilings. You should pay your cleaner by means of the *Chèque Emploi-Service Universel* and not cash in hand, which is illegal. You ask for this special chequebook at the bank. It is designed to take into account the social security contributions that you, as an employer, must pay, and insurance to cover the employee. You have to fill in the details for your casual labourer and send the covering note (*volet*) off in the envelope provided. This is all something of a palaver, but avoiding it and paying cash in hand leaves you as an employer liable to prosecution. See Chapter 19'.

Top tips

- French supermarkets are very well appointed but goods and brand names differ from those in the UK.
- Small traders such as local butchers and bakers offer a more personal service and individual products, and are usually located in the centre of town.
- French goods are often better quality but at a higher price than items in the UK.
- Sales in France are tightly controlled and major sales usually occur only twice a year.
- Many of the larger commercial outlets are located on the outskirts of French towns, in the industrial zone, rather than in the town centre.
- DIY is a growing market in France, but is still in its infancy compared with the UK. Prices and available goods may differ considerably from UK offerings.
- Catalogue shopping is common in France and there are many different companies offering a wide range of goods, from women's fashion to office supplies.
- Antique items can be bought from, in descending order of price: *antiquités* shops, *brocantes* and *dépôt ventes*.
- When hiring builders or other artisans, check that they have a *Siret* number and don't touch them if they haven't.
- Cleaners, plumbers, etc., may be hard to find in rural France, where there exists a seller's market.

Glossary

Charcuterie – Delicatessen

Boulangerie – Bakery where bread is baked on the premises

Boulanger – Baker, or bakery where bread is baked on the premises from dough made on the premises

Depot de pain – Place where bread is sold (often the *tabac* in villages without a bakery)

Patisserie – Pastry shop

Chocolatier – Chocolate maker

Crèpe – Pancake

Galette au beurre – Buckwheat pancake with butter

Foire des vins – Low price wine promotion

Foire de faïence – Low price promotion on ceramic goods

Rentrée – Back to school

Liquidation totale – Clearance sale

Bourse aux vêtements – Specially organised second-hand clothes sale (more consignment store than jumble sale)

Museau de porc – Pig-snout (paté)

Gesiers – Chicken gizzards

Fromage de tête – Brawn

Zone industriel – Industrial estate/retail park

Grandes surfaces – Hypermarkets/large stores such as furniture stores

Cartes de fidelité – Loyalty cards

Lave-vaisselle – Washing-up liquid

Savon de Marseilles – White soap in liquid, solid and flake form for clothes and floor washing, as well as hand soap

Balai brosse – Stiff broom or yard brush

Alcohol à brûler – Cleaning alcohol. Used to clean items such as white goods and in special lamps to purify the air

Cristal de soude – Washing soda

Anti-transpirant – Antiperspirant

Eau javel – Bleach, which comes in tablet as well as liquid form

Sans danger pour fosses septiques – Safe for use with a septic tank

Commerce equitable – Fair trade

Métier – A trade or craft

Presse – Newsagent

Antiquités – Antiques

Brocante – Second-hand shop

Dépôts ventes – Flea market/junk shop

Boiseries – Woodwork/panelling

Rillettes – Potted meat

Saloir – Very deep pot for salting meat

Vinaigrier – Vinegar maker (pot)

Beurrière – A traditional dish with a water reservoir for keeping butter cool in summer.

Oeil-de-boeuf – Window made from a single block of stone with an oval aperture in the centre

Torchis – Cob/wattle and daub

Siret – A company registration number

Volet – Covering note

5

Post

As any British visitor soon becomes aware, the colour of the French Post Office is yellow, not red: yellow vans, yellow office fronts, yellow stickers on your mail and yellow post boxes (often faded to cream) for your outgoing letters. The Post Office logo is a stylised blue 'is-it-a-bird-is-it-a-plane?' object on a yellow background, which appears on everything from mailbags to caps.

When you're looking for the local post office, it might be under the sign PTT (its former name – old PTT badges are regularly sold on www.ebay.fr), but is more commonly called *La Poste* or *Bureau de Poste*. The listing in the *Pages Jaunes* is under P. Opening hours vary and are posted on the door of the branch. Branches in cities quite often open all day from 8am or 9am until 7pm, but smaller branches may close at lunchtimes and after 4pm, although the last collection may be later. In rural areas you're likely to find the post office shut on Saturday after 4pm, all day Sunday and at least half a day, either morning or afternoon, on Monday.

La Poste is a state-owned company, and is staffed by civil servants. From its inception until 2006, it had a monopoly, but now it is open to competition from firms such as TNT and UPS. It provides a range of services in addition to dealing with letters and parcels, including phone calls, faxing, telegrams and money transfer. You can pay your utilities bill at the post office and use the Minitel service, and some branches now offer Internet services as well. The Post Office is also a bank and offers services such as accounts, pension plans and mortgage facilities. As an unofficial rescue package after the liberalisation of Europe's postal market, it was also granted a licence to provide loans under the aegis *La Banque Postale* in 2006, much to the annoyance of other banks.

In a sub post office, there's likely to be only one counter which handles all business, but in larger branches, different counters may handle different services. Make sure you know exactly where you're heading before you join the queue, and be ready to queue up several times if you have several separate functions to perform.

The French postal service used to have a poor reputation, but services have improved greatly in the past 10 years. Nevertheless, if you're in a rural area, you should allow five days for a letter to get back to the UK, what with bank holidays, weekends and often only one pickup a day. Letters from the UK to France often arrive faster than this, however. Letters in France go by the service *rapide* unless you ask otherwise, and should arrive elsewhere in France by the next working day, and if you're lucky, they'll be in the UK the day after. If time is not important, you can send by service *économique* instead, but prepare for this to take somewhat longer.

There are six zones for sending abroad, details of which should be available at your local post office, along with a current list of tariffs (which are also available online). The UK is in Zone 1, along with the other EU countries. When paying at the counter, ask for *prioritaire* for the fastest service, or *le plus économique* if cost is an issue. All the mail goes by air so you no longer need to use special airmail paper or envelopes, or put a *par avion* sticker on the envelope.

Stamps

You can buy stamps at the post office, in *tabacs*, from vending machines outside the post office and direct from the *facteur* (postman) in rural areas. You can also buy packs of pre-stamped envelopes for standard A4 letters and pre-stamped postcards for use in France only. You can also order stamps online from www.laposte.fr if you want to buy in bulk.

France, like the UK, issues special stamps and first-day covers (see the *La Poste* website at www.laposte.com), and information on new issues is usually posted up in the post office. These stamps are usually larger than the usual *Liberté* red or blue stamps. Note, incidentally, that window envelopes in France have the window on the right, not the left as in the UK – if you're going to send out business letters, you'll need to switch your letterhead design to the other side.

Postboxes and letterboxes

The French do not usually have front-door letterboxes as seen in the UK. Instead, you should install a letterbox either by your door, or at the boundary of your land (i.e. at the gate). Letterboxes are meant to have a slot at least 23cm wide and 2.4cm deep, and be positioned so that the postman or woman can deliver the mail without having to get out of their van. Until recently, this meant buying the standard dark green or cream box as sold in every DIY store (with instructions on correct positioning), but perhaps spurred on by the British invasion, the French are now taking to using olde worlde cast-iron postboxes in the shape of houses or milk churns, sometimes even labelled 'LETTERS' in English. If you choose the latter option, make sure your *facteur* has a copy of the key, so he can post items that are too big to go in the slot (there is no need for this with the 'universal' postbox as it has a standard lock that the *facteur* can open).

In rural areas your *facteur* will also pick up your letters if he or she happens to call at the right time, and can even sell you stamps. It pays to establish a good relationship with your postman if at all possible, and he will expect a Christmas bonus in the shape of a decent fee in exchange for the latest Post Office calendar.

Postboxes for your outgoing letters can be found at the post office, or set into a wall or pillar somewhere in most villages. They are not as conspicuous as the red British postboxes. If in doubt, look on the church wall, at the *mairie* or at the railway station if there is one. Rural pickups are usually only once a day and the letter slot is small, so if your packet is urgent or oversize, you'll need a main post office. Here, there may be several (large) slots for delivery – usually within the *département, autres destinations* including overseas, and *tarif réduit*.

Top tips

- The brand colour of the Post Office is yellow – look for the yellow sign with a blue logo.
- *La Poste* no longer has a monopoly on mail delivery, but competition has not yet shown itself to any great degree.
- Post offices offer many services, such as photocopying and money transfer.
- The post office also functions as a bank – there are over 12 million post office account holders in France.
- Most French people own a 'mailbox' type of letterbox, on a stand near their gate, rather than having a letterbox cut in the front door.
- Postboxes in most French villages are usually sited near the church and are dark cream in colour.
- The postman or woman (*facteur or factrice*) can sell you stamps and pick up your outgoing letters if you wish.
- Postmen in towns often deliver by bike or scooter, while those in outlying districts usually drive vans.

Glossary

La Poste/Bureau de Poste – Post office

Pages Jaunes – Yellow Pages, business directory

Rapide – Quick

Économique – Cheap

Prioritaire – Priority

Le plus économique – The most economical

Par avion – By air/airmail

Tabac – Tobacconist – often a cafe and/or bar, too. These also sell newspapers, lottery tickets, phone cards etc.

Facteur/factrice – Postman/postwoman

Autres destinations – Other destinations, i.e. non-local, including overseas

Tarif réduit – Reduced rate

6

Utilities

In France, electricity and gas were formerly supplied only by the state-owned company *Électricité de France* (EDF – www.edf.com). This was formed in 1946 by the nationalisation of a number of private suppliers.

EDF has never had a complete monopoly – even in 1946, individual villages were not obliged to sign up with EDF and some chose to opt out – and in parts of Deux-Sevres, Vienne and the Charente Maritime, electricity is supplied by local departments of works. Also, the marketplace is now officially open to competitor companies such as *Poweo*. Nevertheless, the fact has been that until July 2007 domestic users did not have the option to shop around for a supplier, so little data exists on competitors.

The French environment agency *ADEME* (*Agence de l'Environnement et de la Maîtrise de l'Energie*) can advise you on local providers and also on ways to cut your energy consumption. Visit www.ademe.fr and click on the *Nos délégations régionales* button to find your region. Once in regions, click on the *Plans du site* button for a list of categories (you need *particulier* for domestic usage).

Electricity

Most electricity in France is nuclear-generated, with the main generators being sited inland, though there are also reactors in places such as the Cherbourg peninsula and Brest. As at 2006, EDF was planning to build a new-generation reactor at Flammanville, which was being vigorously opposed by environmental groups.

France is the biggest electricity supplier in Europe and French electricity generally costs less than it does in the UK (in fact, France sells on some of its surplus to the UK). Many smaller French homes even run on electric central heating. This is generally only a viable option, however, for well-insulated modern homes built to a high specification.

The French electricity supply is three-phase and runs at 220/240 volts. This means you can use your UK appliances without problems, but not, for instance, American appliances that require 110 volts. Americans are best advised to sell their existing appliances and buy new ones in France. However, the French supply was formerly 110/120 volts, so if you are moving into a building that has been unoccupied for a long time, the system may have to be upgraded.

It may need upgrading anyway, particularly in older properties, because you may find the power rating (*puissance*) isn't high enough for your needs. One sign of this is that the cut-off switch in your fusebox trips whenever you use too many appliances. You can easily have your power rating upgraded by your supplier (it should be printed on your electricity meter), but be aware that this could mean an increase in your standing charge, and if you own something like several *gîtes* (self-catering holiday cottage), it can push you over the domestic limit and into the commercial arena, with attendant tax implications. Bear in mind that a renovated barn or stable may never have had power installed at all, or you may have bought a new build – in this case, you need to discuss your power requirements with EDF direct before moving in.

To calculate how much power you think you will need, note the power consumption of all your domestic appliances and add up any that you might be using simultaneously – and don't forget to allow for the water pump if you're on well water. The maximum rating allowed is 36kw and the lowest is 3kw, but most domestic dwellings with the normal range of white goods (washing machine, dishwasher, etc.) use an 18kw supply.

It now gets yet more complicated because with EDF you can choose from a range of tariffs (see the EDF site, which has an English-language version).

Option Base gives you a supply of between 3kvA and 18kvA. The standing charge depends on the amount of power you request, and the price per kilowatt hour remains the same all year round. This option is suitable for those with fewer electrical appliances but may be particularly useful while you're renovating a property.

Option Heures Pleins, Heures Creuses gives you a supply of between 6kvA and 36kvA. The standing charge is higher (much higher) than with *Option Base* but the night rate per kilowatt hour is cheaper than the day rate (you get eight hours at the cheaper rate). This is the most popular option and is useful if you have night storage heating, or are willing to run your washing machine, dishwasher, etc., only at night.

Option Tempo offers a complex system, with six levels of pricing per kilowatt hour that vary according to the time and the day of the week. Days are classed into blue (low price), white (medium price) and red (high price), and you can't check which day is which until after 3pm the day before. This might mean, for instance, leaving the washing for a blue day. Useful only if you're willing to stay on top of it, though the introduction of SMS alerts probably helps.

EDF can take a consumption inventory for you so that you can estimate your consumption in advance, and also offers a special rate for those on low incomes – see *Tarif de Première Nécessité* on the EDF website. Most people pay their electricity by direct debit (*prélèvement*) but you can also pay by cheque or directly at the bank, though the days when this is permissible are becoming more limited, perhaps in order to encourage customers to use direct debit.

Connecting to the grid

When you buy a property you should have the electrics checked by a French-registered electrician. Even if you're installing your own system, you can only be connected to the grid once you've been granted a certificate of conformity approved by *Consuel* (*Comité National pour la Securité des Usagers de l'Electricité*). Any aged system you inherit is also quite likely to have problems, primarily lack of power. Note that the French homes use a branch system, not a ring main – these are illegal and invalidate your house insurance.

Dodgy supply

In rural areas the electricity supply can be unreliable, partly because all the cables run above ground and are vulnerable to weather conditions. You can expect power surges and brownouts, and even short-term failures, so it's wise to protect your major electrical items with surge protectors, and your computers with uninterruptible power supplies (UPS units). If you live in an area such as the Limousin, where vicious weather rushes in from the Atlantic, you can also expect lightning storms and strikes which can cause power loss. Make sure your electrical goods are insured against being grilled.

You may find that your French property has a *disjoncteur*. This is a circuit breaker that kicks in whenever your power system is overloaded, such as when you're running too many appliances or when there's a storm. Although it may seem inconvenient to lose power every time lightning flashes, it is infinitely preferable to having all your systems fried. When the switch trips, if it's been caused by the weather, wait for the storm to pass and turn off as many electrical items as you can before flipping the switch back on.

In all rural properties it is worth keeping an emergency pack handy (i.e. somewhere you can find it in the dark) with the following inside:

- Candles and nightlights (nightlights are useful for atmosphere but no good for reading by).
- Matches or a lighter.
- Torch and spare batteries (a wind-up torch is a useful option).
- Transistor radio if required (you'll have no other access to news or music).
- Camping gas or oil lamp if possible – this gives a much stronger light than torches or candles.

Plugs and sockets

French sockets take French plugs, which have round pins rather than oblong, and do not have fuses. Large appliances such as washing machines, which need 16 amps, have a 'female' socket for the earth, but all in all, there are few earthed appliances in France. Items such as table lamps, which need only 6 amps, usually have no earth.

You can buy adapters to use English appliances in French sockets, but they are not widely available in France – it's best to buy these in the UK. Also, be prepared to spend a lot of time installing new plugs on your electrical items – this is a better option for anything you're unlikely to be taking back to the UK.

Bulbs

Most French lights have fittings for large or small screw bulbs, but you can also find bayonet bulbs in the supermarket and other outlets. If you have an item (an Ikea lamp, for instance) that require a specific type of bulb, it's a good idea to buy replacement bulbs in bulk in the UK and bring them over. This is also a good policy to follow if you buy a lamp in France with a specific type of bulb – buy a couple of spares at the same time in case the bulb is no longer in stock the next time you want one.

Power-saving, mini-fluorescent bulbs are now widely available in France, and work out extremely good value over time. Note, however, that you can't use a power-saving bulb in a light with a dimmer switch. You may find that bulbs blow more often in France due to the power surges.

Wood

This is a lengthy section, because not only is wood regarded as a very serious fuel in France, many British people have not previously dealt with wood, particularly if they are moving from a city.

Perhaps around a quarter of France is forested compared with 7 per cent of the UK, which makes wood a viable option. Woodburners are widely available and extremely efficient (clean-burn, double-combustion) and wood is also used as a common method of cooking and heating, via hot-air ducting systems or by running a back boiler that feeds radiators.

There are several disadvantages to wood: it's heavy, it's dirty, it emits particulates, you need somewhere to keep it dry and you need somewhere to dispose of the ash. The advantages are that it's often cheap compared with other fuels, you pay upfront and therefore can keep an eye on your consumption, and because wood is a renewable energy, there are generous tax credits available if you install a wood-fired central heating system. See www.ademe.fr for details. Although wood is considered to be carbon-neutral in terms of CO2 emissions, the particulates it emits are a cause for concern and there is a growing anti-wood lobby in the US and Canada.

It's possible that you can obtain wood from local forests via your *commune* (ask at the *mairie* or town hall) but, in practice, you're more likely to buy it from a local farmer who supplies wood on the side. This is likely to be arranged by word of mouth and to be a cash-in-hand transaction (*liquide*), and don't faint if the price is in old francs!

Wood is priced in *stères* (one cubic metre) or *cords* (three cubic metres) and if your deliveryman is coming any distance, he's likely to want you to buy at least a *cord*. Most fireboxes take logs of about 50cm length, though the larger varieties take up to 70cm. If you need something smaller, specify this clearly when you order, as the price may be higher.

Wood prices vary with the season (lower in summer, higher in winter) and availability, so ask around to see what other people are paying. You can make considerable savings by buying wood well in advance, in metre lengths and cutting it yourself, collecting it yourself, or by keeping an eye on the local paper where a farmer might advertise a one-off sale, for instance from a tree he's cut down on his land. You can also obtain cheap offcut wood from sources such as lumber yards (collection only). If you don't want to cut the wood yourself, make sure to order it cut to length and dried.

Softwoods such as pine should only be used as kindling because they coat the inside of the flue with tar. Hardwoods burn for much longer and with much greater heat output. Species include oak, ash, beech, pear, chestnut and cherry. Chestnut has a tendency to explode, but this is only really a problem if you have an open fire or firebox (the 'Ben Franklin' type of stove). Birch burns short and fast, but is very useful for getting a fire going.

For more ideas on types of wood and their heat output, visit www.stovesonline.co.uk.

Ideally, firewood should be a couple of years old by the time you use it. It should be cut in the spring and spend at least one summer outside, cut, stacked and exposed to the sun and wind before being brought into your barn or woodshed. This process, known as cording, helps to reduce the lignin in the wood, which is what holds the fibres together. Try to bring it into the house at least one day before you burn it (a week is better), because if its humidity level is over 20 per cent, you'll get a lot of smoke and smell, but not much heat. Your logs shouldn't touch the sides or back of the stove, as this can cause the plates to crack and although they are not difficult to obtain, they are quite expensive.

You should have your chimney swept, or sweep it yourself, every year (if you don't, you'll probably invalidate your house insurance). The French word for this is *ramonage*. You can search in the Yellow Pages, ask your plumber or electrician (who probably offers this service or knows a man who does), or you can buy special cleaning logs at the supermarket called *bûche de ramonage* which are designed to clean the flue. Alternatively you can buy a chimney sweeping brush, known as an *hérisson* (hedgehog), and prepare to get your hands dirty.

Woodburners

Woodburners (*poêles à bois*) come in a range of shapes, types and kilowatt outputs. To calculate how many kilowatts you need, calculate the cubic metreage of your room or house and allow 0.05 kilowatts per cubic metre.

Well known French makes include Deville, Godin and Supra.

The *insert* or *foyer* type of woodburner is designed to conduct hot air around the house by means of a ducting system, and is usually built into a chimney designed for that purpose. If you are not planning to duct the air, you might want to consider another heating option, as these stoves do not work very efficiently without their two-speed fan, which is noisy.

The latest woodburners are double combustion, much more efficient than older designs, and may even offer built-in fans to redistribute their heat from the bottom, raising the floor temperature and lowering the ceiling temperature in the room. They come in a range of designs, both modern and traditional, with or without built-in log storage or even plate-warming shelves. Godin produces an antique-looking range of upright cylindrical stoves that are indistinguishable from their true antique models. Cylindrical models, however, can be more difficult to light and are choosy about the wood being very dry, as the logs burn from one end to the other and not across the centre. You also have to use logs that are relatively short and straight.

If effect is more important than performance, you can pick up antique woodburners in most *brocantes* and salvage yards. Although these may not offer the same kind of heat efficiency, they can be very beautiful, with mica doors and a range of enamel colours no longer obtainable in modern ranges. Bear in mind, however, that older stoves emit more particulates, which can be an issue for people with breathing difficulties.

Unless the stove is specifically designed to be multifuel, you cannot use coal in a woodburner as it burns too hot and can crack the plates.

Water

Mains water in France is in the hands of private companies such as Vivendi and most people choose to be metered in order to keep an eye on their consumption. If you move into a house that already has a meter, ask the water company to read it before you use it, or you could end up paying the previous tenant's bill. If your house doesn't have a meter, the charge for installing one is not refundable. You don't have to stick with the current water company, of course, and can choose a competitor if you prefer – look under *eaux* (distribution, services) in the *Pages Jaunes*.

If your property is older or isolated you may well find that you are on well water. If your house falls within a certain distance of the village centre, you may be able to connect to the mains water fairly easily. You have to bear the cost of installation yourself, including the laying of underground pipes, so if you want to join the mains, ask for a quotation from the local water company before proceeding.

The advantages of mains water are that it should be potable, it should be clean and the pressure should be correct. The main disadvantages are its cost, which varies enormously according to region and availability, and that it can be simply cut off by the water company in times of drought. Water shortages have been more common in recent years as the summers have become hotter and the winters drier, so this is something to bear in mind.

The advantages of well water are that it's cheap, with the electricity to run the pump the only cost consideration, which means that you can have deep baths every day if you want; and you're exempt from the restrictions that affect mains water during times of drought (though you still can't irrigate and it would be sensible to conserve water anyway if the water table's low, as your own source might dry up).

Its disadvantages are that: it's usually not potable, which means lugging home mineral water from the supermarket every week (which sometimes reduces the cost benefit); it may have sediments that colour the water and therefore your clothing, washing machine, etc. and if you suffer a power cut, you're left without water because there's no pump.

However, it's sometimes the case that mains water isn't potable either, particularly if you're at the end of the village network, so joining the mains may not be as advantageous as you might imagine. Many householders in rural France adopt a dual approach and use mains water for the house and well water for the garden and toilets.

When you buy your property, it's a good idea to have the water tested. This costs up to €100 and you just ask for the kit at the pharmacy – it comes with full instructions. If you're on mains and your water tests as non-potable, you should be able to negotiate a discount with the water company.

It is generally assumed in France that you will want to conserve water, so new baths tend to have water-saving designs and toilets are usually dual-flush. If you ever have to buy a hot-water boiler and tank (often the tank is integral to the system), check the size of the cistern. Many are only 95 litres, which feels a little scant to the average British consumer, especially if you have a large bath.

Sewage

Rural properties often have a septic tank rather than mains drainage, though urban properties are normally on the mains. Make sure to check first, however, before you buy, as more than one British buyer has found themselves with technically illegal greywater drainage directly into the street, which then has to be replaced at some expense.

As of 1992, the local *mairie* (or town hall) has been responsible for the disposal of local waste water and the general effect of this has been that properties within the village boundaries are expected to join mains drainage at their own expense. Those outside the boundary, along with every single property in France, will have to have their septic tanks checked to make sure they come up to current standards. This has meant, and will mean in the future, considerable expense for homeowners whose tanks were installed years ago and are now considered too small, too close to a well or otherwise inadequate.

Septic tanks need to be emptied periodically. How often depends on their size, but at least every 10 years would be normal. Your plumber should know of a firm that can do the job, and if your tank is down a steep slope, beware of winter weather – the first time our tank was emptied the tanker couldn't get back up the hill and had to pump out the contents into our neighbour's orchard!

Rubbish collection

Most rural villages have a rubbish collection once a week, which may either be from outside your property (at the end of the lane or driveway), or via the large lidded *poubelles* placed strategically around the village. You're usually asked not to put out your rubbish too far in advance of collection, as it is a magnet for vermin. Rubbish collection is usually charged for in your local taxes.

Villages also often have recycling bins, usually at least for glass and plastic, and supermarkets also have them in the car park. The supermarket variety might also include a skip for waste paper and a bin for used clothing in good condition.

You can usually bonfire garden refuse, provided you're not constituting a nuisance (obviously, if you have close neighbours, it pays to ask their permission first). However, bonfires are often not permitted in the countryside during the summer months, in case of wildfire – ask at your *mairie* for local regulations.

Large rubbish can be disposed of at the local dump (*déchetterie*), which is usually open a couple of mornings a week. A list of permitted items is usually posted on the railings outside, and as in the UK, there are plenty of Stig-of-the-Dumps hanging around the place waiting to pick up bargains. You can't generally dispose of hazardous waste this way, so ask at your *mairie* if you have, for instance, printer cartridges or chemicals to dispose of. Out-of-date medicines or medicines of current date but unused, can be taken to your local *pharmacie*.

Gas

Cities and towns in France have mains gas, currently supplied mainly by Gaz De France (GDF). Privatisation of the market began in 2004 for business customers and was extended to residential customers from 1 July 2007. Outside towns and cities, most people rely on bottle gas, either butane or propane.

Cookers and portable heaters run on butane and many cookers are designed with space for a standard 35kg gas bottle at the side of the oven. This can be a convenient option, as it means you can position the cooker anywhere in the kitchen. If there is no space for a bottle inside the cooker, you'll need to house the bottle either in the cellar or outside. Butane should be stored where it cannot freeze, so if it's outside, make sure it's in the correct kind of bottle. Bottles are usually colour-coded, but ask when you buy to be sure you've selected the correct one as different manufacturers' bottles are different colours.

You can buy butane from many outlets, such as feed stores or the petrol pumps at the local supermarket. The normal procedure is that you buy the first bottle at full cost, then when it's empty, you return it and the cost of the deposit is knocked off your next bottle. It needs to be the same type of bottle, however, and from the same manufacturer (such as Antargaz). It's necessary to have at least two bottles on the go at any one time, however, as you're BOUND to run out at some time when you can't replace the bottle – usually in the middle of a dinner party. Picking the bottle up and shaking it usually gives you a few more minutes of gas.

New cookers are usually designed to run on mains gas (*gaz de ville*), so if you are running on bottle gas, inform the vendor at the time of purchase and arrange for the valves to be altered before delivery. Bear in mind that this may hold up a purchase by up to two weeks.

French cookers

French cookers are often about two inches lower than their UK equivalent, and more of a 'range' design, with a central burner for a wok or long fish kettle. The difference in height is to enable you to see easily into pans on the back burner. The high-end ranges such as the Bocuse by Rosières have a large flat plaque on one side so you can push pans from one heat area to another without lifting them.

French cookers do not have an eye-level grill, as the French prefer to grill using ribbed cast-iron griddle pans, or by using a downdraft extractor grill. This means you can't see the side you're cooking (like cooking on a barbeque), and it makes it impossible to cook dishes such as cheese on toast. You can get round this, however, by buying a microwave with a grill feature.

Butane is also often used for portable heaters, but gas-fired boilers and central heating systems usually run on propane. This is available in large tanks of 70kg, which can be delivered by your plumber but these are extremely heavy and cumbersome to move, and must be stored outside for safety's sake. Most people who have a bottle gas-fired central heating system opt to have a gas cistern installed in the garden if this is at all possible. You can buy this, or rent it at an annual rate from a gas supplier, but the latter is quite an expensive option and having a gas tank in the garden will also increase your insurance premiums because of its explosive capability. The tanks are also very large and ugly, and can be quite difficult to disguise effectively while still ensuring access for refilling.

About a quarter of French houses opt for oil-fired (*fioul*) central heating. Oil is not as cheap as mains gas, but is less expensive than bottle gas. The oil can usually be delivered next-day, and it is stored in a large tank (*citerne*) in the cellar or outhouse. It is generally available in different qualities (I buy premium), and is a comparatively dirty fuel – the system should be checked and cleaned annually. Note that if you buy an oil-fired Aga or Rayburn from the UK, the oil pressure is different and the stove will require a refit.

Coal

Coal is not a popular fuel option in France, and it ranks below Germany, Poland, the UK, Spain, the Czech Republic and Italy in terms of European coal consumption, partly because it switched most of its power stations to nuclear a couple of generations ago. Most wood-burning stoves in France are not multifuel, and it may be difficult to find anyone who can deliver coal to your property in any case. However, if you have a multifuel burner and you want to track down a coal supplier, look under *vente charbon* in the *Pages Jaunes*.

Renewable energy

France has signed up to the European Union pledge to meet 21 per cent of its energy needs via renewable sources by 2010, but appears to be falling well short of its targets at present. For the time being, renewable options often remain expensive options to install.

ADEME at www.ademe.fr has information on various types of renewable energy, including solar, wood burning, biomass and geothermal energy. It also has a downloadable PDF about windpower (*eoliens*), in French.

ADEME principally encourages wood burning as the main French renewable energy source, because it provides employment, leads to good forest management and wood is readily available.

One ADEME campaign is *Plan Soleil*, under which you can obtain a (modest, and reducing) subsidy for installing solar-driven hot water or heating systems. Between 2000 and 2006, 27,000 French households took advantage of *Plan Soleil* to install a CESI (*chauffe-eau solaire individuel*) – a solar-driven system that supplies 50-70 per cent of their hot-water needs.

Plan Soleil is available everywhere in France, including the north.

For information on windpower in France, visit www.suivi-eolien.com/anglais. This website covers news and views of windpower in France, and also shows a map of the windiest areas in France, which, not surprisingly, are mainly the coastal regions.

Phones

Due to market deregulation, getting connected to both landline and mobile phones is now more complicated than it used to be. France Télécom (FT) is the default option, though it may not be the cheapest, and is well worth considering if you are new to France and/or do not speak the language well. You can always change service provider later.

Installing a new line

Although the phone market is partially deregulated in France, FT still owns the lines. When you move into your new property in France, if there is no existing phone line, go to your local FT office with proof of address and your passport, and ask for an estimate of the installation cost.

In my rural property, installation took several weeks because FT had to put in six telegraph poles down the driveway, but usually it is quicker than this. Business lines are given priority over private lines, so if you are intending to run a business, make sure to stress this (you will have to pay a professional tariff, however, so check your options carefully). Phone lines generally run overground in France but you can ask for yours to run underground if you find this unsightly, though there is an extra charge for the ditches to be dug.

Taking over an existing line

If there is currently a line, you just need to change the account to your name and then you'll be given a new phone number (the phone number always changes when a property changes ownership or tenancy). This normally takes a couple of days. As you would in the UK, check that the previous owner/occupier has paid their bill up-to-date.

Market deregulation

FT used to have a monopoly on service provision, but it now has rivals in every direction. Accordingly, the company itself now offers additional services such an Internet service provision (via Orange, formerly Wanadoo) and television over broadband. This makes your choice of provider more complicated than previously.

Once you've got your phone line up and running, take a look at alternative phone service providers such as Cégétel and NeufTélécom. All such providers advertise in the English-language press, and it's worth seeing if their offers correspond with your needs (friends and family, international calls, etc.)

If you require broadband (ADSL), you can upgrade an existing phone line free of charge via FT: you can then opt to make your phone calls via the Internet, using Voice over IP. (For Internet Service Providers see Chapter 8.) If you think you will require ONLY broadband and VoIP, and do not want a landline at all, you can contact an ISP such as Alice (formerly Tiscali) and they will handle the line installation for you. It will still be done by France Télécom, but you will not deal with them directly.

In reality, some people end up with a mix of providers. In our extremely rural location, ADSL provision is not available and we have to settle for very slow speed wireless broadband for Internet access, obtained through wireless provider Altitude Télécom, while our phone landlines are rented from France Télécom. We make our phone calls through Cégétel. This, obviously, means getting three sets of bills, but though complicated, it is at least cheaper.

The FT office

If you decide for the time being (probably the simplest option) to go with FT, it's best to be up to speed with your needs before you pay your visit to the office – work out how many phone lines you need for the property, whether they are for business or personal use, whether or not you need broadband, how many phone sockets you have or may require, and what kinds of handsets you want to buy.

Most handsets in France are cordless. FT make their own, and other leading makes include Siemens, Sagem, Philips, Logicom, Alcatel and Thomson, all of which can be ordered from office supply catalogues such as JPG (see Chapter 4), or from retailers such as Conforama. Your existing British handsets may work on the French system but not properly, and in any case, are not approved for such use (the same applies to modems and fax machines).

Bills

You are billed for your line rental every eight weeks and can pay for it in a number of ways, though most people choose *prélèvement automatique* (direct debit), especially if they have a holiday home, as this prevents any problems with late payment. To set up a DD you'll need to take along an RIB when you visit the FT office.

If you don't wish to pay by DD, you can pay by cheque or at the post office, but if you to and fro between France and the UK, you do risk missing a bill. Should you ever miss a payment, you won't be cut off straightaway but instead your service will be progressively reduced and you will be sent warning reminders before the service is removed entirely.

If you opt for phone service provision through a third party, you may be *groupe* (still pay line rental to FT) or *degroupe* (pay your line rental to the third party provider), depending on your geographical location. If you are *groupe*, you will receive bills from FT and your service provider, while if you are *degroupe*, you'll only receive bills from your service provider.

Directories

Once you have a phone number it normally appears in the local *Pages Blanches* directory, which also appears online at www.pagesjaunes.fr.

Depending on where you live, the *Pages Blanches/Pages Jaunes* may be one or several volumes. In Paris, there are seven (five white, two yellow), but in my rural area the phone directory is a single volume, with the domestic numbers running from front to back and the yellow pages running from back to front. If you wish, you can opt not to have the printed version delivered to you, for ecological reasons. All the numbers, France-wide, can be accessed online.

You're supplied with a free copy of the *Pages Jaunes/Pages Blanches* every year, for every phone line that you have, but it only covers your *département*.

This can be awkward if, like me, you live right on the border of one *département* and tend to do your shopping in the other. You can order directories for other *départements* from the post office for a fee, but I usually do a swap with friends in the other *département* who are in the same boat.

If you wish to be ex-directory, there are several levels to choose from:

- *Liste orange* means your details aren't made available to businesses.
- *Liste chamois* exempts you from inclusion in printed or online directories.
- *Liste rouge* means your number is not given out even by Directory Enquiries.

Mobile phones

There are three main providers of mobile phone services in France:

1. France Télécom (trading as Orange, www.orange.fr)
2. SFR (which has links to Cégétel, www.sfr.fr)
3. Bouygues (www.bouygues.fr)

They are all in fierce competition with one another, constantly expanding their networks, issuing new tariffs and changing their contracts, and before you decide on a provider, and even when you have one, it pays to keep an eye on the market via the ex-pat forums and specialist French websites to get a feel for how the offerings compare.

You can buy mobile phone handsets almost anywhere, including online and via catalogues, or mobile phone shops can set you up with both a handset and a contract, as in the UK, in which case you usually get the handset cheap or free. Handset makes are the same as in the UK – there are the familiar names such as Ericsson, Nokia, and so on, but also include makes such as Sagem.

Top tips

- Electricity in France is usually supplied by state company EDF, though it no longer has a monopoly.
- Nearly all electricity in France is nuclear-generated.
- The electrical supply in rural areas generally runs via overhead cable and is subject to surges and brownouts.
- Wood is a major source of fuel in France, with some houses being run on wood-fired central heating.
- Mains water in France is privatised and run by companies such as Vivendi.
- In rural areas, many properties currently function on well water, though there is a drive to bring houses within the village boundaries onto the mains supply.
- Towns and cities have mains sewerage but many rural properties continue to rely on a septic tank.
- Recycling is very popular in France, with nearly every village boasting bins for glass, paper and plastic.
- Not all French villages collect rubbish from your house or lane – you may have to take it to a central collection point.
- Mains gas is usually supplied by state company GDF, though it no longer has a monopoly.
- In rural areas, many houses are not on mains gas and rely on other forms of cooking fuel, including wood-burning cookers.
- Coal is scarce in France and renewable energy is still in its infancy.

Glossary

Puissance – Power rating

Gîte – Self-catering holiday cottage

Prélèvement – Direct debit

Disjoncteur – Mains electricity circuit breaker

Liquide – Cash

Stère – One cubic metre

Cord – Three cubic metres

Ramonage – Chimney sweeping

Bûche de ramonage – Special cleaning logs designed to clean the flue

Hérisson – Literally "hedgehog" but also a chimney sweeping brush

Poêle à bois – Woodburner

Brocante – Second-hand shop

Eaux – Water distribution/services

Pages Jaunes – Yellow Pages, business directory

Potable – Drinkable

Mairie – Mayor's office

Poubelle – Dustbin

Déchetterie – Local refuse centre (dump)

Pharmacie – Pharmacy/chemist

Gaz de ville – Mains gas

Fioul – Oil-fired central heating

Citerne – Large tank

Vente charbon – Coal supplier

Eolien – Windpower/windfarm

Chauffe-eau solaire individual (CESI) – Domestic solar-driven water heater

Pages Blanches – White Pages, residential directory

7 Internet

Broadband coverage is generally better in France than in the UK, as it is mandated by the government. However, the situation is changing all the time, so the following can only be taken as a general guide.

France lagged behind the UK somewhat at the start of the Internet boom because many houses already had Minitel terminals with which they were well satisfied. Now, however, the French are among the world's most frequent online purchasers. This isn't to say, however, that they are buying from French companies – French trading regulations still mean that the websites of many French companies are only shop windows and you still cannot buy their goods online.

There are many French Internet service providers (ISPs) including: Orange, Cégétel, Neuf Télécom and Tiscali. For full details of current providers visit: www.lesproviders.com, www.budgetelecom.com or look in any French Internet magazine (found in the local *presse*). Which Internet service is best for you depends, as in the UK, on your needs, expenditure and location.

Providers offer a variety of packages, with some charging a flat monthly fee for unlimited access, while others offer add-ons such as television and telephone services, so it pays to shop around. Even after you've signed up, you can expect to be cold-called regularly by other providers, keen to steal your business. Annoying as this may be, it can often alert you to bargains you weren't aware of.

Which provider you choose also depends on what's available in your area. Most *départements* aim to offer broadband coverage in the high 90th percentile, but if you're in a very rural area you might find that your local connection is at a far lower speed than those available in cities. You might even have to rely on wireless connection, in which case your providers will be limited to suppliers such as Altitude Télécom. Providers always quote their highest speeds, so be careful not to be misled in this regard – the difference can be in the order of magnitude of 20 times between landline city and wireless country speeds.

Some ISPs offer reduced prices or more services if they can connect to you independent of the national provider. This is called *degroupage*. To find out if you are *degroupée*, visit: www.degrouptest.com and run the tests provided.

Most broadband providers provide you with a modem box as part of your package – often with a fancy name such as the Alice Box. This may be a combined modem/router. However, if you don't need, or can't access broadband and you still have a British modem, you can use this on the French system, though it may require an adapter in order to receive faxes. You can obtain a telephone adapter at: www.bigdishsatellite.com. The easiest thing to do, however, is to buy a French modem – then if a problem arises, at least you know it's not the modem or cable.

To remain current on the changes in French Internet access, check out websites such as www.livingfrance.com, or www.angloinfo.com, and consider joining the forums. Here, you can access up-to-date information on technological changes nationwide and ask any individual questions you may have.

Buying goods online

If you want to buy books, CDs, videos and DVDs online in France, a good first port of call is Amazon France (www.amazon.fr). However, the company does not have Homes and Garden or Toys and Games sections.

Books on Amazon

Amazon France now has over 800,000 English-language books listed and free delivery kicks in at a much lower rate than with Amazon UK. See Books in Culture section for further information.

CDs on Amazon

There is no problem ordering CDs in France, and the French are big fans of English music, so you can often find your favourite bands just as usual. You can, however, often get better deals from Amazon UK Marketplace resellers if you're willing to wait longer for delivery.

DVDs on Amazon

DVDs from Amazon France are Zone 2 and therefore playable on a French or UK player. However, they may be the French edition, which means they may lack certain features such as English subtitles for the deaf, or extras such as documentaries and director's commentaries. The choice of languages may also be different from the UK edition, so ensure that English is definitely an option before you buy. Bear in mind that films often have a different title in French (for instance, '*Il faut sauver le soldat Ryan*' for 'Saving Private Ryan'). The same subtitle problem applies to French-version DVDs you buy in shops or any other online vendor.

DVDs from .com or any other US vendor are generally Zone 1 and can only be played on a multizone DVD player.

Videos on Amazon

French videos are *Secam*, which means they won't play on a PAL video cassette recorder (if you have brought one over from the UK). You're very unlikely to find English-language videos on Amazon.fr and will probably have to order from .co.uk.

Other items, other vendors

There are, of course, thousands of other online outlets worldwide where you can obtain a wide range of goods for delivery to France. eBay.co.uk is a godsend for expatriates, particularly for items such as clothing. French clothing styles can be very different from British styles (for instance, the full, long skirt beloved of so many Englishwomen is not worn much by the French). French clothing prices, especially in the countryside, can also be far higher than in the UK (which has benefited from a drop in real pricing in the past decade). However, French goods are usually of high quality and often very stylish.

If you want new, rather than used, clothing from eBay, you need to specify BNWT (brand new with tags) on the UK site or NWT (new with tags) on the US site when you search for items. You should also take full advantage of individual eBay vendors' online shops. Be aware, however, that since 9/11, US postal regulations have become so tight that many US-based eBay vendors are no longer willing to sell to customers in Europe.

Many UK companies have online shops and will deliver to France. They include such leading brands as Marks and Spencer, The Body Shop, Neal's Yard, Boden and Orvis. When ordering online, be careful to take delivery charges to France into account, as costs can vary widely – it's usually worthwhile to buy several items at one time. For online stores that only deliver to the UK, it can be handy to come to some sort of deal with a UK-based friend or relative whereby they send the goods on. This particularly applies to heavy items or electrical goods, as companies will not generally supply to a country where they cannot fulfil their guarantee.

Top tips

- Rural provision of broadband in France can be much slower than in cities.
- Wireless provision will cover where there is no landline.
- Companies such as Amazon and eBay are good ports of call for goods that are expensive or difficult to obtain in France.
- Many UK companies now have an online presence and will deliver to France.
- For those that will not, come to an arrangement with a UK-based friend or relative.

Glossary

Presse – Newsagent

Département – Geographical area similar to a county. France is divided geographically into 100 *départements*

8

Media

What do the French read?

There are numerous French newspapers, but the French are not as avid newspaper readers as the English. Foremost among the French papers are 'Le Figaro' and 'Le Monde', which are both well-respected and long-standing publications, with 'Le Monde' covering the liberal viewpoint, while 'Le Figaro' is more conservative. Other newspapers with a wide circulation include the left-wing title 'Liberation' and French finance paper 'La Tribune'.

The French are also fond of their regional newspapers and one of these, 'Ouest France', is actually France's biggest selling daily paper.

More French people read magazines than read newspapers, and the newspapers also publish weekly magazines (spin-off titles such as 'Mme Figaro' have a wide readership). Magazines include current affairs publications such as 'Le Nouvel Observateur', 'Marianne' and 'Paris Match', which cover ground that might be covered by newspapers in the UK, while many of the women's magazine titles are familiar from the UK, such as 'Elle' and 'Marie Claire'.

Reading French newspapers and magazines is a very good way to improve your French, particularly if you choose a subject in which you are interested, and there is a magazine to cover virtually every subject.

There is no real French tabloid press as such, due to France's strict privacy laws. It is, for instance, very difficult to publish a picture of someone without their written consent in France. However, celebrities and gossip are both covered in 'Hello' magazine territory.

You can buy newspapers and magazines at the *presse* or *tabac*, in the supermarket and at most railway stations.

Books

Most French towns have a few shops selling books, such as the local *tabac/presse*, which will generally sell bestsellers and books of local interest. Availability of books is strictly controlled by the government to prevent small businesses going out of business, and there are no discount bookshops. Books, therefore, are comparatively expensive compared with UK prices.

English-language newspapers and magazines are available in any town that has a significant British population, and can usually be found at the local supermarket or *presse*. If in doubt, ask – if enough clients ask, the proprietor will generally consider ordering the papers in. Common titles include the 'Daily Express', 'Daily Mirror' and 'Guardian'.

You can order your daily paper by subscription, but this is a very expensive option, as the papers have to be airmailed. Costs are often over £2 for a paper with a 50p cover price in the UK.

You can also order a subscription to weekly print editions of many English newspapers, including the 'Weekly Telegraph' and the 'Guardian Weekly'.

Many English readers nowadays prefer to read their newspaper online, which is far cheaper. Online editions usually offer a selection of articles from the various sections rather than the whole newspaper. The whole paper is usually only available on subscription and you cannot buy a single edition, so subscribing to more than one UK newspaper can prove expensive. As technology gains pace, online papers are becoming more interactive, with 'look-alike' editions coming on-stream, and versions that download to your mobile phone.

Online offerings include:

- Daily Mirror: www.mirror.co.uk and its sister sites: www.sundaymirror.co.uk and www.people.co.uk
- Guardian: www.guardian.co.uk, which also has a subscription-only online paper that 'looks' like the real thing at: www.guardian.co.uk/digitaledition
- Telegraph: www.telegraph.co.uk

English-language books

Those who like to browse around real-life bookshops for their English-language books will have to trek to the nearest large town or a city such as Paris, which has several, including the famous Shakespeare and Company.

English-language books are expensive in France, partly because they are not VAT-free as UK buyers are used to, and it's more economical to order books online. Amazon France (www.amazon.fr) has hundreds of thousands of

English-language titles, which are economically priced and offer next day delivery for items that are in stock (though many are not in stock and have to be ordered from the US or the UK). Free delivery also kicks in at a much lower level than in the UK.

For titles that are not obtainable on Amazon France, you can order from www.amazon.co.uk, which offers fast delivery. Even ordering from Amazon.com doesn't entail too long a wait. Although ordering from Amazon Marketplace resellers can cut costs enormously, delivery can take much longer.

eBay (.com or .co.uk) is another good source for books, but you can find it hard to get your money back if a book should go missing in transit. There are also myriad second-hand resellers online, such as AbeBooks (www.abebooks.com), which specialise in out of print or hard to find publications.

You are liable for import duties on books ordered from outside the EU, but French Customs don't stop all books coming into the country. Bear this extra cost in mind, however, when calculating the total purchase price.

Public libraries

Joining your local library can prove a good way to improve your French. Most French libraries outside the major cities don't possess English books, but a good French coffee-table book on a subject that interests you can always prove a worthwhile route into learning French. Libraries often have DVDs and CDs as well as books, but expect rural libraries to have extremely limited opening times – often only a few hours a day and a few days a week.

Television

French terrestrial television has a poor reputation compared with UK television and, unfortunately, it is largely deserved. If your taste runs to wall-to-wall gameshows, dubbed American series – often decades old – and reality TV, then you're quids-in.

Quality drama, arts and political analysis are harder to find, but the Arté channel is very good, and France 2 has a good reputation for news, particularly the 19-20 evening programme from 7.00pm to 8.00pm.

Most programmes on French terrestrial television are in French, including those made originally in English, which are generally dubbed. Subtitles are rare, but occasionally Arté runs films in *version original* (VO), so if a film was made in English, it may be shown in English. Don't get your hopes up too high for films from the 1980s and before, however, as at this time, the original print bought by the network was often dubbed – this means that although it may be listed as VO, it will be in French.

The new digital offerings give you a greater variety of channels free of charge, but for a wider selection you'll need a cable or satellite package. These provide a greater variety of arts programming, such as the Paris Première channel (theatre, film, music) and Mezzo channel (classical music and jazz). The two largest providers, TPS Satellite and Canal Satellite, recently merged their offerings.

French satellite packages usually offer 100 or so channels, most of them in French. You usually have an option to view films in VO, which means you get to see them in their original language. However, although this is useful for English-language films, it isn't much help for films from Germany, Italy, Japan, etc. Documentaries, television dramas and soaps, etc., are usually dubbed.

French satellite packages include just a handful of English-language channels, such as BBC World (news), BBC Prime (repeats), CNN International, Bloomberg, MTV and Fashion TV. The latest addition is France 24, a 24-hour news station giving the French take on international affairs.

Having exclusively or primarily French television can be a good way to learn the language, but eventually most Britons, even the best-intentioned, fall back on a UK satellite package. You can access the UK-based free-to-air programming on the Astra2 satellite (which broadcasts Sky Digital), and this includes channels such as the following: BBC 1, 2, 3, 4, CBBC, BBCParliament, BBCNews24, Skynews, ITV 1, 2, 3, 4, ITV News, Euronews, CNN, SC4-Digidol, Extremesports, The Vault, LiveTV, Rapture, ChartshowTV, MotorsTV, Hollywoodclassics, cartoons, BBC Radio 1,2,3,4,5,6,7, World Service and ClassicFM.

However, Sky's licence only covers the UK and Ireland so this sort of package does not give you legal access to the encrypted channels such as Sky One and Sky Cinemas. For these, you'll have to pay extra.

You can find satellite installers for your region by logging onto www.angloinfo.com and going to the correct site for your area, or by reading the adverts in publications such as 'French Property News'. They should be able to inform you of the options available in your area.

Radio

French radio is, again, an ideal way to learn French, but if you prefer English-language radio, the World Service is available on short wave (www.bbc.co.uk/worldservice). You can also listen on FM at the following frequencies:

- Antibes Radio Riviera 106.3FM
- Cannes Radio Riviera 106.5FM
- Menton Radio Riviera 100.5FM
- Nice Radio Riviera 100.7FM
- St Tropez Radio Riviera 100.9FM
- Villefranche Radio Riviera 100.9FM
- The Breeze (various towns) 88.4FM

You can also receive English-language radio channels via many satellite television packages, and many are also available by live streaming on the Internet, for instance BBC Radios 1-7 (see www.bbc.co.uk). For this, however, you'll need to check that your broadband connection is fast enough.

Cinema

If you want to watch English-language films, in English at a French cinema, you're best off in a large city such as Paris.

Outside the cities, most English-language films are dubbed into French, though you do get occasional VO programming. Search on www.cinefil.com for details – you'll need to type in your departmental number in order to search, and films are labelled VF (*version française*), VO, N (*nouveauté*) or A (*avant-première*). In general, English-language films made for a mass audience – particularly children – are distributed in a French print and are NOT available in VO.

Cinemas are likely to be multiplex and free seating (i.e. you can sit anywhere), while the words *Grande Salle* or *Salle Prestige* outside a cinema indicate a high-end auditorium. As in the UK, *matinée* and Monday screenings are often cheaper, and so are screenings on Wednesdays, because of school half-day closing. Tickets are cut-price for children under 18, students with a valid student card, the unemployed, and pensioners.

You may be able to join a cinema club if you live in a city, which may give you access to more VO films, though these will not necessarily be in English.

France, is, of course, famous for its film festivals, especially Cannes (Cannes Film Festival), and Deauville (American Film Festival), and there are also a number of film magazines, including 'Première' and 'Studio'.

If you decide to try watching French films, or English-language films dubbed into French, start with action films with strong plots that don't rely on words – these are by far the easiest to follow.

Top tips

- The French prefer to read magazines rather than newspapers.
- Books are expensive compared to UK prices.
- English language books can be ordered from Amazon France at www.amazon.fr
- French terrestrial television has a poor reputation, which is largely deserved.
- Cinemas showing English-language films are rare outside the large cities.

Glossary

Presse – Newsagent

Tabac – Tobacconist – often a cafe and/or bar, too. These also sell newspapers, lottery tickets, phone cards etc.

Version original (VO) – In native language (films and television)

Version française (VF) – Dubbed into French (films and television)

Nouveauté (N) – New, particularly in regard to films

Avant-première (A) – Sneak preview

Grande Salle/Salle Prestige – Indicates a high-end auditorium (seen outside cinemas)

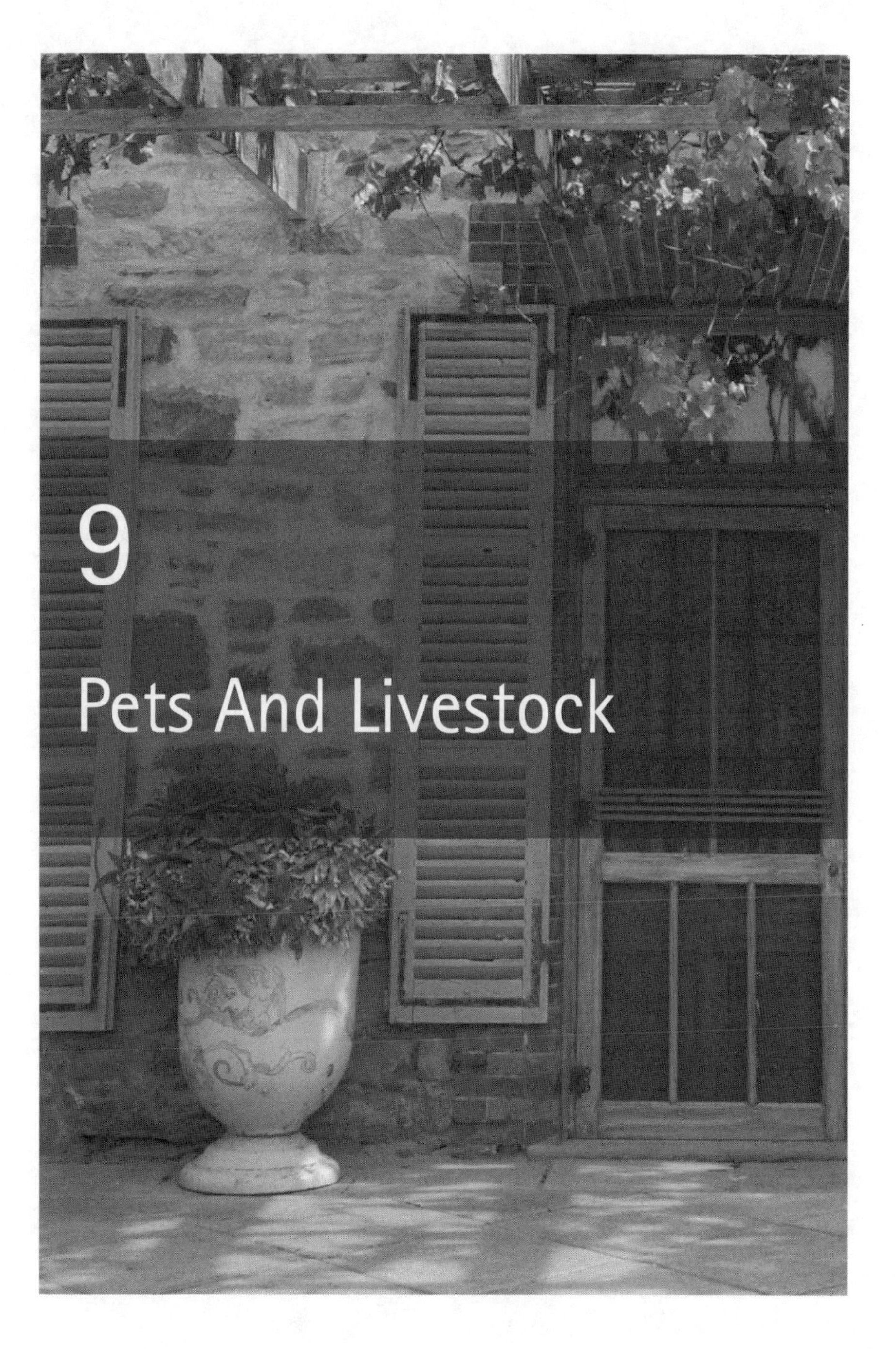

9

Pets And Livestock

French attitude to pets

The French are generally either completely ga-ga or completely unsentimental about their animals. Over one in two French households has a pet and, particularly in cities, dogs – and sometimes cats – are often pampered beyond belief. The Poodle remains, unsurprisingly, the French dog of choice, but is closely followed by the Labrador, though next-up is the pocket-sized Yorkie.

The majority of French dogs and cats (and rabbits, rodents, birds and pet fish) live in rural areas or small towns. However, in rural areas dogs are often kept as guard animals or for hunting rather than for companionship and may be kept permanently caged or tethered, much to the distress of the visiting British. Neutering is also uncommon in these cases. Country cats, meanwhile, are often regarded as essentially wild, and left both unvaccinated and un-neutered. Cat flu and feline AIDS are rife in many areas of France, so make sure your pets are inoculated if they are allowed outside.

If you go for a walk at night in a French village, you are liable to set every dog in the neighbourhood barking, and if you walk your dog in the countryside, you're quite likely to never meet a fellow dog-walker unless they're a fellow Brit. However, walking your dog around the neighbourhood is a great talking point, and an excellent way to meet your French neighbours.

In towns and villages most people walk their domestic dogs around parks, gardens and the local *plan d'eau*, where regulations usually stipulate that your dog should be on a lead (especially if there are ducks on the pond). The French are not as fond of dangerous breeds of dog as the British, but be aware that some breeds such as spaniels and setters, which are regarded as domestic in the UK, may be given a wary eye by French passers-by, who regard them as *chiens de chasse* – hunting dogs. "*Il n'est pas méchant*" is a useful phrase to have ready to reassure nervous pedestrians.

As most British visitors will already know, French towns and cities have a high proportion of dog excrement on the pavements, although it is technically illegal to allow your dog to soil the pavement. If you're out with your dog, take a pooper-scooper with you – if you don't clear up, you're liable to a fine. Many parks have dog-toilets and some streets in towns and villages have dog-poo bins, with names like *Toutounet,* which also dispense plastic bags.

Identification of animals

Under France's *Code Rural*, all 'domestic carnivores' (that's dogs, cats and ferrets) must be identified once they reach a certain age. Identification may be by tattoo (*tatouage*) of a seven-digit number in the animal's ear, or by means of a microchip (*puce*) inserted subcutaneously. The task must be performed by a vet or other representative of the French ministry of agriculture and fisheries.

Dogs

ALL dogs older than four months, born since 6 January 1999, must be identified.

ALL dogs must be identified when they are bought or sold.

ALL dogs in any *département* where rabies is present must be identified.

ALL dogs introduced into France, whether from the European Union or elsewhere, must be identified.

Cats

ALL cats must be identified when they are bought or sold.

ALL cats in any *département* where rabies is present must be identified.

ALL cats introduced into France, whether from the European Union or elsewhere, must be identified.

Ferrets

ALL ferrets in any *département* where rabies is present must be identified.

ALL ferrets introduced into France, whether from the European Union or elsewhere, must be identified.

Buying and selling pets

Puppies and kittens cannot be sold under the age of eight weeks, and all animals must have a veterinary health certificate before they are sold. However, this is not necessary if you are giving the animal away. For instance, at a local market in springtime, you may find people giving away the latest crop of kittens *"à bons soins"*.

Travelling with pets

For travelling between France and the UK, see page 27 and contact DEFRA for more details.

If you wish to travel with your dog or cat within France, it's a wise move to obtain a full set of vaccinations and make sure their flea and tick care is up-to-date. Most hotels and campsites will accept dogs, provided they are chipped, vaccinated and 'well-behaved'. You can also take your pets on a train (see Chapter 12) for a small fee. Dogs, if well-behaved, are also usually welcome in restaurants, even high-end ones, though it pays to ask in advance.

If you want your pet to stay in kennels, consult the local *Pages Jaunes* or ask your vet for a recommendation. It obviously pays to make a visit in person before committing yourself, and be aware that kennels generally won't take pets that aren't up-to-date with their vaccines, including rabies, and (for dogs) kennel cough.

Pet sitters are starting to appear in France. The best place to look for one is at the local veterinary *cabinets*, or in '*30 Millions d'Amis*' magazine (which also has a website at: www.30millionsdamis.fr).

Where to obtain pets

You can buy pets from a breeder (search online as a first option), your vet, some local markets, local rescue centres (SPA) and from the local paper. The advantage and risks of each are the same as in the UK. If you're looking for a pedigree animal, you'll need a registered breeder, but if you just want a mutt, then the vet, paper or rescue centre is the usual port of call.

Be aware that spaying and castrating animals costs a lot of money in France, which means that in rural areas every spring and summer there is an endless supply of farmyard kittens, many of which are drowned when owners cannot be found for them. Once you are up to your ideal cat quota, STOP! More than one Brit has been suckered into picking up every waif and stray in the neighbourhood and ending up with tens of animals they can't afford to feed or house.

Visiting the vet

French veterinary surgeries are usually very well equipped and staffed and some vets are even trained in homeopathy, just like French doctors. However, in rural areas, some vets are not used to small animal practice, so shop around and see who has the kind of attitude you're looking for if you don't want your domestic animals treated like livestock.

Veterinary fees in France are generally modest compared with those in the UK, but call-out fees for home visits are substantially higher than attending the *cabinet* in person. Fees are posted somewhere in the waiting room, and there is usually a notice with information about puppies and kittens for sale, adverts for drugs, and legislation affecting animals. You can also buy animal feed and treatments, car carriers, dog cages and all manner of peripherals (if you want something, ask if there's a catalogue available).

At the vet's, domestic animals are normally given a dossier containing a *carnet de santé* that lists all their treatments and inoculations, flea and tick treatments, etc. Annual vaccination for cats and dogs is not obligatory in France, but bear in mind that some diseases common in France are not well known in the UK. These include:

Leptospirose: can be carried by wild animals such as *ragondins* (muskrats).

Piroplasmose: babesiosis, a tick-borne disease that can kill within days or so damage the liver that the dog dies, seemingly unrelatedly, many years later. The vaccine is expensive and not effective against all strains, so you may prefer to simply keep your dog flea and tick-free.

Heartworm: endemic in the south of France.

Rabies: there is the occasional rabies scare in France, usually in the south.

The full range of operations, cancer treatments and everything else you would expect can normally be carried out in France, and most surgeries are well equipped with operating theatres, recovery areas, x-ray departments and blood testing laboratories. However, be aware that it can be difficult to find a vet out of hours in rural areas, and near-impossible to get a callout for a domestic animal – if a pet should fall sick, you may need to make an emergency dash to a vet in a larger town.

Pet food and other goods

Pet food can be found in a variety of locations, including veterinary surgeries. Most surgeries sell just one particular brand of high-end food such as Royal Canin or Hill's SciencePlan, so it pays to visit each *cabinet* in your area to see what's on offer – any item from the range can usually be ordered.

You can also find animal feed at DIY stores such as Mr Bricolage, including rabbit pellets, salt licks and chickenfeed. Also on sale will be dog leads and chewy bones, and bits and tethers for small livestock. The leading commercial food brands for domestic animals, such as Whiskas and César, can be found at the supermarket, along with French brands such as Frolic. Supermarkets also offer own-brand foods for dogs, cats, rabbits and birds, along with pet beds, cat litter, dog shampoo and toys.

You can find a wider range of these items, and in larger sizes, at DIY stores, where you might also find kennels, travelling cages and wooden rabbit hutches. Most towns also have one or more *toilettage canin* outlets (Poodle parlours), where you can take your dog (or cat) to be washed and trimmed: many also do home visits. Poodle parlours also sell leads and harnesses, plus other pet accoutrements.

At all of these outlets (other than the supermarket), if you are looking for something in particular, it's worth asking if there is a catalogue available. Mail order is very quick in France and next-day delivery is often possible.

What to do if you lose your pet

Inform your vet and local mayor straightaway, and offer a reward (it's not a bad idea in any case to make sure your dog has an identification disc with *recompense* on it, along with your phone number). Your pet will already have a microchip or tattoo, so if you make it worth their while, someone will bring your pet to the vet. You can also, as in the UK, take out an advertisement in the local paper. Be aware that in rural areas, cats are often shot by hunters, who regard them as competition, and many dogs are stolen in France every year. In this regard, it can help to have both a tattoo and a *puce* (chip) if your dog is a pedigree breed, as its identification is then more difficult to remove.

Abandoned and abused pets

Sadly, pets are abandoned in great numbers all over France every year, in spite of a government awareness campaign. The French sometimes leave their pets at the side of the road when they go away on holiday, while the British may do likewise when they find their local taxes are higher than they expected and they suddenly need to cut costs. Some British who return to the UK also simply leave their pets to their fate in France rather than pay for the necessary inoculations. Meanwhile, hunters will often abandon a hunting dog that can't find the prey or keeps getting lost, so coming across an abandoned animal is unfortunately not an unusual occurrence.

If you can corner the animal, get it caged and call the local SPA (*Société Protectrice des Animaux*) and also inform your mayor and the gendarmerie. You need not expect anyone to be especially interested, however, so be prepared to keep or rehome the animal yourself. Local farmers who spend all day alone on a tractor are sometimes grateful for the company of a dog if you ask around.

If you see an animal that you feel is being abused (including a dog trapped in a car on a hot day), phone the local *gendarmerie*. Animal abuse is illegal in France, and the police are, for instance, empowered to break a car window if the animal's life is endangered. Farming and fisheries regulations are also strictly enforceable for livestock, so if you see any that are living in parlous conditions, report it – food hygiene and safety rules are golden in France.

Dangerous dogs

If you believe you know of a dangerous dog, inform the local police and your mayor. There are strict regulations pertaining to dangerous dogs, which may not be owned by minors or anyone with a criminal conviction, and which must be kept muzzled and on leads in public. See Chapter 2 for information on which breeds are considered dangerous.

Rescue centres

The SPA (www.spa.asso.fr) is run on a local and regional level and is not a national body like the RSPCA. It promotes animal welfare via its website, its magazine '*Animaux*' and a newsletter. Sadly, however, it only has about 38 rescue centres nationwide (in contrast, the RSPCA has hundreds of outlets and over 50 rescue centres), which means that overcrowding is common and euthanasia is often the only option for many of the animals that arrive there.

Non-SPA rescue centres vary in quality, but may have different regulations, such as a no-kill policy. Some have been set up by British ex-pats. If you find an abandoned animal, ask at your local veterinary surgeries and look online to see if there is an independent rescue centre in your region.

A list of French rescue sites can be found here: www.viva-vous.net. Type *refuges* into the search box.

Livestock

The keeping of livestock is heavily regulated in France. Animals must generally be registered, tagged in some form, their slaughter must be declared, and they must have 'passports' in order to be transported. You may not sell the produce from animals you raise (eggs, meat, skins) without registering as a business, though you are allowed to give it away.

Livestock regulations are enforced by the GDS (*Groupement de Défense Sanitaire*), which provides information (in French) here: www.gds38.asso.fr. To find out the regulations on identification, type *identifications bovins/ovins/équidés* etc. To find out the regulations on ear tagging, type *boucles* into the search engine and choose *formulaires de boucles*. The GDS is a national body, but another body which takes responsibility at departmental level is the EDE (*Établissement Départemental d'Élèvage*).

Sheep and goats

Since the advent of Foot and Mouth (*fièvre aphteuse*) disease in 2001, French regulations on sheep and goats have been tightened. All animals must now be tagged, or owners face a hefty fine. Tags are yellow plastic with two sets of numbers, and the animal must carry this tag for the whole of its life. It must also be registered, and its papers must accompany it whenever it is moved, bought or sold. When you have the animal put down or slaughtered, this must also be officially declared.

Horses and donkeys

Horses are not tagged in the ear in France. 'Passports' with a description of the horse's markings are now obligatory, as throughout the Europe Union since January 2008, all horses must now be microchipped (this formerly applied only to horses intended for consumption).

Cattle

Cattle are currently identified by ear tags with numbers, but due to the large amount of these that simply fall out each year, different *départements* are trying different designs, including buttons that incorporate a microchip (*puce*). Animals must be tagged in both ears, and must also be registered with the national database.

Fowl

Regulations on domestic fowl are fluid, because of the possibility of HN51 bird flu arriving from Asia. To stay abreast of regulations in your *département*, visit the www.grippeaviaire.gouv.fr website regularly. If you want to keep a few chickens for the eggs, ask your *mairie* for the local regulations – often these only apply to nuisance (such as a cockerel annoying your neighbours) or the size of the chicken coop you're planning to install. If bird flu arrives in your region, you can expect to be required to keep your fowl under cover rather than free range but need not take any more drastic measures until ordered to do so.

Rabbits

Many French people keep rabbits for the pot rather than as pets. French hutches are normally made of concrete and slot together like a house of cards – they are cleaned by blowtorching. A combination of grass and kitchen scraps should keep eating rabbits healthy enough to be slaughtered at the optimum age of three months. If you're keeping rabbits as pets, consult your veterinarian for advice on vaccinations, etc.

Top tips

- In France, all domestic carnivores (dogs, cats and ferrets) must be identified once they reach a certain age. This is normally done by microchip or tattoo.
- Before you can sell an animal, it must be over eight weeks old and have a veterinary certificate. You can, however, give an animal away without a certificate.
- Travelling with your pets within France is quite easy. Many hotels, holiday cottages and campsites take dogs, though they usually require them to be chipped and vaccinated.
- Spaying and castrating pets is expensive in France. In rural areas, very few animals are neutered.
- Veterinary surgeries are well staffed and equipped but vets outside towns may not be used to small animal practice.
- You can buy pet food at the supermarket, DIY outlets and the veterinary surgery.
- The French animal rescue association is the SPA, but it is underfunded and has few centres compared with the RSPCA.
- The keeping of livestock is heavily regulated in France because of the food production chain. Make sure that you know the requirements for your particular livestock types.

Glossary

Plan d'eau – Public pond or boating lake

Chiens de chasse – Hunting dogs

Il n'est pas méchant – He is not mean/vicious

Tatouage – Tattooing

Puce – Microchip

Département – Geographical area similar to a county. France is divided geographically into 100 *départements*

À bons soins – To a good home

Pages Jaunes – Yellow Pages, business directory

Cabinets – Practice, as in veterinary, etc.

Carnet de santé – A dossier issued by the vet for a domestic animal, which lists all their treatments and inoculations, flea and tick treatments, etc.

Ragondins – Muskrats

Toilettage canin – Dog grooming

Recompense – Reward

Société Protectrice des Animaux (SPA) – Society for the Protection of Animals (equivalent to RSPCA)

Gendarmerie – Military body charged with police duties among the civilian population (effectively acts as the police force in many areas, including small towns, but differs from the civilian police force in being under the jurisdiction of the ministry of defence)

Fièvre aphteuse – Foot and mouth

Mairie – Mayor's office

10

Gardens

Gardening in France can be very different from gardening in the UK. First and foremost, it's affected by climate. France's continental, mountainous and Mediterranean climates are not something experienced by the British gardener, and even in the areas designated as maritime, the weather can be more extreme than in the UK.

Everywhere in France you can generally expect summer temperatures to be higher than in Britain (sometimes VERY high, depending on your area), winter temperatures to be lower and winds to be stronger. This means you can also expect plants to grow larger than their UK equivalents.

To gain a good idea of what will grow in your area, take a walk around your neighbourhood and see what is in other people's gardens. Even in rural areas the French are far from the vegetable-loving flower-haters of repute, with every inch of ground laid out to *potager* – nearly every French garden contains flowers in joyous profusion, often with a startling and uninhibited use of colour, and in spite of formal French tradition, the more relaxed 'English' style of garden is greatly admired. Nationwide, joining the '*Villes Fleuries*' competition has transformed many French villages, which are now brilliant with colour all summer long as they compete for the coveted four roses designation. Towns and villages hoping for a place usually have a '*Ville Fleurie*' sign on the outskirts of town, and even the outlying farms join in.

In my area (Basse-Normandie), a quick glance around shows that camellias are particularly popular, as are shrimp-pink willows grown as standards, tea roses and bedding plants of every variety, while no window box goes without its geraniums. Colourful hedges are also very common. Often these are of one variety of bright evergreen such as photinia fraseri Red Robin, but the most popular are the *haies fleuries* – flowering hedges. These consist of robust shrubs such as weigela, variegated cornus, amelanchier and ceanothus, designed to offer a succession of colour throughout the season. Also popular are *haies de oiseaux*, which offer shelter and winter food for the birds.

Importing plants

You are allowed to bring plants with you from the UK to France. There are currently no restrictions on houseplants, but there are restrictions on certain shrubs. If you are moving to Corsica, this is a protected zone for Fire blight, and it is probably best not to take garden shrubs with you at all (for details of Fire blight host plants, visit the DEFRA site at: www.defra.gov.uk). Great Britain is also host to the fungus Phytophthora ramorum, which affects shrubs such as rhododendrons, camellias and viburnums. You may not export any members of these plant families without a commercial licence and health certificate – if Customs spot a plant in your car, it will be impounded and destroyed.

Buying plants in France

The French buy their plants from the same sorts of outlets as the British: plant nurseries, garden centres, supermarkets and other outlets such as grain stores and DIY shops. All such outlets also sell seeds and bulbs, though the range may be limited.

Plant nurseries

The cheapest option for plants is probably the plant nursery. It can often be difficult to tell from the outside whether a nursery is retail or trade only – just going up and asking is usually the best bet. You can expect the plants in nurseries to cover acres of ground, be potted up for the most part and there is usually little labelling. If you establish a good relationship with a nurseryman, however, this is the best place to order specific varieties you want. Bare-root trees are usually only available from November to March, and can be less than half the price of potted trees.

Garden centres

Garden centres such as Baobab are a relatively new phenomenon in France. The plants are more expensive than from a plant nursery, but the layout is more familiar to the average Briton and you can stock up on items like tools, paving and chipped bark at the same time. Plants are usually well labelled and include planting instructions – remember that heights and spreads are in metres.

Supermarkets

The seasonal supermarket offers on items such as lavender plants, roses or fruit trees are generally a good way to stock up on cheap, ordinary plants.

Bare-root fruit trees are a particularly good bargain. Always buy as soon as the stock arrives as storage conditions are far from ideal.

Other outlets

Outlets such as DIY stores and feed stores often sell plants, usually at competitive prices. Expect to find good fill-in and bulk plants such as heathers, leylandia and common shrubs like viburnum. You can also buy plants from mail-order catalogues such as *Jacques Briant* (www.jacques-briant.fr) – check in the back of a gardening magazine for details and be aware that the colours in catalogue photography are often startlingly oversaturated.

French savvy

When you want to buy plants in France, go armed with a French plant dictionary or handbook (not an English one translated into French). This is because although the species you come across are likely to be the same, the varieties will probably be different and it can be hard to work out expected heights and widths. For instance, the Cox's Orange Pippin apple tree isn't generally known in France (nor is the apple available in the shops), but you may find *Reine des Reinettes* or *Clochards* instead, which have a similar taste.

A French gardening book will also give you the correct planting instructions for your region, and cover items such as citrus fruits, vines, persimmons and olives, which are greenhouse plants in the UK but can be grown outside in many areas of France. One useful book if you want to grow fruit is '*L'abc du Verger*' by Jean-Yves Prat.

There are also many French gardening magazines available at the *presse*, including '*Mon Jardin*', '*100 Idées Jardin*', '*La Main Verte*' and '*Top Jardin*'.

UK mail order

France currently lacks a Plantfinder-type publication (though there are useful links here: www.cheminsdelarose.fr), so if you are in need of specific plants that your nurseryman can't supply, you can order them from the UK. The RHS Plantfinder can be found online at: www.rhs.org.uk. Nurseries vary as to whether they export to France or not, but many are happy to send over bare-root plants in the off-season (the cost of importing pot plants is prohibitively expensive).

Tools and equipment

France has excellent ranges of gardening tools but certain items may not be readily available, or may be different in design. French spades and forks, for instance, tend to be very flat (and often quite flimsy), though the curved, English style is becoming more common. Handles that you slot your hand through are usually not available either – French handles tend to be T-shaped. The Dutch hoe with a hollow blade that you use by pushing is also something I've never seen in France – French hoes have a solid blade and you work them by dragging. However, ranges such as *Rexel* are very high quality and electric items such as chainsaws, strimmers and shredders are seriously tough. Look out for makes such as *Ryobi* and *Karcher*.

French DIY stores and supermarkets often stock frighteningly strong weedkillers, slug repellents and poisons – check the ingredients and warnings on packaging if you are concerned about children, animals or the environment.

When you're starting a garden from scratch, it may take some shopping around at different outlets to find all the items you might find in one place in the UK. For instance, gravel chips and slabs might only come from a builder's merchant; reclaimed railway sleepers from the local DIY shop; your strimmer from a shop specialising in bikes and garden equipment; and your plants from several different nurseries and garden centres. Often, items aren't on display and have to be ordered – it is always worth asking, though some items, such as coco shell and biodegradable matting, often aren't available outside the cities.

A rewarding opportunity

Gardening in France presents some challenges but can also be fantastically rewarding, particularly if this is your first chance to plant up a large area. If you take an interest in your garden, this will also generally be respected by your neighbours, who may be keen to swap seeds and cuttings with you. Local gardening clubs are a good way to meet your fellow citizens and can give you access to private gardens that are only open to the public for a few days each summer. Often this is in order to host a *bourse aux plantes*, which is not, as it might sound, a plant swap, but is what might in the UK be termed a plant fair.

Part-time living

If your home in France is a holiday home, it's a good idea to pay someone to maintain your garden while you're away, at least to keep the grass cut and the brambles in check. Apart from anything else, this makes your property look cared for and occupied, which reduces your risk of being burgled.

If you know that your home will only be occupied for part of the year, take care to plant up your garden accordingly. This means choosing low-maintenance options such as hard-standing wherever possible, and shrubs and trees that don't require much TLC.

One useful tip is to plant every plant through a layer of plastic sheeting (known as *toile de paillage*), topped with bark or gravel – this reduces weeds and prevents too much temperature fluctuation in the soil. You should also aim for structure and foliage colour rather than flowers, with a good percentage of evergreen planting. If you holiday only at certain times of the year, choose plants that flower in the seasons when you'll be present – the summer, or Christmas for instance. It can be very irritating to turn up at your holiday home to find nothing but bare twigs and dying blossoms all over the garden when you know that two weeks earlier it looked splendid.

French gardening glossary

arroser – water

bêche/bêchette – hoe/hand hoe/spade

désherbent – weedkiller

fourche/fourchette – fork/hand fork

toile de paillage – plastic mulch (usually green and woven)

tremper – soak

cassissier – blackcurrant bush

cerisier – cherry tree

cognassier – quince tree

framboisier – raspberry bush

griotte/guigne/bigarreau/cerise – different types of cherry

grosellier à grappes – red or whitecurrant bush

groseillier à maquereau – gooseberry bush

kaki – Sharon fruit

mirabelle – a type of very small plum

néflier – medlar

noisettier – nut bush

poirier – pear tree

pommier – apple tree

Reine Claude – greengage

tailler – prune

Top tips

- Gardening successfully in France means being aware of your local climate.
- To see what will grow in your area, look in your neighbour's gardens.
- You are allowed to bring houseplants with you from the UK, but for garden plants, check with DEFRA.
- The French buy their plants mainly from nurseries – garden centres are an innovation.
- A French gardening book is invaluable, particularly if you want to grow fruit or vegetables.
- Some UK nurseries will supply to France – check the RHS Plantfinder for details.
- French tools are excellent but their hoes and spades are a different shape to UK ones.
- Dangerous poisons for rats, mice, moles and so on are readily available in France.
- If your French house is a holiday home, design the garden to be as low-maintenance as possible, and for impact specifically in the seasons when you visit.
- If you are away a lot, it is worthwhile hiring someone to maintain your garden, perhaps as part of a house-and-garden contract.

Glossary

Potager – Vegetable garden

Haies fleuries – Flowering hedges

Haies de oiseaux – Hedges which offer shelter and winter food for birds

Presse – Newsagent

Bourse aux plantes – A plant fair

Toile de paillage – Plastic sheeting/mulch, usually green and woven

Arroser – To water (as in plants)

Bêche/bêchette – Hoe/hand hoe/spade

Désherbent – Weedkiller

Fourche/fourchette – Fork/hand fork

Tremper – Soak

Cassissier – Blackcurrant bush

Cerisier – Cherry tree

Cognassier – Quince tree

Framboisier – Raspberry bush

Cerise/bigarreau/griotte/guigne – Different types of cherry

Grosellier à grappes – Red or whitecurrant bush

Groseillier à maquereau – Gooseberry bush

Kaki – Sharon fruit/persimmon

Mirabelle – A type of very small plum

Néflier – Medlar tree

Noisettier – Nut bush

Poirier – Pear tree

Pommier – Apple tree

Reine Claude – Greengage

Tailler – Prune

11

Car travel

Car travel in France

French roads

France has an extensive road network. On maps, roads are labelled A for *autoroute*, N for *nationale* or D for *départemental* (*nationale* and *départemental* tells you which body is in charge of maintaining them). N roads are always the equivalent of a UK A road, but seeing D on a map is no indication of what to expect – some D roads are on a par with UK A roads, and some are mere country tracks.

French motorways are generally toll roads, built by private companies, and are well surfaced and maintained. If you're making a long journey, take the tolls into account – you may find it cheaper to fly or take the train. There are also tolls on certain bridges and tunnels, as in the UK. See the AA website at www.theaa.com for current details.

French motorways and N roads usually offer a rest break roughly every 15 minutes of driving time. These are called *aires* and range from full service stations on motorways – see www.autoroute.fr for a list – to a bit of grass at the side of the road on a country D road (*aires de service* are handy for motorhome owners, as it usually means a place you can park up, get water and empty the chemical loo). Motorways are often emptier than you might expect because many people prefer to avoid the tolls – outside of the south, they are often a pleasure to drive on.

French dual carriageways are often motorway standard, with crash barriers and central reservation planting – the French frequently have extensive and beautiful roadside planting, including pollarded trees. In contrast to motorways, the dual carriageways and N roads are often busier than you might expect, because drivers are avoiding the motorway tolls.

French minor roads are often in better condition than English B roads, although they deteriorate fairly rapidly and tend to show the marks of annual patching. In areas where the road is bordered by hedges, these are cut annually with a special machine – watch out for signs saying *élagage* (pruning), as the machines may block the road. Long grass is cut back twice a year, usually in May and September – watch out for signs saying *fauchage* (reaping).

French drivers

France has a reputation for having some of the world's worst drivers and, sadly, it's close to the truth. France has about the same amount of road surface as the UK, but nearly twice the road deaths, and French drivers often drive with a carefree disregard for speed limits, drink limits and so on.

However, the situation is improving. Road deaths have fallen since the 1970s, and there is a solid government campaign against drink-driving – the idea of the designated driver has taken root in the French psyche and the penalties for drink-driving are higher than in the UK.

Be aware that French drivers do not flash their headlamps to indicate that they are giving way (such as on a narrow road or a hill), or in thanks – headlamps are used solely as alerts, either to say "Give way, I'm coming through", or "*gendarmes* ahead". If you are flashed by a succession of cars, it is almost certainly the latter.

Driving

Driving in France for the first time can be very unnerving if you haven't driven on the right before. As you leave the port or airport area, there are numerous warning signs telling you to Drive on the Right! – but once you've left locale you're on your own. Repeat the above as a mantra whenever you reach a junction and be very circumspect about overtaking if you're in a right-hand drive vehicle.

Most accidents occurring to British drivers take place when they turn right and cross lanes out of habit – this can be particularly easy when you've refuelled, pulled into a lay-by or are turning onto a quiet road where there is no other traffic to give you a clue.

Driving on the right is tiring until you get used to it, so allow for this and plan your journey accordingly, with frequent rest breaks. Remember too that France is a big country and it can take a lot of time to get from A to B – your road atlas or map may not be the same scale as you're used to in the UK, and allow a sensible target of kilometres per day if you are heading into the distance. Many driving accidents are caused by a driver falling asleep at the wheel, so monitor your tiredness levels, and bear in mind the effects of any medication you may have taken (do not drive if you took anything for motion sickness on the plane or ferry).

If you are planning to live in France permanently, you will probably be much more comfortable in a left-hand drive vehicle, as this gives you a better sightline when driving: passengers in a right-hand drive car can also feel very uncomfortable at the proximity of oncoming traffic. Learning to drive from the left-hand seat is generally easy for anyone right-handed, as the gear lever position is more instinctive. However, some Britons prefer to retain their existing car as something familiar at a time when they have already made major changes in moving country. For importing your UK car to France, see page 148.

French country driving can be a lot of fun, as traffic is usually light, but watch out for farm vehicles, which can be a source of frustration when you're stuck behind them for miles on end. Very wide vehicles on any road have to have both a car in front and a car behind, both labelled *convoi exceptionnel* or *grand largeur*) to warn approaching drivers that the road may effectively be blocked and that speeds may be down to a crawl. Nevertheless, even without this warning you can be caught out by the width of some farm machinery such as harrows, which may be much wider than the tractor towing them. Always slow down when approaching a tractor, particularly in low light levels, as the farm implement at the rear may not only may be difficult to see, it may also be bouncing about wildly. It is, incidentally, sometimes legal for a farmer to drive a tractor between fields even when he has lost his normal licence, so do not assume that the driver in charge is necessarily competent, or even sober!

Priorité a droite remains the standard on French roads unless otherwise indicated, meaning that traffic joining from the right has priority, no matter what the respective size of the roads. One sign you should watch out for, especially on country roads, is a triangular red-banded warning sign with a black X on a white background. This means traffic merging from the right has priority.

If you have priority, the sign is the same as the road junction sign in the UK – a thick black vertical arrow with a thin black horizontal bar.

Most minor joining roads now have stop signs or give way signs (*vous n'avez pas la priorité*, or *cedez le passage*) indicating that drivers should give way to the major road. Despite this, watch out for local people ignoring this and coming straight out at you from the right – *priorité a droite* is a deeply ingrained habit in France. It is especially dangerous at roundabouts, as not all joining roads have to give way to traffic already on the roundabout – and people also quite often ignore the give way signs.

A white pillar topped with a red stripe means you should watch out for farm traffic coming from the right – and be aware that a farmer perched up high may not see you.

Traffic congestion on French roads can be serious at certain times of the year and when it is expected to be particularly severe, the government issues 'red day' travel advisories, telling people to stay at home if their journey isn't absolutely necessary. Congestion days usually include the major bank holidays (*jours feriés*), 15 July (people travelling after the Bastille Day celebrations) and 15 August. However, the majority of the French take a holiday in August, so many major roads, including the motorways to the south and the roads around Paris, are chock-a-block throughout high summer.

Navigation

There is no substitute for having a good French road atlas in the car. The AA publishes them, as does Michelin. Larger-scale local area maps in the *Carte Bleue* series are also very useful, as these show even minor roads.

You can plan your route ahead of time with a service such as Google Earth, Mappy or Map24 (in French). A GPS that covers France is also very useful, but be aware that if you switch the electronic voice to English it may have little understanding of French pronunciation – roads with numbers are fine, but roads with names, such as rue de Bretagne might come out as rue de 'bretaggny'.

Rules and regulations

Driving a UK vehicle

If your lights are aligned for UK driving you must fit deflectors to avoid dazzling oncoming drivers. Details are available at the ferry port and deflectors are on sale, with instructions on where to place them (it varies according to the make and model of your vehicle).

Breakdown

All drivers in France must carry a spare set of headlight bulbs and a red warning triangle or hazard warning light, to warn following traffic in case of breakdown. It's also wise to carry high-visibility vests for every passenger, as is compulsory in Spain. Items such as these are available as part of a French driving kit sold at UK ports, which also contains headlamp stickers. The kit is also available in most French supermarkets.

Speed

When you see French speed signs, remember that they are in kilometres. If two speeds are indicated, you must obey the lower speed in poor driving conditions (rain, fog, etc.).

Throughout France, the maximum speeds in the dry are:

- Motorway: max 130kmph, min 80kmph
- Dual carriageways with central reservation: 110kmph
- Roads outside built-up areas: 90kmph
- Towns: 50kmph

All speed limits may be altered due to wet weather or other conditions. In practice, on motorways, the limit is often 110kmph, while approaches to towns, such as industrial estates or scattered housing, often have a limit of 70kmph even where the road is open and straight. Whenever you are in a French town or village, the maximum speed limit is 50kmph when you're between the place-name signs, but speeds may be set even lower – 30kmph isn't unusual on a tight bend or near a school, for instance. If you see a 20 or 30kmph sign with a speed bump, SLOW DOWN – these are very high and can easily trash your suspension if you take them too quickly.

If you have been driving for less than two years, you cannot go over 110kmph on any French motorway, regardless of the speed limit that applies.

Speed traps and cameras are common in France, and meet with the same degree of irritation and disdain as in the UK. Speed cameras are well flagged in advance by a sign warning you of *contrôles automatique* but the camera itself is often set quite low and hidden by vegetation. Carrying a speed camera detector in your car is illegal in France but you can find an up-to-date list of cameras at the French government site: www.securite-routiere.gouv.fr

The *gendarmes* often set up mobile speed traps at the entrance to villages, and they can fine you on the spot.

French road signs

Many French road signs are familiar to UK drivers, such as 'Stop', or picture signs showing deer, cattle, etc. The shapes and colours of warning signs, instruction signs and information signs are also standardised across Europe. However, here are some word signs you may come across:

Accotements non-stabilisés – soft verge

Allumez vos feux – put your headlights on

Cedez le passage – give way (usually at junctions)

Chaussée deformée – bumpy road ahead

Convoi exceptionel – extra-wide vehicle ahead (seen on the back of other vehicles)

Élagage – pruning machinery in road ahead

Fauchage – scything taking place ahead

Gravillons – loose chippings

Halte péage – stop at the toll station

Pas de salage – danger of slippage (i.e. the road has not been gritted)

Pensez de nos enfants – children in the area, slow down

Verglas – surface ice forms in cold weather (looks like the UK sign 'slippery when wet')

Virage – tight bend ahead

Vous n'avez pas la priorité – give way (usually at roundabouts)

Picture signs unfamiliar to UK drivers

A blue circle with a white tyre means you can only enter this road with snow chains on your tyres.

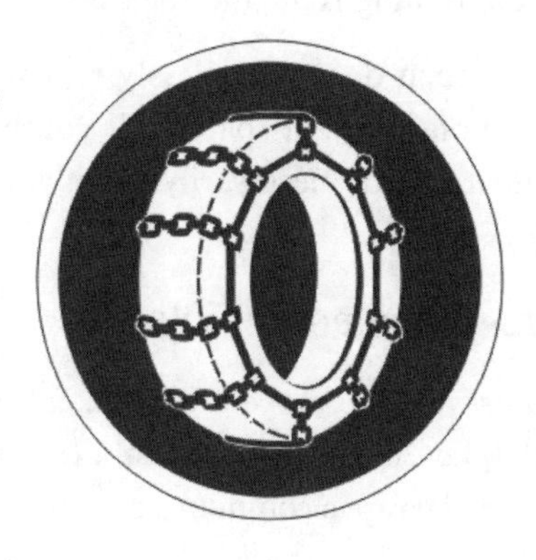

A yellow diamond sign means your road has priority over joining roads.

A yellow diamond sign with a black line through it means your road no longer has priority over joining roads.

A comprehensive list of French road signs can be seen at: www.drivingabroad.co.uk

An indispensable book to have when driving anywhere in Europe is the Haynes publication 'Driving Abroad' – this gives detailed country-by-country guides plus general tips on remaining safe.

Destination signs

Destinations are listed on French road signs in descending order from furthest away to closest, with distant towns and cities shown in white on green and local towns and villages in black on white. If you know you're close to your destination and the turning is coming up soon, get into the habit of reading from the bottom up or you could miss your junction. Junctions are marked with a large green drum with white arrows pointing to the continuing road and the turnoff.

The French do not endlessly repeat destination signs to remind you that you're on the right road, so if you haven't seen the destination again for a while it doesn't necessarily mean you've missed your turnoff.

Two-wheeled vehicles

Motorcycle and moped riders in France must wear an approved crash helmet and bikes over 125cc must drive with their headlight on at all times. Motorbikes are a common sight on motorways, but mopeds are not permitted.

French children are allowed to ride mopeds from the age of 14 – a necessity in rural areas – and you will also see many pushbike riders. Pay attention, particularly to the latter, as many do not wear high-visibility clothing, helmets, or have lights on their vehicles. The death rate for children on mopeds is high.

You have to be 14 to ride a moped of up to 50cc, 16 to ride a bike of up to 125cc, 18 to ride a bike over 125cc and 21 to ride a bike over 34 horsepower. A standard car licence entitles you to ride a motorbike up to 125cc, once you've been driving for two years.

Garages

French roadside garages usually sell diesel, petrol and liquid petroleum gas (*GPL*) at the pumps. Diesel is called *gazole* or *diesel*, while petrol is called *essence* and the similarity of the word *gazole* to *gasoline* has caused many a British driver to fill up with the wrong fuel. Think before you pump!

Petrol is unleaded only and sold in two grades – 95 and 98 (premium) and is often cheaper at the local supermarket than from a garage. Supermarket pumps are usually self-service, while garages may be either self-service or have attendants. Rural garages are often one-man bands and are not open at lunchtimes or in the evenings. This is not a problem for most French because many petrol pumps take *Carte Bleue* credit cards and can be used automatically. However, they do not always take credit cards issued by foreign banks, so take care not to get stuck in the middle of nowhere having run out of petrol. It's wise to keep a jerry can of petrol in the boot of the car (though be aware you can't take this on a ferry).

Buying a car

Most French drivers drive French cars and there are sound reasons for you to do likewise if you live in France. They are left-hand drive, and the local garages will be familiar (and generally affiliated) with certain makes, such as Renault, Citroën or Peugeot. The engineers are therefore familiar with that firm's range of vehicles and any attendant problems, and if your car needs a part, it is more likely to be in stock – if you own an unusual vehicle, it can take weeks to obtain a spare part. Any decent-size garage will also be equipped with the diagnostic systems appropriate to its affiliate brand – which is very important with modern cars.

If you have bought a home in the countryside, you should buy a diesel vehicle. Not only is this cheaper to run, it is almost impossible to resell a petrol engine car in rural France where everyone drives diesel.

New cars in France are cheaper than in the UK, but many French still buy from over the border in Belgium, where prices are yet lower. Investigate the warranties before you buy, as these vary greatly from manufacturer to manufacturer.

Second-hand cars, in contrast, are often more expensive than in the UK. When buying a second-hand car, take the same precautions as you would in the UK. Buying out of the paper comes with the same risk factors, and it's wise to buy from a local dealer or garage instead – here, you usually get a car that's been serviced and valeted, and has a three to six-month guarantee.

When looking for a car, UK-based websites such as Top Gear (www.topgear.com) or Honest John (www.honestjohn.co.uk) can be invaluable for obtaining up-to-date reviews, along with road tests and lists of what to look out for in both new and used vehicles. Bear in mind, though, that pricing and depreciation may not be relevant, nor will details about dealer service. You can check a car's European safety rating on the EuroNCAP site at: www.euroncap.com

If you are searching for a particular vehicle (I, for instance, recently wanted a Citroën C5 estate), make out a specification, including price, and take it to your local garages – they are all part of dealer networks and will usually be happy to track down the right vehicle for you, if the sale is near-enough certain.

You must register your new car with the local *préfecture* within 15 days, though if you buy from a garage, they will do this for you. French number plates begin with the number of the *département* in which the car is registered and need to be changed over within the same timeframe. Again, your local garage can do this for you (and by the way, you're not allowed to keep the old plates).

Importing a vehicle

If you wish to import your existing car from the UK the procedure is quite straightforward. But it is even more straightforward not to do it at all and save yourself a lot of effort.

As mentioned elsewhere, driving a right-hand drive car in France brings its own set of difficulties, but it's worth bearing in mind the issue of maintenance and servicing too. Most brands sold in the UK are also found in France but the models may be slightly different (so spares might be an issue with more exotic cars). And the vast majority of garages in France are franchised to the major French makes – Renault, Citroën and Peugeot. Selling your British Ford or Vauxhall in the UK and buying a French brand will, in the long run, make your life easier.

However, if you are attached to your British car, you can put it on French plates without too much trouble providing it is unmodified and a well-known make and model.

Contact your local *Direction Régionale de l'Industrie de la Recherche et de l'Environment (DRIRE)* for details of what you need in the way of documentation and a re-registration form (*demande de certificat d'immatriculation*). These days, most *départements* allow you to download the forms from their websites. The documentation you're likely to need is:

- The receipt for your car when you bought it (*certificat de vente ou facture*) or proof of origin (*justification de l'origine du véhicle*).
- The car's registration document (*certificat de circulation précédent* or *titre de circulation étranger*) colloquially referred to as the 'logbook' in the UK, or a certificate of permanent export issued by the DVLA.
- *Certificat fiscal* – this is issued by your local tax office. You will need to show the above two documents and possibly a *certificat/attestation de conformité* (see below).
- Proof of address (*justicatif de domicile*) – a recent phone or electricity bill is fine.
- Proof of your identity, such as a passport.
- A test certificate (*contrôle technique* – the French equivalent of the MoT, a UK MoT is not acceptable) less than six months old for any vehicle more than four years old.
- A manufacturer's construction certificate (*certificat/attestation de conformité*).

That last one can be tricky. For common, modern cars, you just need to visit the DRIRE with all your documentation, and the Vehicle Identification Number (VIN), and they will carry out a computer search. If your car comes up, the DRIRE will issue the certificate – for a fee (currently €30). Otherwise, you will need to contact the French branch of the manufacturer with full details of your vehicle, including VIN, date of manufacture, engine size and type, and anything else you think will help. If you're lucky, and that exact model was distributed in France, then they will give you the certificate – in return for a bill of anything up to €150 (and you will still have to pay the DRIRE).

But it isn't always that easy. For example, we had a short wheelbase Nissan Patrol – a model that was distributed in France but not with the same engine, which was only used on UK models. Nissan could issue only a 'partial' attestation. Completing the process would have meant taking the vehicle to the DRIRE for an examination (and another fee). In the end, it proved more complicated than it was worth, and we simply sold it.

The lesson is, if you have any doubts about how easy it will be to register the car, visit the DRIRE first. This may be worth doing even before you have brought the car to France. If it turns out to be impossible to register, you don't want to be stuck with a vehicle that is much harder to sell and much less valuable in France (because it's right-hand drive and on foreign plates) and for which you've already paid the cost of a ferry trip.

When all your paperwork is in order, go to the *préfecture* to obtain the registration certificate (*Carte Grise*). Once that is issued, you can insure the vehicle and any decent size garage should be able to make up your new plates.

The driving licence

In France, you're allowed to drive a standard road car from the age of 18. If you have a UK driving licence, you should apply for a European one if you are intending to live in France full-time. This is not because the French do not recognise the UK licence – they do – but because the DVLA will not renew a UK licence with a foreign address.

You should always drive with your licence on you – apart from anything else, it's a useful form of ID if you're stopped, or for use in shops, restaurants, etc., when you're asked for a *piece d'identité*. Most French people also keep the *Carte Grise* – the vehicle's logbook – in the car at all times, tucked behind the mirror or in the glove compartment. However, if you do this and the car is stolen, it makes it easier for the thief to sell it on, so you may prefer to travel only with the insurance document in the car.

Learning to drive in France

If you're planning a move to France and don't yet have a licence, it's wise to learn to drive in the UK before you leave, as the French option could prove more expensive and time-consuming. In France, you'll have to undergo at least 20 hours of instruction with a registered instructor and pass a theory test in French before you take your practical driving test. Nor can just anyone accompany you in the vehicle, they must either be a qualified driving instructor, or over the age of 28, have had a clean driving licence for three years and be approved by your insurance company. This can make it more difficult to build up practice hours by driving with a spouse or friend, as is commonly done in the UK. If you choose to take your test in France, your *permis B* licence may need to be extended if you tow a vehicle over a certain weight.

French drivers start out with 12 points on their licence and LOSE points for infringements – the reverse of the situation in the UK. Infringements cost between one and six points, depending on their seriousness, but if you commit no new offences for three years, all your points are reinstated. You can also 'win back' four points by taking a driving awareness course (*stage de sensibilisation*). If you are unlucky enough to lose all 12 points, your licence will be suspended for six months and you'll have to take an exam to get it back again. Under exceptional circumstances, however, you can be banned altogether. Speeding offences can be fined on the spot.

There are special cars that you can drive without a licence in France. Called *voitures sans permis*, they are often seen in rural France driven by the elderly. Noisy, slow (top speed 60kmph) and two-seater only, they are really only an option if you're not allowed to drive anything else. They are not a cost-saver, as even a second-hand one costs more than a low-spec Renault or Peugeot. However, they can be useful if you haven't yet passed your test or have lost your licence. Note that due to a change in regulations, drivers born since 1988 and who have been banned cannot now drive *voitures sans permis*.

Traffic lights and pedestrian crossings

French traffic lights are normally at the height expected in the UK, with another set lower down at about 6ft. Sometimes, however, the only light visible is one strung above the road, and these are very easy to miss.

The lights show red, amber and green as in the UK, but the sequence is different. They change from green to amber to red to indicate stop, but to indicate start, they change without warning from red to green, without going through amber. A flashing amber light, seen alone, means proceed with caution – this is sometimes seen on pedestrian crossings on bends, heavy plant exits, etc.

Traffic lights are few and far between in rural France – where I live there is only one village with a traffic light, which has been installed for use by driving instructors teaching students.

Pedestrians don't have right of way on zebra crossings unless they've placed their foot on the crossing, or have clearly signalled their intention to cross (and if you don't stop in this case, as a motorist you can be fined €750 and docked four points). However, most French drivers don't give way to pedestrians on crossings, and many pedestrians wait until the road is clear before proceeding. Don't slow down for a pedestrian before checking your rear view mirror as you could find other traffic cannoning into you, or – even worse – overtaking you right on the crossing.

In picturesque towns and villages there are sometimes *passages cloutés*, which are signalled with brass knobs in the road, or cobblestones, and are not highly visible. These have the same regulations as zebra crossings.

Renting a car

The major rental firms such as Budget and Hertz have a presence in France and often offer quite competitive rates compared with the UK. Check with your insurer to see if you're covered – if you're insured to drive any vehicle there should be no problem, and if you have French insurance, you can usually switch insurance temporarily from one vehicle to another. Cars can also be hired from most local garages, which will usually lend you something off the forecourt. If your usual car is in for repairs, most rural garages will lend you a (clapped-out old) vehicle as a *voiture de remplacement* free of charge while yours is in the shop. In some cities such as Paris, non-drivers can hire *voitures sans permis*, much to the fury of other road users. Self-drive vans are available from car rental firms, garages and sometimes from the local supermarket.

Parking

Car parks are called *parkings* in French, indicated by the usual white P on a blue background. This may indicate a designated parking area or underground car park. However, the term for 'parking' is *stationnement*, which is what you will see on lamp posts detailing the hours within which you're permitted to park. In many busy town centres, parking areas are painted blue, which indicates short stay only. You can buy a parking disc (*Disque Bleue*) from supermarkets, which permits you to park in the blue zone – just turn the dial to the correct time and the disc tells you how long you've got. In Paris, there are red zones where parking is not permitted at all and in any case you cannot stay in one place for more than 24 hours. Watch out in cities for streets where the parking switches from one side to another halfway through the month – indications are usually on the streetlamps.

Top tips

- When in doubt, assume *priorité à droite*.
- When joining a roundabout, remember that traffic is coming from your left (plus also, possibly, your right!)
- Speeds are in kilometres – if you're in a British car, use the inner markings on your speedometer.
- Many motorways are toll roads in France – travelling from north to south could cost as much as £50 in tolls.
- Freight must keep to the slow lane.
- Farm traffic may often be wider than it first appears.
- You are not permitted to drive in France under the age of 18.
- Second-hand cars are often more expensive in France than in the UK.
- Traffic lights change from red to green without going through amber.

Glossary

Autoroute (A) – Motorway

Nationale (N) – National road maintained by the state (equivalent to a UK A road)

Départemental (D) – Local road maintained by the *departement.* Some D roads are on a par with UK A roads, and some are mere country tracks

Aires – Rest points on A and N roads

Aires de service – Rest points where you can park up, get water and empty chemical toilets

Élagage – Pruning (machinery in road ahead)

Fauchage – Scything (taking place ahead)

Gendarmes – Police

Convoi exceptionnel/grand largeur – Abnormal load/wide load

Priorité a droite – Traffic joining from the right has priority

Vous n'avez pas la priorité – Stop/give way as you do not have priority (usually at roundabouts)

Cedez le passage – Give way (usually at junctions)

Jours feriés – Bank holiday

Contrôles automatique – Speed camera

Accotements non-stabilisés – Soft verge

Allumez vos feux – Put your headlights on

Chaussée deformée – Bumpy road ahead

Gravillons – Loose chippings

Halte péage – Stop at the toll station

Pas de salage – Danger of slippage (i.e. the road has not been gritted)

Pensez de nos enfants – Children in the area, slow down

Verglas – Surface ice forms in cold weather (looks like the UK sign 'slippery when wet')

Virage – Tight bend ahead

Gaz de Pétrole Liquéfié (GPL) – Liquid petroleum gas (LPG)

Gazole/diesel – Diesel

Essence – Petrol

Préfecture – The local administrative office which looks after vehicle registration, among many other things

Département – Geographical area similar to a county. France is divided geographically into 100 *départements*

Demande de certificat d'immatriculation – Re-registration form

Certificat de vente ou facture – The receipt for your car when you bought it

Justification de l'origine du véhicle – Proof of vehicle's origin

Certificat de circulation precedent/titre de circulation étranger – A vehicle's registration document

Certificat fiscal – Tax certificate

Certificat/attestation de conformité – A manufacturer's construction certificate

Justicatif de domicile – Proof of address

Contrôle technique – Test certificate (the French equivalent of the MoT)

Carte Grise – Registration certificate (similar to the V5 or 'logbook')

Piece d'identité – Proof of identity such as passport or driving licence

Permis B – Driving licence

Stage de sensibilisation – Driving awareness course

Voitures sans permis – Cars that you are allowed to drive without a licence

Passages clouté – Pedestrian crossing denoted by a change in road surface

Voiture de remplacement – Courtesy car

Parking – Car park

Stationnement – Parking space/the act of parking

Disque Bleue – Parking disc which permits you to park in blue (no-wait or short-wait) zones

12

Public transport

France has a multi-pronged public transport system consisting of trains, planes, buses and the underground.

Trains

The national railway network comprises SNCF (*Syndicat Nationale de Chemin de Fer*), which runs the national railway service, and RFF (*Réseau Ferré de France*), which runs the network of lines. The SNCF has two further subsidiaries – TER SNCF, which runs the regional rail system (local trains), and TGV, which runs the high-speed trains. The SNCF carries over 800 million passengers a year, the majority of them in the Paris and Ile de France areas. The rail network therefore centres on Paris as a hub, and to travel cross-country may involve going through Paris.

French trains are usually clean, efficient, safe and well-maintained, and French passengers expect high standards, becoming furious at small delays that English passengers might take for granted. Train travel in France is cheap compared with the UK, but also needs to be compared with the price of toll roads when you're considering a journey through France – the tolls can add up very quickly and make train travel look even more attractive in comparison. TGV fares are also comparable with air travel (which has generally dropped where TGV routes have been introduced).

France is justifiably proud of its TGV trains (*trains à grande vitesse*, or high-speed trains). These constitute the fastest regular passenger rail service in the world and run at up to 200mph (though on high-speed lines only, which are not available throughout the whole TGV network).

TGV trains offer first- or second-class seating and some are double-decker (duplex). They all have a buffet car serving drinks and food, and there are phones onboard, which is handy, as use of mobile phones isn't permitted. You have to book your seat in advance (although you can buy just a few minutes ahead of your journey, at the station) and standing passengers are not allowed. This means that trains are often crowded, but never overcrowded, usually running at about 70 per cent capacity. The introduction of duplex trains in the mid-1990s increased capacity by almost half without reducing the speed of the network.

TGV trains run non-stop between most major French cities, and link outside the country to matching high-speed networks in Switzerland, etc. However, the TGV network does not by any means cover all of France – it runs in a rough, open spider's web from Paris to the north, east, south and west, with the remainder of the country filled in by normal-speed trains and local networks. However, the network is being constantly expanded, with new routes set to come online every year or two.

The regular train network is also fast and well-appointed, with the TER (*train express régionale*) service covering mainline stations. Slower than the TER trains are the omnibus trains that service the suburbs, some of which are electric.

Stations

French railway stations usually have a restaurant nearby, often quite good quality, and a snack bar in the concourse, along with drinks and chocolate machines, though France differs somewhat from the UK in not generally having shop concessions along the concourse. Other facilities might include a coffee bar, drinks bar and photocopying.

Trains

All French trains are non-smoking and the use of mobile phones is forbidden, though TGV trains do have phones on board which you can use with a phone card.

Fast trains generally have a restaurant car and/or steward service, while on TGV trains and *corail* (electric) trains you can order a tray meal when you book your ticket. As in the UK, French train food is expensive and not very high quality.

Luggage can be stored in large racks at the end of each carriage and there are also small overhead luggage racks above the seats. Although security announcements usually ask for people to keep their luggage with them, in practice this is often impossible and the large racks are often packed – it definitely pays to padlock or otherwise secure your luggage, as theft from them is relatively easy.

Toilets are usually situated near the large luggage racks, but may not be available on suburban services. You may find there's an antiseptic gel dispenser in the cubicle rather than soap and water.

Sleeping accommodation is provided on night trains, consisting of three types: reclining seats – which are free but have to be reserved in advance; *couchettes* – mixed-sex accommodation with sleeping bags provided; and the higher-class and much more expensive *voiture-lits* or sleeping cars, which sleep 1-2 in first class or 2-3 in second class and have an attendant and washing facilities.

There is an overnight Motorail service running from Calais to destinations in the south, which takes cars and motorbikes but not caravans. Cars are handled notoriously roughly and fares are expensive, but it is much quicker than driving. Sleeping accommodation is as above.

Buying a ticket

You can buy train tickets at railway stations, from automatic vending machines at the station, from travel agents, by phone (tel: 08 92 35 35 35) or online at: www.voyages-sncf.com. You must buy your ticket and have it validated before you get on board a train – you can do this by pushing it into a machine on the concourse, which time-stamps it.

There are two basic tariffs for fares, the full-fare white tariff, which covers peak periods and public holidays, and the off-peak blue tariff. If you start your journey during a blue period and finish in a white period, you only have to pay the blue fare, but if you travel completely in the white period with a blue ticket, you're liable to an on-the-spot fine.

Discounts are available for a huge variety of reasons and it pays to carefully go through the options available. For instance, there are automatic discounts for over-60s travelling off-peak, which can be made even greater with a railcard (*Carte Sénior*). Children under 11 travel for half price, and those under four who don't require a separate seat travel free of charge. Young person's railcards are also available (*Carte Enfant* + or *La Carte 12-25*) which give various discounts for the person travelling, family members and even the dog. Family railcards are also available if you have three or more children under 18, which offer discounts of 30-75 per cent, depending on how many children you have, but you have to be a French resident to obtain one.

Couples, groups, students, commuters, regular travellers and the disabled are all entitled to a range of reductions, available via season tickets, discount cards, etc., and you can also make savings by including overnight stays, hotel bookings, buying on a national holiday, booking well in advance, or building up train miles (*s'miles*). Make sure to ask the operator for the cheapest method of travel possible, or examine SNCF's website VERY carefully – if you look under *Cartes et Abonnements* there is a test you can take to see 'what kind of traveller' you are. The SNCF also publishes *Le Guide du Voyageur*, which is packed with information and is available from railway stations.

You must pay for your dog to travel by train if it weighs over 6kg – the charge is a half-fare, second class. But if you can fit your pet (any kind) in a box 45cm x 30cm x 25cm, it costs €5 one-way. One family cat or dog can travel free with holders of a *Carte Enfant+*.

Planes

International flights into France mostly come into the Paris airports – Roissy-Charles de Gaulle and Orly, which handle around 75 million passengers a year, but there are also international flights to around 30 other cities, many in the south, such as Marseilles, Toulouse and Nice, or in tourist areas, such as Bordeaux.

Low-cost carriers keep expanding into France (there are over 44 at the time of writing) and Paris is very well served, but rural destinations change frequently as competition is ruthless and routes that do not make the grade are axed. Some French airports only link to airports in the south of the UK. The best way to check on current availability is to browse the Internet for 'low-cost flights to France', and visit the individual sites of carriers such as Ryanair, BMIBaby, Flybe, etc. There is also an up-to-date list of all budget international carriers going to France on www.attitudetravel.com. Note that fares differ widely in price according to the time of year and between carriers, and watch out for add-ons such as airport tax.

Domestic flights within France are mostly run by Air France, which is state-owned and has a virtual monopoly on the intercity routes – a number of other French carriers have gone out of business in the past ten years, although Air Turquoise, which shuttles between Reims and the south, and a number of airlines serving Corsica are still extant for the time being. Low-cost carrier easyJet also runs domestic flights Paris-Toulouse and Paris-Nice.

However, Air France does have competition in the form of the TGV network, which is constantly expanding, and this has helped to reduce airfares on domestic routes. The 'Open Skies' deal between the US and the EU may also change provision in ways as yet unknown.

Underground

Métro

Métro systems now exist in Lille, Lyon, Marseille, Toulouse and Rennes as well as Paris, but Paris remains the best known. Opened in 1900, it's one of the world's earliest, and now boasts over 300 stations, and transports over 4 million travellers on a daily basis. Stations are labelled with a large 'M' over the top, and some of those designed by *Guimard* are a distinctive *Art Nouveau* feature of the Parisian landscape.

Métro trains run every 90 seconds or so, almost all day long, and there is a flat fare no matter how far you travel (all journeys are single). You can buy tickets singly or in books of 10, called *carnets* from *Métro* stations, *tabacs*, bus terminals and ticket machines (which take credit cards or coins). However, if you're travelling in Paris all week, it's worth getting a *Hebdomedaire* or *Carte Orange* ticket which lasts from Monday to Sunday (you'll need a passport-size photo for the pass), or a *Paris Visite* multi-day pass if you're a visitor (you don't need a photo for this one). Tickets are fed into a turnstile machine at the stations, and there are random ticket inspections on the trains themselves. Rather than buying tickets, some Parisians now use the *Navigo* smartcard, which is being gradually rolled out across the *Métro* system – similar to the Oyster card used in London.

You can work out your journey by logging onto the RATP website at: www.ratp.fr, buying a map from a station or newsagent, downloading a map from www.isubwaymaps.com, or using the maps inside or outside the *Métro* station. Some stations also have computerised journey planners, where you enter your destination station and the machine tells you how to get there. Bear in mind that some station connections are a tad complicated, with a number of lines converging at once, and there are passenger walkways to get from one line to another – the *Métro* is not a friendly environment for the physically disabled, and has many tunnels, stairs and escalators to contend with.

All trains are non-smoking and there are the usual seats for pregnant women, war wounded and the civilian blind, though there is no wheelchair access. There are also folding seats (*strapontins*), which you're not meant to use once the train gets crowded. The doors close automatically with a warning signal. To open them, newer models have push-buttons, but older models have a lift-up handle.

Some *Métro* tunnels are not as claustrophobic as the London Underground – some have walkways right along their length and are well-lit – but the lack of air conditioning, and revolting smell from the rubberised wheels of the rolling stock can be dreadful in the summer (though apparently it makes them go faster).

RER

The *Réseau Express Regional* (RER) is the Ile de France's underground commuter service from the suburbs into Paris and is run by SNCF independently from the *Métro* system. It runs on a combination of old regional railway lines and newer dedicated underground lines and is therefore maintained partly by SNCF and partly by RATP (*Régie Autonome des Transports Parisiens*, the body responsible for running the *Métro*).

Stations are often deep-line and very spacious (*stations cathédrales*) and trains drive on the left, like SNCF trains, rather than on the right like *Métro* trains, even when using *Métro* track. Overall, it is faster than the *Métro* because it has fewer stops, though the trains run less frequently than *Métro* trains, and there is access for wheelchairs.

Divided into four sectors labelled A-E, the network serves nearly 250 stations in and around Paris, including the new Disneyland station at Marne-la-Vallée-Chessy, Versailles and the Paris airports.

The RATP website has an English-language section which allows you to plan your journey, explains the benefits of various offers such as the *Cartes Amethyste, Emeraude* and *Orange*, offers a list of local vendors where you can buy tickets, and shows maps of the RER network, *Métro* network, the Parisian zones, and the night bus network (*Noctilien*) that replaces the RER during its shutdown period (12.30am to 5.30am).

Buses

All French cities have bus (*autobus*) and/or tram services, often reasonably priced to encourage users to leave their cars at home. One of the latest tram schemes is in Nice, and will involve re-pedestrianising some city areas, and creating public transport that is friendly for disabled users. For information on services local to your area, log onto www.angloinfo.com.

In Paris, bus tickets cost the same as *Métro* tickets, and can be used on either form of transport. The same passes, such as *Carte Orange* also apply (see *Métro*, page 163).

Outside urban areas, France's transport planning system favours the train, particularly the TGV. This is perhaps why France does not have a national bus company, but there are some international bus companies running long-distance coach services, mainly in the south, and Eurolines (National Express) operates services from the UK to many French cities, including Paris.

Rural bus services between villages and towns are either rare or non-existent and where they do exist, they are often either school buses or services run by SNCF to fill gaps in the rural rail network. Rural and long-distance buses are called *autocars* (they are generally coaches), and if there is a bus station, it's usually right by the railway station. In practice, most people in rural France either drive or expect to be picked up from the railway station by someone who does.

Cross-Channel services

Ferries

There are several cross-Channel ferry operators, though the market has tightened in recent years and has seen P&O hand a virtual monopoly to Brittany Ferries on many of the longer routes.

LD Lines and its sister company *Transmanche Ferries* operate services from Portsmouth and Newhaven to Le Havre and Dieppe, while other low-cost operators have opened up on the shorter routes, including SpeedFerries, SeaFrance and Norfolkline, running services between Dover and Dunkirk/Calais/Boulogne. Condor Ferries runs services from Poole and

Weymouth to St Malo, but goes via the Channel Islands (passengers may disembark here and continue their onward journey later).

All ferries provide cabins and, depending on the length of journey, may also offer reclining seats, suites, cinemas, a range of restaurants, swimming pools, etc. You are usually required to book either a reclining seat or a cabin if you are taking a night crossing, if they are available, but if they are not, people will happily bed down all over the ferry – seasoned travellers are notable for their sleeping bags, blankets and blow-up pillows.

Which type of crossing you choose depends on your priorities – if cost is the main issue then the shorter crossings are much cheaper, but are more crowded, have fewer facilities and often entail more driving. If you consider the crossing as part of the journey, then it is usually worth paying for a cabin, where you can shower, lie down to relax, and store your belongings during the crossing, leaving you free to explore the boat unencumbered.

If you want to compare providers, search online for 'ferries to France', or look at sites such as Direct Ferries (www.directferries.co.uk), which gives an at-a-glance chart showing all the services between France and the UK, including ferries to the Channel Islands. Prices vary enormously between providers and the time of year, and it is almost impossible to work out the cheapest fare without inputting a putative combination of date, time and persons travelling – very irritating if your crossing dates are flexible. Generally speaking, however, it pays to travel with a full car rather than an empty one, and membership of a property-owner or frequent traveller club is usually worthwhile.

All ferry services may be cancelled in bad weather but just how bad it has to be depends on factors such as the height and times of the tides and the draught and tonnage of the boat. Occasionally, ferries are re-routed, but in this case passengers are informed before boarding and given sweeteners such as a free cabin and money to cover extra fuel costs, while a coach is laid on to take foot passengers back to the original destination port.

Eurotunnel

Eurotunnel operates a car-train service through the Channel Tunnel. The firm offers crossings from Folkestone to Calais, with the journey taking just over half an hour and you can embark either as a foot passenger or take a vehicle, including caravans and trailers. Booking is usually necessary, and there are incentives for frequent travellers and those travelling off-peak – see www.eurotunnel.com for details.

Eurostar trains for foot passengers only, which run through the Channel Tunnel, start at London St Pancras and go to Calais and onwards to Lille, Paris, Brussels and Avignon, along with selected ski resorts and Disneyland Paris. Eurostar also links to the TGV and other parts of the French rail network, and you can buy a connecting ticket.

CASE STUDY: Transport

Mark and Sandra Bradley moved from Nantwich in Cheshire to a village in France's Pays de la Loire region three years ago. They were experienced in living outside the UK, having spent much of their lives as ex-pats, in Ireland, Nigeria and Iran, but had been back in England for many years.

Sandra doesn't drive, but the couple say this did not affect their choice of residence. They wanted to live in a village in any case, rather than the isolated countryside or in a city, so local amenities within walking distance were already on their wish-list.

Their village has these in abundance but they also admit that they drive into their nearest large town, Mayenne, on an almost daily basis, as it is only a few minutes away. They also use their car for leisure purposes, though they intend to reduce this, in order to reduce their eco-footprint, which is something that concerns them.

"If Mark was ill or something," says Sandra, "and couldn't drive, I'd just do what I did in the UK – call on our network of friends. Other than that, I have no problem with taking buses and taxis."

The Bradleys are both retired and have invested in *Cartes Seniors*, which entitle them to substantial discounts on train services. "We've travelled to places such as Nice on the Med, and Valence on the Rhône, and also to Paris," says Mark.

"We get a minimum of a third off standard ticket prices and at selected times a 50 per cent reduction is available. And then on top of that, reduced prices are often still applicable on special offers. The train is our preferred method of travel around France, not just for the reasonable costs but also for other considerations such as the level of service."

Overall, the Bradleys don't feel that a car is strictly necessary where they live and if need be they'd be content with public transport. "The car is a convenience that we would rather have," says Sandra. "But there is a thrice-daily bus service from the village into town. And with better planning and increased use of local shops we could get everything to satisfy our daily needs right here. Lots of people in the village do."

Top tips

- The French public transportation network is focused around train travel, in particular the TGV (high-speed trains).
- The TGV network covers most of France, with slower-speed, but still fast networks joining the dots.
- Paris is the major hub for international flights, but there are around 30 international airports in France, many of them in the south.
- Where domestic flights are concerned, Air France has a near monopoly and prices are quite high – many people take the TGV instead.
- There is no French national bus or coach company, but some international companies do provide long-distance bus services throughout France.
- You can book a coach journey through France with National Express.
- Cross-Channel ferries run from ports in the south of England to the north coast of France, with some going via the Channel Islands. Journeys take between one and eight hours.

Glossary

Trains à grande vitesse (TGV) – High-speed trains

Train express régionale (TER) – The train service covering the mainline stations

Corail – Electric train

Couchettes – Bunk-style beds (sleeping bags are provided)

Voiture-lit – Sleeping cars (have an attendant and washing facilities)

Carte Sénior – Over-60s railcard

Carte Enfant +/La Carte 12-25 – Young person's railcard

Carnets – Book of 10 Métro tickets

Tabac – Tobacconist – often a cafe and/or bar, too. These also sell newspapers, lottery tickets, phone cards etc.

Hebdomedaire – Weekly

Carte Orange – A ticket which lasts from Monday to Sunday

Paris Visite – A multi-day pass for visitors

Métro – French public transport system, which is predominantly underground train lines. The Paris Métro is the most well-known

Strapontin – Folding seat

Noctilien – Night bus network which replaces the RER during its shutdown period (12.30am to 5.30am)

Autobus – Bus

Autocars – Rural and long-distance buses (generally coaches)

13

Money

Currency

Since 2002, the French currency has been the euro, in common with Germany, Spain and many other mainland European countries. In the days of francs it was quite easy to do the average franc/sterling conversion in your head, allowing 10 francs to the pound, but euros are, on average two-thirds of a pound, though the exchange rate, of course, varies. In many supermarkets and shops, the franc price of goods is still printed alongside the euro price, so you can double-check the value of the item against your sterling benchmark.

Be aware that many French people, particularly those over 50, still think and speak in francs. People over 60 still often give prices in OLD francs, which are ten times higher than the new francs, which can certainly make your eyes water when pricing up the winter woodpile!

Vocabulary

Monnaie means change, not money – the French word for money is *argent*. You may also hear *petite monnaie*, literally small change. Nearly everyone calls eurocents *centimes*, not cents. When referring to cash money, the French generally use the words *liquide* or *espèces*.

Cash economy

France remains a much more cash-driven economy than the UK, and many people do nearly all of their purchasing in cash or by cheque, which are used much more frequently than in the UK. French cheques do not require a cheque card, but if you pay by cheque over €50 (and sometimes even for less) you may be asked for ID. For this reason, it is always useful to carry your passport on you if you don't have a *Carte de Séjour*.

Many outlets do not accept international credit cards but only a *Carte Bleue* held on a French account.

Changing money

You can change money at banks or *bureaux de changes* all over France. *Bureaux de changes* are found mainly at air and sea ports, and in the larger cities and have the advantage over banks of being open at the weekend. If you have foreign currency in notes, you may also be able to exchange it in an automatic cash machine at a port (these machines also exist on the ferries). To check if you're getting a fair rate of exchange, visit www.xe.com, which gives the current rate of the day.

Importing and exporting money

If you are a French resident, you can hold accounts in the UK or offshore, and import and export money out of France without limitations. If you send or receive cash, however, you should let Customs know if the sum is above €1,500. Also, if you travel out of France holding more than €7,500 in French banknotes or other legal tender (such as bearer bonds), you must declare it.

If you want to transfer sums of money from the UK to France on a regular basis, or have big one-offs such as a property to pay for, you could try a company such as Travelex, which specialises in Britons buying property overseas – visit www.travelex.com and choose United Kingdom from the drop-down menu for more information. Using a money transfer company of this kind, you can 'lock' the exchange rate at which you buy for up to two years into the future, which is an insurance against the exchange rate worsening (however, if it changes in your favour, you can't change it).

If you want to use your UK bank, you can negotiate a commercial transfer rate and periodically move the money by bank transfer (*virement*) to a French account, where you can simply withdraw it from cash machines as normal. Allow 5-7 days for the transfer to take place and be prepared to submit a raft of information including the name of the bank, name of the branch, account name, account number, bank code, branch code, BIC number and IBAN number. If your UK bank is Swift-affiliated (you can check at www.swift.com), you may also be asked for the Swift number – this is the same as the BIC number. Swift stands for the Society of Worldwide Interbank Financial Telecommunications and offers a fast transfer, which should mean that your money transfers within 24 hours.

You can also move large sums of money by bank draft (*chèque de banque*), but this is a slower option that uses registered post. If you're transferring from the UK to France, you also have to wait for the draft to clear, just like a cheque. Smaller sums can be moved by Western Union or international money order.

Top tips

- The French currency is the euro.
- France is a more cash-based economy than the UK and many transactions are made in cash rather than by credit card.
- French cheques do not usually need a cheque card for amounts under €50.
- If you are not known to the shopkeeper, you may be asked for ID when paying by cheque.
- You can change sterling to euros and vice versa at most air and ferry ports.

Glossary

Monnaie – Change

Argent – Money

Petite monnaie – Small change

Liquide – Cash

Espèces – Cash

Carte de Séjour – Residency permit

Carte Bleue – French debit card

Bureau de change – Foreign exchange counter

Virement – Bank transfer

Chèque de banque – Bank draft

14 Healthcare

The social security system

The social security system in France – *La Sécu* – is comprehensive but complicated. It includes the health service, pensions cover, unemployment benefit and other benefits such as maternity, permanent disability, child benefit, etc. Contributions are collected by URSSAF (*Union de Recouvrement des cotisations de Sécurité Sociale et d'Allocations Familiales*), but sections of the system are run by numerous other bodies, including the *Caisse Nationale d'Assurance Maladie* (CNAM), *Caisse Régionale d'Assurance Maladie* (CRAM) and *Caisse Primaire d'Assurance Maladie* (CPAM), along with a host of others. All of these agencies are normally referred to by their abbreviations.

To find out how to enter the social security system in your particular circumstances, phone the French Health Insurance Advice Line on 08 20 90 42 12, where the staff are very helpful. If your French is up to it, you can also find details about the social security system at www.service-public.fr, which has many links to other government ministries, and at www.ameli.fr. Don't expect to understand it all at once – many French people don't. (At the time of writing, *Assurance Maladie* (the *ameli* site) had withdrawn its English pages.)

One thing that may surprise Britons is that the French do not have a social security number equating to the UK national insurance number that you receive when you are 16 and then retain throughout your life. The system requires, instead, that everyone is covered by a different agency according to their individual circumstances. Children and students are dependants to the age of 20 and are covered by their parents' social security cover; salaried workers (80 per cent of the French) are covered by their employers; the self-employed are covered by whichever body (of many) is responsible for their particular line of work; the retired are covered automatically; and the low-waged are covered by the CMU (*Couveture Maladie Universelle*). There are also separate social security *régimes* for civil servants and agricultural workers.

As a British citizen, you are not automatically entitled to health cover or social security benefits in France. For instance, you cannot receive unemployment benefit until you have worked, nor if you're self-employed. And although you have the right of free entry into France – even if you are unemployed – you are not entitled to stay longer than three months if you are a 'charge on the system' – i.e. you can't support yourself and your family.

In order to get into the French system, therefore, at least one member of a household will need to register with a relevant body. The other members can remain as dependants, or *ayant droit* – a common position, for instance, for housewives.

Whom should you contact for social security cover?

- If you're salaried, your social security is covered by your employer.
- If you're self-employed, you contact URSSAF, or the *Chambre de Commerce* or *Chambre des Métiers* for your region, if applicable. Overall, though, if you contact URSSAF, they will do everything else for you.
- If you're retired you need to obtain forms E121 or E106 from the UK, depending on your circumstances. If you're in receipt of a state pension, you're fully covered for healthcare in France. If you're retired but not yet receiving a state pension, you'll need to start paying into the French system straightaway in order to receive any French state pension – take professional advice on this, as if you don't pay in enough, you won't receive anything at all. See Chapter 20.
- If you're unemployed, contact www.jobcentreplus.gov.uk before you move to France.

Whatever your circumstances, if you have two or more children, visit the CAF website at: www.caf.fr to check if you are eligible for family allowance.

Healthcare in France

France's health system has long been the envy of Europe, and for British visitors the difference between the French service and the UK's NHS is sometimes very noticeable indeed.

France has virtually no waiting lists for operations or hospital beds. And if you're unlucky enough to find yourself hospitalised, your discomfort will probably be greatly eased by the usual two-to-a-room standard of accommodation (that's if you don't get a room to yourself), excellent food, and lack of pressure to leave following surgery.

However, the dream standard is under threat. All national health services cost their governments money, and the French health service has been losing money hand over fist for decades. France spends more of its GDP on health than on defence, with much of the bill going on medicines, many of which are thought to be prescribed unnecessarily. The government of Jacques Chirac, accordingly, made some reforms during the early 2000s that were designed to encourage the French to think more carefully about their healthcare and to use the health service as a resource rather than a panacea.

The reforms met with considerable resistance. Not only are the French traditionally a nation of hypochondriacs, used to being prescribed a carrier-bag full of medicines for virtually any ailment, they are also used to visiting several doctors until they get what they want, and to referring themselves to specialists for treatment without a reference from their family doctor. It's quite common in a family for each member to have a separate GP, with perhaps one choosing a GP specialising in gynaecology, another choosing one who's trained in homeopathy and the children seeing a paediatric specialist. Most women have a separate gynaecologist, and many French people also see a 'psy' – psychologist or psychiatrist.

Under the new reforms, patients are now required to register with a particular GP, as in the UK system, and cannot see a specialist under the national health system without a GP's referral (unless they wish to pay privately). Even here, however, the government was forced to back down somewhat and exempt psychotherapists and gynaecologists from these new measures. You can also change GP at any time, without giving a reason. Just go to your new doctor and ask for the form (the *Déclaration de Choix du Médecin Traitant*) and send it off to your *caisse* (social security agency).

Under the French health service, treatment is only subsidised, not fully funded, by the state and there is a sliding scale of reimbursement, from 100 per cent for items such as maternity care to zero per cent for some 'comfort' medicines. To complicate matters further there is also a set governmental tariff of charges for treatment, which your local doctor, dentist or hospital is not obliged to stick to. Medical practitioners who are labelled *conventionné* have agreed to charge the normal state tariff for services and this is something to watch out for when you choose a doctor, otherwise you could find yourself paying far more than the normal consultation fee. Details on whether the doctor or dentist is *conventionné* should be posted in reception – if you can't see it, ask for it.

Mutuelle

The majority of your medical cover is paid for by the social security system, with which you must register if you live in France. Which *caisse* you join depends on what you do for a living (see Chapter 19). You're reimbursed for treatments (doctor, dentist, etc.) by sending off your *feuille de soins* (reimbursement form) to your *caisse*. Your doctor will just hand the form over at the end of the consultation.

On average, unless you are unwaged, retired or disabled, you can expect to be reimbursed about 65-70 per cent of what you've paid out, which leaves you with a considerable gap. This is why just about every French person who can afford it takes out insurance to cover the rest. The real name for this is *assurance complementaire maladie*, but it's nearly always referred to as *mutuelle*.

Mutuelle is offered by large general insurers, but is usually more competitively priced from a specialist *mutualiste*. Tariffs can be confusing, especially for a Briton who doesn't understand the system, because reimbursement will often be as high as 200 per cent of the government tariff for treatments. This is to cover the higher charges that are sometimes found in the larger cities. Your *mutuelle* insurer will send you an *attestation* card every quarter, and you should carry this around with you to use with your *Carte Vitale* (see below) – just knowing your *mutuelle* number is not enough.

The Carte Vitale

The *Carte Vitale* is a credit-card-sized card containing all your social security details, including your *mutuelle* cover, and it has now replaced the majority of the *feuille de soins* or reimbursement forms that people formerly had to fill in. The *Carte Vitale* is used at hospitals, pharmacies, dentists and nurses *cabinets* and doctors. However, at the time of writing, not all doctors were fully in the system and all required payment upfront, whether they took the *Carte Vitale* or not. (If they did, your reimbursement was automatic, and if they didn't, they gave you a form to send off.) If your doctor still gives you a form, you can ask your pharmacy to post it for you and save you the job.

At the pharmacy, they run the card through the machine, and fees for any medication you've been prescribed go direct to social security and your *mutuelle* insurer in the correct proportion – you no longer have to send off a prescription reimbursement form.

There is now a forfeit for all doctor's consultations (i.e. you pay out €22 and get back €20), a measure designed to help fill the coffers of the health service painlessly.

Note that if only one half of a couple is working, the other can remain as a dependant or *ayant-droit* on the other's insurance, as do any dependent children. In this case, each adult gets a *Carte Vitale*, but there is only one *mutuelle attestation*. This can occasionally cause glitches if you use a pharmacy that is outside your normal *département*, because the computer system won't have all the information it needs to process your details – you need both the *Carte Vitale* of the principal assured person AND the *attestation*.

Emergency services

Be prepared for emergencies before they arise by finding out the location of your nearest hospital with a casualty department – not all hospitals have them, just as not all hospitals have paediatric and maternity departments.

The French emergency services are highly efficient and provide an effective combined response to emergencies. Overall, responsibility lies in the hands of SAMU (*Service d'Aide Médicale Urgente*). SAMU has a website in English at: www.samu-de-france.fr/en which explains the history and aims of the service. It provides doctors to work in casualty departments of hospitals, runs ambulances and air ambulance services and also operates mobile intensive care units that attend the sites of major road accidents, explosions, etc.

What to do in an emergency

The emergency number in France, as in the rest of Europe, is now 112 (as listed on your mobile phone and equally valid in the UK). However, the old numbers listed below still work.

- If you know for certain that the issue is life-threatening, dial 15, and you'll go straight through to SAMU. There, a doctor will question you and send an appropriate response. Suspected heart attack, stroke, poisoning, and major blood loss all come under this heading.
- If you're not sure if the emergency is life-threatening, dial 18. This takes you through to the fire brigade, which is the hub for all local emergency services and is linked with the ambulance service. Fire brigades have their own ambulances and doctors, and have resuscitation equipment on board. The operator will question you and decide which team to send. Childbirth and accidents involving blood loss come under this heading.
- If you are sure the emergency is not life-threatening, call the local ambulance service (*ambulance municipal*), listed in the phone book, or one of the services listed under 'Ambulances' in the Yellow Pages. The latter are private services, so there may be more than one listed – use of them is covered by most people's *mutuelle* health insurance.
- If in doubt, phone the local *gendarmerie* (emergency number 17) which will put you through to the correct service.

It is a good idea to keep all the local emergency numbers by your telephone or programmed into the handset – there is nothing like stress for causing you to forget all the numbers you most wish to remember.

If you live in an urban or suburban area, you can also benefit from France's network of specialist emergency doctors, *SOS Médecins*. This organisation has an English language website at: www.sosmedecins-france.fr/en which explains their background, ethos, etc. and also has a map showing where your local SOS centre is. Your local centre should also be listed in the Yellow Pages.

What to expect

Within minutes of your emergency call, you can expect a car with doctors, defibrillators, oxygen, etc. on board, possibly with the fire brigade's ambulances bringing up the rear.

Many French ambulances are not vans, as in the UK, but estate cars (often Citroën C5s), which are very nippy on narrow roads and enable doctors to get to the scene of an emergency quickly. However, it can be an unpleasant experience to be slid into one of these headfirst to be taken to hospital. Fire brigade ambulances are red, usually vans, while those of SAMU are white with a blue star on the side. You might also see ambulances labelled SMUR – these are the mobile intensive care units operated by SAMU.

You may find that you are not taken to the local hospital, but will go to the nearest one with a casualty department, which may be further away.

You don't have to pay for ambulance and fire brigade services at the time; fees are billed and reimbursed under the normal healthcare system. And no hospital can deny you treatment in an emergency, even if you don't have any money on you. If you are a British national you will at some point be asked for your EHIC card (see page 194) but if you are a resident in France, your *Carte Vitale* will usually take care of everything.

Emergency hotlist

☎ In an emergency, dial 112

☎ If the emergency is life-threatening, dial 15

☎ If the emergency is not life-threatening, or you're not sure, dial 18

☎ If you need the *gendarmes*, dial 17

Ambulance services

Ambulance services are private in France, and you're quite likely to be asked which company you want to use if, for instance, you need to be transferred from one hospital to another. In rural areas, it's quite common for the same company to run the ambulance service, local taxi service and somewhat unsettlingly, the local hearse!

Hospitals

French hospitals are generally extremely clean and well-equipped, although there are exceptions in the larger towns and cities. Sadly, however, the rate of 'superbugs' such as MRSA is no better than in the UK. Hospitals with casualty departments may be few and far between in rural areas and you may have to travel some distance for specialist services such as maternity or paediatrics.

The expected 'standard' of accommodation is two patients to a room. Single occupancy is also quite common but cannot be guaranteed, and is one reason for taking out *mutuelle* insurance: you can then ask for your own room at no extra charge. A room will typically have its own bathroom, or at least a toilet and hand basin, a television, which may be free or for which there may be a deposit to pay (it's for the remote), and a phone, calls from which have to be paid for. It should be pointed out that there do still exist older-style hospitals in French cities which fall far short of this dream standard and have large wards similar to UK hospitals.

French hospitals expect you to supply toiletries yourself and the list is usually posted inside the bathroom. It generally includes towels, washcloths, soap, eau de toilette (they're very specific about this), and anything else you need such as talc, pyjamas, dressing gown and slippers. Note that washcloths (*gants de toilette*) are not square flannels, but are designed for you to insert your hand into, and are for the use of the nursing staff so they can bed-bath you easily – you can buy them at the supermarket.

When you check into hospital, expect to be asked for your *Carte Vitale* and details of your *mutuelle* insurance, including your *attestation*. The hospital tariffs, including 'hotel' charge and single-occupancy supplement are normally displayed near reception.

When referred by your doctor you might find yourself in a private clinic at no extra cost. Private clinics and state establishments run alongside each other in France and there is little difference in quality – in fact state institutions may prefer to use a local private clinic's facilities rather than build their own specialist units for certain ailments.

Clinics may have a religious affiliation, in which case the main differences you'll notice are things like crucifixes and religious paintings on the walls (these are forbidden in state hospitals, due to France's separation of church and state), and you might get a visit from the hospital almoner to check on your spiritual welfare. Unless it's run by a religious order (where the staff might be nuns) the doctors, nurses and other hospital staff are quite likely to be the same people as at the main hospital.

French hospitals may run more tests than you see in the UK, and take 'biopsies' – tissue samples – quite readily. This is nothing to worry about and is partly due to the lack of cost-cutting measures: the French would rather be safe than sorry. Your test results are your property and you'll be given a copy, which you need to keep safe. This also applies to x-rays and ultrasounds – fun for scaring your friends with at dinner. They may also keep you in for longer, or keep you in merely for observation where a UK hospital would send you home. This can be reassuring, scary or irritating, depending on your circumstances.

Hospitals don't have pharmacies on the premises – if you visit one for emergency treatment out of hours, you may need to visit the *gendarmes* to get the *pharmacie de garde* (on-duty chemist) to open up for you. If you're outside your *département*, make sure you hand over the *Carte Vitale* for the head of the family and not a dependant.

Doctors

All French residents are now obliged to sign up with a *médecin traitant*, i.e. your own GP (*generaliste*). You're still not obliged to actually use this doctor, but if you use a different one, you'll only be reimbursed for 60 per cent of the fee rather than the usual 70 per cent. This is to discourage patients from 'shopping around' for second and third opinions, which was a bad habit in the past.

Visiting the doctor currently costs €22 for the standard tariff, which you can pay by cash or euro cheque. At the end of the consultation you're given a form (*feuille de soin*) to claim back the money. However, do check before having treatment that the doctor you're seeing is *conventionné* (see page 181). About 92 per cent of GPs are signed up and you are only likely to run into this issue in the major cities, but the tariffs should be clearly displayed on the doctor's desk or at reception. Rather than posting off the *feuille de soins* yourself, you can ask your local pharmacy to do it for you when they hand over your prescription.

To find a GP, look in the *Pages Jaunes* under *médecin generalist* or visit your town hall or *mairie*. It's also useful to get a personal recommendation, especially if you're looking for an English speaker. If you possibly can, choose a GP who is based in the same *département* as you. Doctors in France do pay house calls, but although your own GP may be content to visit *hors département*, the case may be different if you have to call the locum, especially out of hours. On the other hand, you may prefer a doctor outside your *département* if he or she is nearer geographically, or the hospital to which he or she generally refers patients is closer or better equipped than anything in your own *département* (doctors usually refer patients to hospitals in the same *département* as the surgery, though not always, as it depends on what speciality you may need).

Opening hours for GPs vary, but 9am-12 noon and 2pm-6pm is typical, and you can usually get an appointment the same or the next day. Saturday mornings are often 'free house' when you can turn up without an appointment and just wait. If your local surgery is closed, the answerphone should give you the locum number or, failing this, contact the local *gendarmerie*.

Many French doctors speak English, but don't expect them to use it, as the French are often shy of speaking English unless they speak it very well. Therefore you may find it's useful to have with you a decent dictionary, or a specialist book such as the 'Glossary of Medical, Health and Pharmacy Terms' by AS Lindsey, which covers both English and French terminology. It can also help to take along a friend or spouse who speaks French, as it's easy to miss vital things or even forget your French when you're unwell or in a stressful situation.

Luckily, French medical technical language is largely similar to that in English, as most medical terms derive from Greek or Latin (a myocardial infarction, for instance, is an *infarctus du myocarde*), but there are also some faux amis to watch out for, such as *colle*, which means cervix in French – i.e. the 'neck' of the womb, not the neck of the body, and *drogues*, which means hard drugs, not medicines.

Be aware that the French are not as shy about the body as the English. You're quite likely to have a physical examination at the surgery and your doctor will probably not leave the room while you undress, nor ask for a nurse to be present. Temperatures are sometimes taken rectally, not orally, and you may be prescribed medicines via suppository rather than by mouth, as this is the fastest way to get drugs into the bloodstream. Also, if you go for something like a gynaecological check-up, you're quite likely to be expected to strip completely naked and stay that way for a considerable length of time – take a t-shirt up onto the couch if you're sensitive about this kind of thing.

Also, don't panic if a French doctor refers you to hospital for something you thought was quite minor – it doesn't mean you're seriously ill, it's simply that French doctors emphasise preventative medicine and are not so used to watching a budget as UK ones.

Prescriptions

Doctors still traditionally prescribe (some would say over-prescribe) a lot of medicines in France, and have a habit of using brand names. If you are prescribed a drug, therefore, you may find that the pharmacist replaces it with a generic one. It doesn't mean you're not getting the right treatment, it's simply that the pharmacists are more familiar with the generic medicines than the doctors are, and are using them in an attempt to save money. If you insist, you don't have to accept the substitute medicine, but bear in mind that your reimbursement will be for the generic medicine, which means you could end up paying considerably more money for a brand-name drug. Cost-cutting aside, you're quite likely, nevertheless, to emerge from the pharmacy with a bag full of antibiotics, wipes, sterile dressings, eye *lavages*, etc., according to your ailment.

Not all of these prescription items are reimbursed at the same rate. Essential medicines are reimbursed at 100 per cent (and are labelled accordingly), white-label medicines considered 'important' for your treatment are reimbursed at 65 per cent, and blue-label 'comfort' medicines are only reimbursed at 35 per cent. If you don't consider all of the items necessary, or don't have insurance cover and would rather not spend the money, think about managing without some of them – but speak up before the pharmacist peels the labels off the items and attaches them to the prescription form.

Pharmacies

Since doctors charge a fee (which is reimbursable, but which you still have to pay at the time) for many French people the pharmacy is the first port of call when they're sick, particularly as pharmacists offer first-aid treatments such as stitches. Pharmacies also perform services such as blood pressure testing, and staff are trained to recognise poisonous mushrooms and dangerous snakes. Many medicinal items are available over the counter in France which are prescription-only in the UK.

French pharmacies are individually owned – there are no chains like Boots – and can be identified by the green cross sign. This flashes when the pharmacy is open. Typical opening hours are: 8.30-12 noon, 2.00-7.00pm, with most rural pharmacies closing for lunch. If you're having the last consultation of the day at the doctor's surgery and need a prescription, the doctor can ask the pharmacy to stay open for you. On Sundays, there is usually a duty chemist (*pharmacie de garde*) open somewhere – details should be displayed on the doors of your normal pharmacy.

If you have any questions to ask about your medicines, the pharmacist may prove more helpful than a doctor whose time is at a premium. Pharmacies are also the place to buy brands of toiletries that aren't available elsewhere, and you can expect all the staff to be very clued up and informative about the products on offer. Each pharmacy in a town will stock different brands of toiletries and make-up, so it's worth shopping around.

Complementary medicine

Many medical treatments seen as 'alternative' in Britain are considered mainstream in France, particularly acupuncture and homeopathy. Many doctors and even some dentists offer homeopathy and all pharmacies stock a wide range of homeopathic and herbal treatments.

All 'alternative' treatments, including treatment at spas (balneotherapy and thalassotherapy), are refundable by the French health service if they've been prescribed by a doctor, but not to 100 per cent. In fact, *médicine douce*, as it's called in France is widely seen as under threat and many doctors and dentists are campaigning for it to be reinstated to its former 100 per cent reimbursement level.

Dentists

Dentistry is reimbursed at a rate of around 70 per cent, except purely cosmetic work such as teeth whitening, which may be at your own expense. Charges, however, tend to be lower than in the UK, to the extent that some Britons from the south-east come over to France specifically for treatment. To make sure you get your reimbursement, you'll need a dentist who is *conventionnée*.

To find a dentist, look in the *Pages Jaunes* under *dentiste*, or ask at the doctor's surgery or the pharmacy – in an emergency, the *gendarmerie* can usually help. If you want dental surgery, you'll need a *chirugien-dentiste*, but there are also other kinds of dentists, such as prosthetic dentists who make false teeth, and many dental surgeons are also qualified as orthodontists. Most are self-employed one-man-bands and do not employ a hygienist but do the dental cleaning and descaling themselves (at my surgery, the receptionist also doubles as dental assistant).

It may come as a surprise, having waited in a brown lino-clad waiting room that hasn't been touched since the 1970s, to find that your rural dentist has extremely up-to-date equipment of the kind sometimes only seen in private practice in the UK.

Many dentists are also homeopaths – for instance, for a saliva stone you might find yourself with a prescription for homeopathic Trifolium Praetense, or for a tooth abscess, you might be given Merc Sol rather than antibiotics.

When toothache strikes...

If you need emergency dental treatment in rural France out of hours, you can really find yourself in a jam, as I found out recently.

It began with a bit of a twinge in a molar one sunny Saturday afternoon. I have trouble with this tooth from time to time, with bone fragments from an old extraction working their way up through the gum, so I did nothing about it for a few hours. But this time it was a big mistake. By Saturday night I was ready to chop my own head off with a chainsaw, but flunking on this option, I opted for downing a huge dose of Doliprane (paracetamol) and going to bed.

When the pills wore off at 4.00am, I knew I was in serious trouble. My face was the size of a sofa pillow; I could hardly swallow, and the pain was indescribable. The problem was, I also guessed that if I made the 23km night-time trek to my nearest casualty department, they still wouldn't treat the tooth. You can't have an extraction if there's no dental department, and when my friend had gone to the same hospital with an abscess, they wouldn't even give her antibiotics, but just sent her home with extra-strong pain relief. That much I figured I could handle alone.

However, having finally realised that it was probably an abscess I took a dose of Merc Sol, from my trusty homeopathic pharmacy. Merc Sol does nothing at all to relieve pain, but it does bring boils and abscesses to a head.

In the morning I was up early, trying to avail myself of the local emergency services. My dentist, of course, was shut, and would be so until Tuesday. Nor could I find any other dentist open. The *Pages Blanches* (included in the *Pages Blanches/Pages Jaunes* directory) showed that the *service de garde* was in Sees, over 70km away at the other side of my *département*, and it was only open from 10.00am until 12.00 noon. In fact, it proved to be just an answerphone, which referred me back to the *service de garde* for my region in Flers. This was only 40km away, but having tried the number for two hours there was no answer.

It was now noon, so I rang Flers hospital and asked for the dental department, but it was shut until Monday.

Seeing my options closing around me, it was at this point that I decided I would have to tough it out and be a grown-up. It was a lower molar, after all, not life-threatening. I decided not to cancel that evening's party, but to let everyone come round as planned, and meanwhile I logged onto the Internet to try every home remedy I could find. These included vodka rinses, teabags on the gums, clove oil, and raw garlic compresses, and they all helped somewhat, along with large doses of Doliprane. Preparing food and tidying up also took my mind off the pain a little, then suddenly, mid-afternoon, after three doses of Merc Sol, the abscess burst, to my enormous relief.

Friends turned up with wine (not allowed) and yet more variations on pain relief (thank God for French pharmacies) and the evening passed without my having to kill myself.

The next day, I tried again to see a dentist but couldn't find anyone to take me (most dental surgeries in my region are closed on Mondays and the few that were open were booked till the following week). On Monday evening I did finally manage to see a doctor (though not mine, who was busy), but he was rather reluctant to do anything other than prescribe antibiotics and mouthwash. "Ooh, that's horrible," he said, backing away. "Have you thought of seeing a dentist...?"

In fact, I didn't actually manage to see a dentist until Tuesday afternoon, three days after my problem had begun, and even this was a 25km drive away. In the event, the wait was probably just as well, as the only treatment she could offer was to scrape the abscess out manually, without anaesthesia, explaining that anaesthetics don't work if an infection is present.

So, is there a moral to this story? Only that perhaps, if you're going to have a tooth abscess, buy a house in a French city, not the countryside. Or at least keep your medicine cabinet well stocked!

Medical examinations

You'll come across these quite quickly if you're employed in France, as most employees have a medical examination when they're hired, and then have one annually thereafter. This is a rather cursory affair compared with a full medical, however, and is mainly to ensure that you can do your job safely.

You can demand a full medical (*bilan de santé*, or 'check-up') free of charge every five years under the social security system once you reach the age of 16 (provided you're paying contributions). This takes two to three hours and usually includes a chest examination, blood and urine tests, an electrocardiogram, hearing and eye tests, a dental and mouth examination and various measures such as height, weight and blood pressure, plus a chest x-ray. Either you or your doctor can ask for more tests, such as HIV or cancer screening. If you're female, once you reach the age of 40, your doctor will probably suggest an annual mammogram.

After treatments such as an operation, you're entitled to see your medical records, and it's quite usual for you to be handed your own x-rays or ultrasounds. Always keep them, because if you have regular checkups for any condition, you'll be expected to bring them along. Visit the *Commission d'Accès au Documents Administratifs* (www.cada.fr) for more information on your rights to view your own documents, including an English translation of the Act of 1978.

Long-term illnesses

All treatments for serious long-term conditions such as diabetes, heart disease and thyroid disease are 100 per cent covered on the French health service and all prescriptions are free. If you enter the country with any such long-term condition, inform the Department of Work and Pensions (DWP) before you leave and try to obtain the correct paperwork.

Not in the system?

All of the above applies to people who live in France and are in the healthcare system, but what if you're not? Non EU-citizens travelling to France are not covered by the EU's reciprocal healthcare agreements, so they must take out private cover. This is offered by only a few insurers and it's very expensive, but www.globalinsurance.net is a good starting point.

Meanwhile, EU citizens who, for instance, to and fro between French and UK properties can find themselves in a no-man's land where they lack full cover. If you're a UK resident, the EHIC card (which replaced Form E111) is obtainable from the post office and will give you basic cover when you're in France. Many French doctors and hospitals were well-versed in using the E111, though they're not so familiar with the EHIC card. Using the EHIC, you'll still have to pay for some treatment at the time you receive it (except emergency hospital treatment, which will be billed direct to the NHS), and you claim reimbursement from French social security in the same way as French residents.

It should be stressed, however, that the EHIC is not a catch-all. It covers emergency hospital treatment but not prescribed medicines, x-rays, lab tests, special examinations, physiotherapy or dental treatment. So if, for instance, you feel a tooth twingeing while you're at your French holiday property, be prepared to pay for treatment. Likewise, most travel insurance will only cover you for emergency treatment, though it can also offer extra benefits such as repatriation.

Many private health insurers are not willing to cover clients on a normal domestic policy if they regularly travel between properties in two countries – the risk is simply too variable. Therefore, if you have an existing private healthcare (PMI) policy that covers you in the UK, don't assume it will cover you while you're in France. You may find you need an extension to your existing policy, or a specialist policy provided by an international health insurer such as Goodhealth International (www.goodhealthworldwide.com).

If you are living permanently in France, you can buy a private ex-pat policy from many insurers. Approach this with caution however, as it is unlikely to work out cheaper than registering under the French system and is thought by most French medical personnel to be technically illegal. Some people, even after they have moved permanently to France, prefer to continue paying their social security in their home country for as long as possible in order to obtain reciprocal cover, but you are unlikely to be able to do this for more than two years. Contact the DWP for details.

CASE STUDY: Healthcare

Steve Mason was glad he was in the French system when he was rushed to his local hospital with acute appendicitis in September 2003.

"We handed over our *Carte Vitale* and that was that," he says. "Within an hour of the diagnosis, I was being operated on."

Steve cannot speak highly enough of the quality of care: "As well as constant, professional nursing attention, I had my own room and bathroom, a TV and a phone by the bed. This was the first time I'd been in hospital in my life, at the age of 45, and it made an incredible difference to me when I was feeling low in the middle of the night."

"They were not in a hurry to get rid of me and were talking about keeping me in for 10 days, but I was well enough to go home after five, which was more than enough for me. When I was discharged, a district nurse came to the house every day for a week to change my dressings. This was great, because I had never had an operation before and it bothered me that I didn't recover as quickly as I'd hoped. I could ask her about anything that was on my mind – the only drawback was that the tests were at 6 in the morning!"

The portion of Steve's care that was not covered by his social security was covered by his *mutuelle* insurer, AGF. Upon entry to the hospital, his wife handed over their *Carte Vitale*, along with the attestation from the *mutuelle*, and all expenses were taken care of. At no point did he have to hand over any cash except for phone calls he made from the hospital. Six weeks after his discharge, his post-op check-up showed him to be in good health.

Top tips

- The French health service is the best in the world, with the government spending more on health than on defence.
- Hospital accommodation is usually two to a room, with toilet and washing facilities.
- The cost of healthcare is not fully funded by the government and most French people buy top-up insurance.
- You have full health cover if you are a child, unemployed, retired, disabled, or pregnant.
- When you visit a doctor, you pay at the end of the consultation.
- Most French people carry a *Carte Vitale*, which eases the burden of paperwork.
- French pharmacists are qualified to perform minor first-aid.
- In emergencies, dial 112.
- The French emergency services are a specialist branch of medicine, co-ordinated by the fire brigade.
- You are entitled to emergency treatment in France if you're a British national.

Glossary

La Sécu – The French social security system

Régime – Designation/regime/system

Ayant droit – Dependant

Déclaration de Choix du Médecin Traitant – The form used to choose or change your GP

Caisse – Social security agency

Conventionné – Medical practitioners who have agreed to charge the normal state tariff for services

Feuille de soins – Reimbursement form for treatment

Assurance complementaire maladie – Medical insurance. Commonly known as *mutuelle*

Mutualiste – An insurer specialising in medical insurance

Attestation – Certificate/card of insurance

Carte Vitale – The French healthcard, which contains all your social security details, including your insurance cover

Département – Geographical area similar to a county. France is divided geographically into 100 *départements*

Ambulance municipal – Local ambulance service

Gendarmerie – Military body charged with police duties among the civilian population (effectively acts as the police force in many areas, including small towns, but differs from the civilian police force in being under the jurisdiction of the ministry of defence)

SOS Médecins – Specialist emergency doctors

Gants de toilette – Washcloths that you can insert your hand into

Pharmacie de garde – Duty chemist

Médecin traitant – Attending physician/GP

Generaliste – General practitioner

Pages Jaunes – Yellow Pages, business directory

Hors département – Outside the *departement*

Médicine douce – Complementary therapy

Dentiste – Dentist

Chirugien-dentiste – Dental surgeon

Service de garde – Emergency service (for dentists, chemists, etc.)

Bilan de santé – A full medical

15

Tax

Taxes in France are quite high, and a constant source of complaint, but this is mainly because of high social security contributions (see Chapter 19). In fact, income tax per se is quite low, particularly if you can take advantage of the many allowances – the average Frenchman with a wife and two offspring pays only about 9-10 per cent income tax. However, at the time of writing, the future situation remained unclear, following the election of Nicolas Sarkozy as president, who was elected partly on a promise to reduce personal taxes. Other taxes also exist in France, such as VAT and wealth tax.

Who is liable?

Both people who are domiciled and not domiciled may be taxed in France.

You are considered to be domiciled if any of the following apply:

- You're resident in France for 183 days in any one year.
- You are principally employed in France.
- Your centre of economic interest is in France.
- Your principal residence is in France.

Domiciled

If you are domiciled in France, you're taxed on your entire worldwide income from all sources, including:

- Wages and salaries
- Business profits
- Professional profits
- Agricultural profits
- Real property income
- Income from transferable securities
- Compensation (certain company managers)
- Capital gains

You pay tax on items such as bonuses and company cars and other items that constitute benefits packages. Pension lump sums that are tax-free in the UK are taxed as income in France.

Not domiciled

If you are not domiciled in France, you pay taxes in France on any income from French sources. This includes:

- Income from property located in France.
- Income from stocks and shares invested in France.
- Capital gains.
- Pensions and annuities held in France.

The item that is most applicable to the British is capital gains tax incurred when selling a French holiday home. This, however, may be partially offset by a tax credit in the UK.

Pensioners

If you're a retired Briton living in France, your UK state or occupational pension is classed as income and is taxed in France, with the exception of government service pensions, which are taxed in the UK. Personal pensions, however, are a new phenomenon in France, and you could easily find yourself paying French income tax on your 'tax-free' lump sum. Take professional advice – preferably before moving over.

Double taxation

France has a double-taxation agreement with the UK, as it does with all other EU countries. This means you are exempt from paying tax twice, no matter in which country you are resident or in which you earn your income.

The double taxation agreement can be complicated, however, and again it pays to take professional advice, as it is easy to imagine that you are not liable in France, particularly if you own other property in the UK or elsewhere. Some high earners choose to move their holdings offshore – your accountant can advise whether it is worth doing this.

How is income tax paid in France?

France differs from the UK in that it does not have a PAYE system and all French residents have to pay their own taxes and submit a tax declaration each year, whether they are employed or self-employed. Families are also taxed as a unit, not as individuals. There is no concept such as 'head of household' and either half of a couple can fill in the family tax return. The tax year runs from January to December.

Most French people hire an accountant to do their taxes because the system is very complicated, even for salaried persons. If you're self-employed or run a business, even more so. The French Chamber of Commerce in London's Westminster can provide details of Anglo-French tax consultants.

✉ French Chamber of Commerce in Great Britain
21 Dartmouth Street
Westminster
London
SW1H 9BP

☎ 00 44 20 7304 4040
Fax 00 44 20 7304 4034
💻 www.ccfgb.co.uk

You can also check the advertisements in the French property press or sites such as Angloinfo for accountants in your area. In my experience, French accountants are not as enthusiastic to find ways for you to avoid tax as UK accountants – they are more concerned with making sure you are compliant.

For tax purposes, 'units' are calculated as follows:

- If you're a single person, you count as one unit.
- If you're a couple, you count as two units.
- If you're a single parent with one dependent child, you count as two units.
- If you're a single parent with an adult child, you count as one-and-a-half units.
- For married couples, the first two dependent children each count as a half unit, then third and subsequent children each count as one unit.
- Except for the above exceptions, each adult over 18 in a household counts as one unit.

Children are considered to be dependent if they are:

- Under 18.
- Disabled (any age).
- Aged 18-25, widowed or divorced AND childless. People in this situation (who must fulfil all three criteria) can apply for a tax exemption on their parents' tax return.

Overall, the system has traditionally taken good care of families, especially those on low incomes or with three or more children, but has disadvantaged double-income couples with no children, who can claim almost nothing in the way of allowances.

No tax is payable on very low incomes, currently set at €7,640 for under-65s and €8,340 for over-65s, but you still have to fill out a tax form.

Your tax return

The tax return is called a *déclaration des revenues* and should drop into your postbox in early spring each year. Your sums will have been calculated on your previous year's income, which might necessitate you changing the figures and sending the form to your accountant. Once the accountant is happy with it, you then sign it and post it back, or deliver it to your local tax office (*Centre des Impôts*). If you need to discuss it, the *Centre des Impôts* is usually very helpful (many French people do not understand their tax returns either and there is often a queue). Once you've filed your first tax return, you can switch to filing online if you feel comfortable with this method, and this gives you an extension to the normal deadline.

Your tax demand

You normally receive your actual tax demand (*avis d'imposition*) in the summer and can pay either in three *tranches* (*tiers provisionnels*) or monthly (*mensualisation* – though there are 10 monthly payments, not 12). Most people opt to pay three times a year, which allows them to invest their income in the meantime. In this case, only the first two payments are provisional – the third is adjusted to take into account your actual income for the previous year and may therefore involve a top-up or a refund. If you pay in ten instalments, this adjustment is usually paid in November/December.

Reducing your income tax liability – employees

If you are an employee, you can claim an automatic 10 per cent reduction for expenses up to a maximum figure of just over €13,000. You can also claim an additional 20 per cent reduction for making pensions contributions (which are compulsory in France) or for owning an annuity. Contributions to life insurance policies cannot be claimed against tax.

Reducing your income tax liability – self-employed

If you are self-employed you cannot claim either of the above allowances but you can reduce your tax liability by joining an *Association Agrée*, which submits your tax declaration for you. You pay a flat fee to join, plus a subscription fee, but if your earnings are over about €12,000, the *Association* more than pays for itself. It also provides a 'green light' through the tax system, as the authorities do not generally query tax forms submitted by an *Association*. The *Association* itself, however, may keep coming back to you asking for more information, and expects you to have kept detailed accounts of expenditure and income.

Income tax reductions and credits

Tax reductions and credits for 'social and economic reasons' can be obtained for:

- Paying into a *mutuelle* for your health insurance.
- Caring for aged parents.
- Paying alimony.
- Paying for help required at home.
- Paying union fees.
- Taking eco-friendly measures such as switching your car to GPL or making your house more energy-efficient.

If you are low-waged, you can also get help to employ a childminder or use daycare facilities so that you can work, though the system also rewards stay-at-home mothers and many French women choose to stay at home after having children.

Self-employment and compliance

The French tax system as a whole is complex, with many allowances depending on your status, but it is particularly difficult for anyone who is self-employed. It is hard to negotiate the minefield – even using software such as *Ciel*, which is approved for the purpose – without the help of an accountant (*comptable*) so it is well worth employing one, although their fees are high compared with the UK.

If you run a *microenterprise* (i.e. you turn over less than €27,000 per year) you are entitled to 'free accountancy' but this will probably only be a couple of days per year. If you are *professional libérale*, you will almost certainly need more than this. However, your accountant will probably save you more money than he or she costs, and will at least make sure you are compliant so that you get no nasty surprises.

It is generally accepted that most French self-employed people do about a third of their work 'off the books' and the tradition was that the tax authorities turned a blind eye to this. However, the situation has tightened and it is particularly important for foreigners to make sure that they are compliant, as there are rewards for informing on malefactors, and offenders can be deported. The French tax authorities have sweeping powers and will investigate you if you appear to have a higher standard of living than you should – such as driving around in an expensive car and eating at expensive restaurants when you're nominally on a low income.

Leaving France

If you leave France and have been paying income tax there, you should inform the tax authorities and fill out your tax declaration (*déclaration provisoire et anticipée des revenus*). You can easily end up overpaying tax when you leave France and may have to claim a refund.

Other taxes

Wealth tax

Described by the French Government as a 'tax on your fortune', the ISF (*impôt de solidarité sur fortune*) must be paid by high net worth individuals. The level is currently set at €732,000 – about £500,000. However, because wealth tax takes into account property, furnishings, antiques and art objects, it is quite possible for British people who have done well in the property market to become liable for wealth tax. Nevertheless, wealth tax is still not a tax to be feared as it is incremental, and even at its highest (when your high net worth is over €15,255,000 – about £10 million) it is still only 1.8 per cent. Ask your accountant for advice.

VAT

Almost all economic activity in France is subject to VAT (*TVA*), which is why you see the letters TTC (*toutes taxes comprises*) written on so many prices. VAT rates are variable but the standard rate is 19.6 per cent. For items such as books, cinema tickets, drinks and take-away food, the rate is 5 per cent, while for newspapers and magazines it is only 2.1 per cent. Children's clothes now have zero VAT and so do 'basic' foodstuffs.

If you run a business in France, you normally have to register for VAT if you turn over about €30,000 or more. However, you can choose to register for VAT even if you make less than this. Claims are simple to make (ask at the tax office – *Centre des Impôts*), and it's sensible to register if you pay out any reasonable level of expenses such as electricity bills, stationary, office equipment or other supplies.

VAT can confuse, and even scare, people because they think they will end up out of pocket. To understand it, it's best to think of it as two separate taxes – the VAT you charge your customers and the VAT you pay on supplies.

When you are VAT-registered you add the tax to what you would normally charge your customers. Let's say you charge a customer €500 for an item or service. If the current VAT rate is 19.6 per cent, their total bill would then come to €598. When you are paid, you pass on the €98 (the VAT part) to the tax office. So you receive exactly the same as you would have done if you hadn't been VAT-registered. It makes no difference to your profits, though it does make your goods or services slightly more expensive for your customers.

Where you gain is on supplies. Suppliers charge you the same regardless of your VAT status. But if you are VAT-registered, you get to claim back the VAT part of the bill. That can reduce your expenses considerably. So, overall, you stand to make more profit by being VAT-registered.

Corporation tax

Only about a third of French companies pay corporation tax, known as the *Impôt sur les Sociétés*, or IS for short. Most of these are limited-liability companies such as *Sociétés Anonymes* (SAs), *Sociétés par Actions Simplifiées* (SASs), and most *Sociétés à Responsabilité Limitée* (SARLs). Business partnerships may also elect to pay corporation tax, while some 'legal entities' such as *sociétés anonymes* (SAs or public limited companies) may be liable according to the nature of their business. Businesses in official areas of economic decline may have some exemptions. See page 267, for more information on company designations. No corporation tax is charged on any company you own outside France.

The current rate for corporation tax is 33.3 per cent and it applies to net adjusted profits after taking into account allowances, inventories, reserves, etc. (This contrasts with 19 per cent in the UK.) You will need an accountant's advice to make the most of your allowances. If you are thinking of setting up a business in France, it might be worthwhile attending a UK-based course beforehand, such as those held by Quorum (www.quorumtraining.co.uk).

For detailed information on French corporation tax, visit the Embassy of France in the US site at: www.ambafrance-us.org/intheus/tax/fit.asp

Other taxes paid by businesses

Almost more of a problem for businesses than corporation tax are the social security payments they must pay for employees. This constitutes about 35-40 per cent of salary and is one reason that some small French businesses find it difficult to hire staff.

Businesses also have to pay local taxes known as *taxes professionelles*, which vary according to location (generally speaking, taxes are higher in the south). The calculation is based principally on the annual rental value of the firm's tangible assets with some additional calculations for the overall salary bill of the company.

Top tips

- France does not have a PAYE system and everyone must fill out their own tax return.
- It pays to hire an accountant to do your tax return, especially if your situation is complicated.
- Tax is paid per household, with each adult and child counting as a unit or part-unit.
- Income tax is relatively low, but social charges can be painful.
- Pension lump sums that are tax-free in the UK are classed as income, and taxed, in France.
- France has a wealth tax for high net worth individuals.

Glossary

Déclaration des revenues – Tax return

Centre des Impôts – Local tax office

Avis d'imposition – Tax demand

Tiers provisionnels – Three tranches/payments (a way of paying taxes)

Mensualisation – Monthly

Association Agrée – A form of trade indemnity association

Mutuelle – Medical insurance

Comptable – Accountant

Microenterprise – A regime enabling the reduction of accounting burden (for companies turning over less than €27,000 per year)

Professional libérale – A professional

Déclaration provisoire et anticipée des revenues – Tax declaration

Impôt de solidarité sur fortune (ISF) – Wealth tax

Taxe à la Valeur Ajoutée (TVA) – VAT

Toutes taxes comprises (TTC) – Including tax (seen on bills etc.)

Centre des Impôts – Local tax office

Impôt sur les Sociétés (IS) – Corporation tax

Sociétés Anonymes (SAs) – Public limited companies

Sociétés par Actions Simplifiées (SAS) – Limited-liability company with greater freedom given to shareholders

Sociétés à Responsabilité Limitée (SARLs) – Multiple-person private limited companies

Taxes professionnelles – Local business taxes

16

Civil matters

French citizenship

You can become a French citizen in three ways – by **birth, marriage** or **naturalisation.**

Birth: if you were born in France, you have an automatic right to French citizenship when you're 18, provided you have spent at least five years in France since you were aged 11. However, you do not have to become a French citizen if you don't want to (opting out was more common in the days of compulsory national service).

Marriage: if you marry a French citizen, you're entitled to French citizenship after one year of marriage, provided you are still living in one household.

Naturalisation: you can apply for French citizenship once you've lived in France full-time for five years. You'll have to prove that you're of good character and that you speak the language well. You apply to the prefect of your *département*, who will contact your local mayor for information about you (as to whether you've broken any laws, etc.) The application will then take 18 months to two years to process. There is no right of appeal if you are not granted citizenship, but if you're successful, it automatically naturalises your spouse and children under 18.

Marriage and divorce in France

France is a secular state, which means there is a separation of church and state (religion, for instance, is not part of the state school curriculum). French marriages are civil affairs and are performed by an *officier de l'état civil* (usually the local *mairie*) at the *mairie* or town hall. However, most French people, being nominally Catholic, then follow this up with a church ceremony. This has no legal basis but at least gives the bride the traditional opportunity to dress up. Religious ceremonies must take place after, not before, the civil ceremony – the rabbi, priest, etc. is not allowed to perform it without proof of the marriage certificate.

If your marriage is legal in the UK, it is automatically recognised under French law, and by default is considered to be under the marital 'regime' of *communauté universelle*. All French marriages are performed under a 'regime', of which there are four:

1. *Communauté universelle* – all assets are jointly owned by both parties and all debts are joint.
2. *Communauté réduite aux acquêts* – all assets from before the marriage are owned separately but joint assets acquired since the marriage are jointly owned (there are exceptions, such as inheritances).
3. *Separation de biens* – all assets are held separately.
4. *Participation aux acquets* – all assets are owned separately unless the marriage is dissolved, in which case all assets acquired during the marriage are considered to be owned jointly.

For a full definition of French legal terms visit:
www.net-iris.fr/lexique-juridique

Many French couples choose not to marry at all and co-habit instead. This can be either *en union libre*, in which case the partners are taxed individually, or in official *concubinage*, which entitles each partner to some, but not all, of the rights of marriage. *Concubinage*, however, can still involve inheritance problems, as partners are not legally relatives and therefore have to pay higher inheritance taxes. You can get around this, and make your partnership more legally recognisable, by signing a PACS agreement (*pacte civile de solidarité*). This is often used in France and is equally applicable to same-sex couples – it entitles you to better property rights and some income tax benefits. See a *notaire* for details.

If you decide to get married in France, there is substantial red tape to plough through, even if you're an EU citizen. One of you will need to reside in the place where you wish to marry for at least 40 days; you will have to post bans at least 10 days before the marriage date, undergo a medical examination that includes blood tests to check for Rhesus compatibility, and provide reams of paperwork, including your birth certificates and proof of residence, all translated by an official translator (*traducteur assermenté*) and dated within the past three months. If you are then held up by red tape, you can easily find yourself having to obtain everything again.

If you're not an EU citizen, it can be even more complicated and you may find yourself required to supply items such as proof that you're not already married and an affidavit at law (*certificat de coutume*) that shows that your French marriage will be recognised in your home country.

Getting divorced

Getting divorced is a common event in France and the procedure was liberalised in 2005 with the introduction of the no-fault option of divorce by mutual consent (*le divorce sur demande conjointe*).

When divorcing, each spouse must have a lawyer, though if you choose the mutual consent option, the same lawyer can act for both of you (for obvious reasons, however, French lawyers advise against this). Your lawyer(s) will draw up an agreement and if both parties are satisfied, it can take as little as four months, though you have to be married for at least six months in order to file the petition in the first place. You do not have to give a cause for the breakdown of the marriage and need only appear in court once. Either or both partners can apply for legal aid.

Other types of divorce are:

- *Le divorce sur demande acceptée* – one spouse gives just cause for the divorce and the other accepts it.
- *Le divorce pour rupture de vie commune* – where a separation has existed for at least six years, or one spouse alleges that the mental faculties of the other, for at least six years, have rendered their life together impossible in the future.
- *Le divorce pour faute* – one spouse is required to prove (by means of witnesses, medical evidence or photographs) just cause for the divorce. Just causes include desertion, ill-treatment, adultery, and criminal conviction on the part of the other spouse. Divorce of this type formerly constituted 40 per cent of divorce cases in France, mainly because the partner 'at fault' could not receive any compensatory lump sum upon divorce. This clause, however, has now been cancelled, easing the way to no-fault divorce.

Divorce cases are presided over by a family judge known as a JAF (*juge aux affaires familiales*) unless they are contested, in which case they must be decided in court. JAFs are required by law to encourage people to reconcile, and can also order a couple to go to mediation.

Divorce bits and bobs

- Upon divorce, French women generally revert to their maiden name unless they need to keep it for professional reasons (in fact, women often use their maiden name in France, especially for items such as medical records).
- Women must wait 300 days before they remarry, unless they provide a certificate showing they are not pregnant.
- Children are considered to be a joint responsibility and maintenance must be paid by both parties.
- Access to the children for the departing spouse is usually granted on the basis of every other weekend and half the holidays.
- Maintenance settlements for women are not normally granted unless the woman is of retirement age or cannot work.
- Prenuptial agreements are valid in France, and are taken into account in any settlement.

For further information on divorce in France, visit:

http://ec.europa.eu/civiljustice

Dying in France

There are sufficient British people dying in France now for the *Association Française d'Information Funéraire* to have an English-language section on its website. Visit www.afif.asso.fr and click on the union jack for details in English.

When a person dies in France, whatever their nationality, the medical death certificate (*certificat de décès*) is signed by the attending physician. If the death is not of known cause, or clearly due to an accident, there must be an inquest to determine the cause.

You must register the death within 24 hours at the *mairie* or town hall of the area where the death took place (which may or may not be your home town or village). Anyone can undertake this task, so for obvious reasons it usually falls upon a family friend or more distant relative, rather than a spouse. You should take along the dead person's ID (a passport is ideal) as well as your own ID, the medical death certificate and the *livret de famille* (family dossier) if relevant.

In small villages, where the death is sudden and is of a British national, it's quite common for the ambulance crew or attending doctors to phone the local mayor, who will come over to the house and do the necessary paperwork. They will also recommend a firm of undertakers (*pompes funèbres*) for you. If your loved one died in an institution, such as a hospital or retirement home, however, the death will automatically be reported by the institution.

If the deceased is a foreign national, you should also inform the relevant embassy. You then have one week in which to inform other interested parties such as banks, insurance companies and so on.

Once the paperwork is done at the town hall, they will issue an *acte de décès* (death certificate). You should make at least six copies of this, as you will need it for all manner of paperwork. If you are both French residents and have children you may end up needing as many as 20 copies. Be aware that the *acte* does not state the cause of death and you may therefore also need copies of the *certificat* if you are intending to export the body back to the UK. Only once the *acte* is issued can the town hall issue a burial permit.

You are not allowed to bury or cremate the body for at least 24 hours after death, but burial or cremation must take place within six days. Embalming must also take place after the first 24 hours, which can become a fraught issue for Muslims as it's contrary to Islamic practice. Note, however, that a body also cannot be repatriated to the UK unless it is embalmed.

Because France is a secular state, there is no requirement to have a religious funeral. France is a Catholic country, however, and cremation therefore remains rare, though it is on the increase. Even five years ago in France it was rare to find a crematorium except in a major city – now, however, the situation is changing, due to changing religious beliefs and lack of space for graveyards.

The mayor of the *commune* where the death occurred has to give consent for a cremation to take place, though this will probably be requested by the undertakers, and it's usual for the cremation to be held at the nearest crematorium to where the death took place, not at the nearest crematorium to where you live. If you want to have the body transferred to a different location, there is generally a fee, though it is usually lower than the UK equivalent.

You can then take the urn away, or the crematorium can store the ashes for up to three months. You cannot scatter the ashes on a public footpath (which includes roads and rivers), but you can scatter them on private land, at sea or outdoors in, for instance, a forest. However, you do need permission from the local mayor if you wish to inter the ashes in any kind of monument. As in the UK, cremation is cheaper than burial.

Plots are now in short supply, so many bodies are interred in vaults rather than underground. If you have access to a plot, you effectively rent it for a period of up to 99 years, or you can choose the commune plot, which is reserved for five years. (At this point the body is disinterred and buried in a common grave.) The plot must be covered by a concrete slab within three months of the funeral, and if you choose to erect a monument, it is up to you to maintain it.

The French decorate the graves of family members for *Toussaints* (November 1) usually with baskets of chrysanthemums.

Repatriating a body to the UK

If you wish to repatriate a body to the UK, you'll need to get in touch with the British Embassy in Paris (18bis rue d'Anjou, 75008 Paris, tel: 01 44 51 31 00, or search the web for 'British Embassy in Paris'). You also need to inform the funeral home of your wishes, so that they can prepare the body (embalming) and coffin (zinc-lined) accordingly. Coffins can usually travel back from France by sea, but some airlines will not take them, due to tighter anti-terrorism measures.

If all goes well, a body can usually be repatriated within seven days, but if the death necessitates an inquest, it can take several months. If the person died unexpectedly, violently or of unknown causes, there will be another inquest in the UK once the body has been returned.

Repatriating a body is expensive and can be complicated, so if you know that you or any member of your family definitely wishes to be interred in the UK, take out insurance. This will give you automatic cover for your bills, along with access to international undertakers, who are well versed in the procedures and understand all the issues involved.

Differences from the UK

- If a death occurs at home, it is quite common for the ambulance crew to leave the body in the house until the undertakers arrive, rather than taking it away.
- Caskets are usually open – if you want a closed casket, ask for one.
- Cremations are usually held at the nearest crematorium to the place of death, not the place of residence.
- You can apply to the prefect of your area to bury a body on private ground. To do so, you will have to present:
    1. A will signed by the dead person requesting this form of interment.
    2. The results of a geological and hydrological survey showing that the interment is not a danger to public health.
    3. A plan of the property, showing the proximity of neighbours, etc.

Top tips

- If your marriage is legal in the UK, it is automatically recognised in France.
- Divorce by mutual consent is available in France.
- A cremation is usually held at the nearest crematorium to where the death took place, not at the nearest crematorium to where the deceased lived.
- Cremation remains rare, as France is a Catholic country, but it is on the increase.
- You can become a French citizen in three ways: by birth, marriage and naturalisation.

Glossary

Département – Geographical area similar to a county. France is divided geographically into 100 *départements*

Officier de l'état civil – Officer of the state (such as a mayor)

Mairie – Mayor's office

Communauté universelle – All assets are jointly owned by both parties and all debts are joint

Communauté réduite aux acquêts – All assets from before the marriage are owned separately but joint assets acquired since the marriage are jointly owned (there are exceptions, such as inheritances)

Separation de biens – All assets are held separately

Participation aux acquets – All assets are owned separately unless the marriage is dissolved, in which case all assets acquired during the marriage are considered to be owned jointly

En union libre – Co-habitation

Concubinage – Common-law marriage

Pacte civile de solidarité (PACS) – Civil union

Notaire – Notary

Traducteur assermenté – Official translator

Certificat de coutume – Affidavit at law

Le divorce sur demande conjointe – No-fault option of divorce by mutual consent

Le divorce sur demande acceptée – One spouse gives just cause for the divorce and the other accepts it

Le divorce pour rupture de vie commune – Where a separation has existed for at least six years, or one spouse alleges that the mental faculties of the other, for at least six years, have rendered their life together impossible in the future

Le divorce pour faute – One spouse is required to prove (by means of witnesses, medical evidence or photographs) just cause for the divorce. Just causes include desertion, ill-treatment, adultery, and criminal conviction on the part of the other spouse

Juge aux affaires familiales (JAF) – A judge who presides over family matters, including divorce cases

Certificat de décès – Medical death certificate

Livret de famille – Family dossier

Pompes funèbres – Undertakers

Acte de décès – Death certificate

17

Children

An empirical British observer might well suggest that the French like children more than the British do. Whether the country is technically child-friendly or not, it's certainly true that you see children everywhere. They accompany their parents to restaurants, even as babies, and are usually welcomed with open arms. Invite French people for dinner and they'll probably bring along their children as a matter of course, along with the kids' food and some videos and board games. In rural areas, children still go fishing and cycling alone or in groups without adult supervision, just as children in the UK did 30 years ago.

Having a baby in France

France encourages childbirth, as its population has never recovered from the blow it suffered when it lost two million young men in the First World War. Consequently, the state does its best to make it possible for couples to have children by providing generous tax and maternity benefits. This is one reason for its exceptionally high rate of childbirth, at 1.9 children per woman.

If you find you are pregnant and do not live in France but, for instance, own a holiday home there and would prefer to give birth in France rather than the UK, then see page 179.

If you live in France and decide to have a baby there, and you do not already have a gynaecologist, ask your doctor to recommend one. Most French women have a gynaecologist separate from their GP as a matter of course, but not all work as obstetricians or in hospitals, so be aware of this if you want to see the same gynaecologist throughout your pregnancy. You may also find that your health insurance covers a private ob-gyn who can take you right through your pregnancy. If you live in the Paris area and are having a baby there, you could consider joining Message, a support group for mothers: http://messageparis.org

Once you are pregnant, your doctor will issue you with a *Déclaration de Grossesse* and details of how to send it to your nearest *Caisse d'Allocations Familiales* (CAF). This will get you into the state system for insurance and benefits. The CAF will send you your *Carnet de Maternité*, which is filled in as you progress through your pregnancy. It even comes with a pass that enables you to require others to give up a seat for you on public transport! From this moment until the end of your pregnancy, you should not have to hand over any money for medical treatment, including the normal doctor's fee, which is usually paid after each consultation.

Your medical expenses during pregnancy are covered by the state, provided that you are registered with the CAF and that you attend all the examinations to which you are obligated (if you don't, you could lose your benefits). However, you can choose to have your baby in a private clinic rather than a state hospital and pay for this on your medical insurance (*mutuelle*). Private clinics are often run by religious orders but you need not be a Catholic, or even a believer, to be a patient in one – some are *conventionné* (agreeing to charge set tariffs for services), and some are even part of the French health system. Check that the ob-gyn of your choice is permitted to deliver in the clinic, however, and be aware that if there are complications with your birth, you might be transferred to the hospital anyway. You are expected to book your hospital bed well ahead of time – not that they will refuse to treat you if your baby comes late or early. You can also usually attend antenatal classes at the same hospital.

Pregnancy and birth are more medicalised in France than in the UK and home births are not common, though they are permitted (doctors are usually happier about it if you have a good educational background and decent standard of living). If you want a home birth, speak to your doctor, who can recommend a midwife (*sage femme*), but note that home births may not be available in your area (i.e. the doctors will not guarantee the health of your baby if you opt for one), they are not fully reimbursed as hospital births are, and some insurance policies will not cover home deliveries. If you simply want a natural childbirth, it's possible that this can be arranged to take place in hospital, and many midwives are trained as homeopaths or acupuncturists.

When you become pregnant, your doctor will give you a leaflet explaining how the French system works and what to expect. Also recommended for French pregnancy terms is: '*Guide de la femme enceinte*', by Marie-Claude Delahaye. This will give you all the vocabulary you should need. You should also obtain an English-language book such as 'What to Expect when you're Expecting'.

Care includes the usual pre-natal checks seen in Britain such as blood tests to check iron levels, hormone levels, syphilis, HIV, toxoplasmosis, etc., but also some that are not known in the UK outside private practice, such as a health check for the father, and 're-education' (physiotherapy) classes after delivery to get you back into shape.

There are numerous antenatal checks that occur during pregnancy and you'll need to attend them in order to obtain your benefits (maternity benefit, free hospital bed, etc.) There are three scans, at three, five and eight months, though some women opt not to have the last one. On the other hand, you can ask for more scans if you feel you need them. Your blood will be tested for immunity to toxoplasmosis and you will generally undergo *échographies* (ultrasound scans) in the fourth month and seventh month to check for abnormalities. Be aware that if you decide to undergo a blood test to check for Down's Syndrome and an abnormality is found, you will be strongly urged to undergo an amniocentesis. At around seven months, you set out your birth plan and if an epidural is a possibility, you also see the anaesthetist.

Although it is now medically encouraged, many French women prefer not to breastfeed. If you wish to breastfeed, inform your doctor ahead of time and get in touch with *Le Lèche League* (www.lllfrance.org).

Standard maternity leave for a first baby is 16 weeks – 6 weeks before birth and 10 weeks afterwards, with an extra two weeks prenatal leave if any complications are found. (This is assuming that you give birth to only one baby.) However, maternity leave changes according to how many children you have, either consecutively or together – for instance, you get 20 weeks off when you have your third child, and 22 weeks off if you ever have triplets. Leave can also be moved around if you have a premature birth. Throughout this time, you are on full pay.

France introduced paternity leave in 2002, which entitles a father to 11 days off on full pay to spend time with a newborn. Parental leave was also introduced, in 1997. This entitles a parent who has worked for a company for at least one year, to take three years unpaid leave and still have a job kept open for them on their return.

A mother usually stays in hospital for five days after a birth, though up to two weeks is not uncommon, and she is trained in all aspects of looking after her newborn – it is quite remarkable to see how calm and confident new mothers in France generally are.

Registration

Once the baby is born it will come as no surprise that the procedure is surrounded by red tape. The birth must be registered (*déclaration de naissance*) within three working days at the local *mairie* or town hall and in exchange you will be given a *carnet de naissance de l'enfant*. Registration can be done by the mother, or anyone else present at the birth, provided they take along the preliminary birth certificate (*extrait d'acte de naissance*) and proof of address. If you have your baby in hospital, the hospital itself will probably undertake the procedure. Once you have registered the birth, you will then receive the full birth certificate (*acte de naissance*) – you can request this online at: www.acte-naissance.fr

Formerly, parents were required to choose the child's name from a short list (usually saints' names). The French got around this by hyphenating names together, hence the preponderance of Jean-Claude and Marie-Christines, etc. found in France. But now you can choose any name you like as long as it isn't 'prejudicial'. As a surname, children are normally given the father's name – if you want the mother's, or a joint name, you have to make a declaration to that effect.

Nationality

If one of its parents is French, a child automatically has French nationality, no matter where it is born. However, no matter what its parentage, any child born in France is entitled to ask for French citizenship when it reaches the age of 18, provided it is a resident of France. Until then, if you are both British, it will take your nationality.

If you are British and wish your child to be registered as a British national, contact the British Embassy in Paris at: www.ambafrance-uk.org

Postnatal care

Your baby will have to undergo examinations every month after birth, or you will lose your eligibility for child benefit. Examinations in the first week, ninth month and 24th month are included in a child's certificate of good health. You'll also be given a follow-up appointment with your gynaecologist eight weeks after you deliver.

Vaccinations are not compulsory in France but they are expected, and your child is liable to be refused entry to a crèche or school without them. They include vaccinations against TB (first month), diphtheria, tetanus, polio, whooping cough and haemophilus B (at 2-3 months), and MMR (measles, mumps, rubella – known as ROR in France) after one year. The Hepatitis B vaccine used to be given at 2-3 months but this has been discontinued after a suspected link with multiple sclerosis.

Child benefit

Couples with only one child do not receive child benefit. However, you will still be better off, because a child counts as a 'half' when calculating your household taxes, so your total income is split between more people. Once you have a second child, child benefit kicks in and applies until the age of 20. Once you have a third child, it increases per head, and from four and above, it becomes really quite significant.

Contact the CAF for details and to stay current – the system is complicated, and includes allowances for when you do not go back to work, allowances according to your income, allowances for dependent children remaining at home and earning a low wage, and grants for handicapped children.

Childcare

France has one of the highest rates of working mothers in Europe at about 80 per cent, and part of the reason is the availability of free and low-cost childcare.

State-subsidised childcare is available at the age of two months and of the 4.36 million children in France aged 6 years or younger, only the 300,000 to 350,000 cared for at home by parents, unregistered childminders or domestic staff are not in receipt of state-subsidised childcare.

Grants are available if you place your child in a crèche or use an at-home childminder, and school places are available free of charge once your child is three years of age.

Many French women use registered childminders (*assistantes maternelles* or *nourrices*). These are women registered to look after one to three children in their own homes. Children should be aged two and a half to three years. *Assistantes maternelles* may be independent or attached to a local crèche and staff must be paid at least the minimum wage. They are paid directly by the parents who use their services.

If you prefer collective care, rather than individual, you can send your child to a crèche or day nursery from the age of ten weeks to three years. These are sometimes set up by employers, or you might have access to one run by the local council, a private crèche or something run by a voluntary organisation. The ways crèches are financed varies, but municipal crèches are partly funded by the CAF, which is responsible for paying out benefits to families and childcare establishments in each *département*. On average, parents pay about one quarter of the real cost, depending on their household income.

There are no regulations governing how the children's days are organised at a crèche or day nursery, but it is compulsory to display a prospectus (*projet d'établissement*) in the building. This gives information about facilities, the staff to child ratio, early-learning activities and welfare provision and so on, along with any specific care offered to disabled or sick children. The children are looked after by a qualified nursery nurse.

Since 2000, childcare outlets have been able to change their hours to fit in with family life, and such *multi-accueil* establishments may open as early as 6.30am and go on till 7pm or even later. Even outside these hours, you might have access to a *crèche de garde* or *duty crèche*.

Local authority crèches are very common in Paris and the larger cities, but rarer in rural areas, where many people still rely on family, and you may find you have to travel a considerable distance. You may also find you can't get in – most women register for a place at the start of their pregnancy. In consequence, some parents have set up their own *crèches parentales*. These can take no more than 25 children, and are subject to the same rules and safety standards as local authority crèches. They are run by the parents, with one parent present at all times, and training is given by childcare specialists.

Crèches familiales are a compromise between a crèche and a childminder and consist of a network of childminders. They are paid directly by the town council, with the cost being divided between the family, town council and Family Allowance Funds. Group activities (*jardins d'enfants*) are organised on a regular basis so that the children can get together for early-learning activities.

Once your child reaches the age of three, he or she can be sent to school and many parents choose this option, partly because it is free of charge.

CASE STUDY: Childcare

Margaret and Ben Simon had their daughter Charlotte in France, in June 1999. When she was 6 months old, the couple began looking for childcare. "This was for work commitments mainly," says Margaret, "but the fact that we knew Charlotte would be an only child also meant we felt it was important that she socialised from an early age."

The options available to them included crèche (which they favoured but where there were no places), a daycare centre and a mother-toddler group, but in the end they came down on the side of a childminder. This was more serendipity than anything else, says Margaret, as there was a registered nanny working in the area.

Charlotte went to the childminder from the age of 6 months to the age of 18 months, when a place became free in the local crèche and the Simons took the decision to move her there. "The relationship with the childminder had deteriorated," says Margaret, "though this was more due to her personal circumstances than anything else, but we also felt more comfortable having a team of people looking after Charlotte rather than just one person. The crèche was also directly opposite a hospital, and in licensed premises, rather than her just being in someone else's home. Crèche was also open all year round and the hours were great. The main disadvantage was that we had to pay slightly more because we were outside the *département* and we also had a 20-minute drive to get there, but we did get tax breaks."

The Simons kept Charlotte in crèche till she was two and a half when, because she was out of nappies, she was able to go to school. They were very pleased with the arrangement. "She still remembers the crèche," says Margaret. "The child-nursery nurse ratio was kept deliberately low (with four children to every nursery nurse) so a relationship could develop. They were very focused on each child's natural development and creative skills, with lots of activities based around music, art, dance, etc., and because it was a state crèche it had municipal funding and grants etc., so it was very well equipped."

"For very young children," says Margaret, "I personally prefer crèche to the more personalised services of a childminder, where minor differences of opinion can take on a greater importance than they would normally. As a child gets older, however, a personal childminder or babysitter can work out well and that's what we do now on the occasions when Charlotte needs it."

Top tips

- Childbirth in France tends to be more medicalised than in the UK.
- Some French gynaecologists do not work in hospitals – be aware of this if you want to see the same person throughout your pregnancy.
- Home births are not common in France, though natural childbirth in hospital can be arranged.
- Women usually stay in hospital for up to five days following birth, but are permitted to stay longer.
- All medical expenses of birth are covered by the state, provided you attend your check-ups.
- Children born to British parents have British nationality by default, but may be able to apply for French citizenship at 18.
- Children are given a *Carnet de Santé*, which you take with you to doctor's appointments.
- Vaccinations are not compulsory but it may be impossible to register your child at crèche or school without them.
- There are many forms of childcare available in France, from childminders to crèches to nursery schools.
- Children can start school at the age of three, which is free of charge.

Glossary

Déclaration de Grossesse – A document declaring pregnancy

Caisse d'Allocations Familiales (CAF) – Family benefits office

Carnet de Maternité – Maternity notebook

Mutuelle – Medical insurance

Conventionné – Charges set tariffs for services, often doctors, dentists, etc.

Sage femme – Midwife

Échographie – Ultrasound scan

Déclaration de naissance – Birth registration

Mairie – Mayor's office

Carnet de naissance de l'enfant – Child's health record

Extrait d'acte de naissance – Preliminary birth certificate

Acte de naissance – Full birth certificate

Assistante maternelle – Registered childminder

Nourrice – Nanny

Département – Geographical area similar to a county. France is divided geographically into 100 *départements*

Projet d'établissement – Prospectus (at a crèche or day nursery)

Multi-accueil – Communal/shared space

Crèche de garde/duty crèche – Duty/emergency creche

Crèche parentales – Creche run by parents

Crèches familiales – A compromise between a crèche and a childminder, consisting of a network of childminders

Jardins d'enfants – Group activities

18

Education

The French education system is somewhat different from the English one, and would probably be more familiar to an American, as it has a similar, grades-based system. Grades, however, are numbered in reverse of those in the US, starting at Grade 12 in nursery school and rising to Grade 1 at ages 18 or 19. For those of a non-academic bent, it also offers a strong apprenticeship system which is 'scholarised' and leads to recognised qualifications.

Maternelle (nursery school) lasts from the age of 3 to the age of 6 and is universally available but not compulsory. Compulsory education begins at the age of 6. From 6 to 11, children attend *Primaire*, then from 11 to 15, they attend *Collège* (secondary school). At 15, if their exam results are good enough, they attend *Lycée* (sixth form, or sixth form college), or undertake an apprenticeship.

Many French children then sit the *Baccalauréat* exam and a high proportion then go on to university. The cream of the crop go to the *Écoles Nationales* (see page 250). University standards are not especially high, but getting into one of the *Écoles Nationales* requires Oxbridge-like exam results.

Currently, there are around 15 million students in the education system, 2 million of them in further education, and fewer than 10 per cent of French children leave school without any form of recognised qualification.

Differences of approach

The French education system is highly centralised, with policy set from above (though local head teachers now have more autonomy than they used to), and all teachers are civil servants whose jobs are protected.

Generally speaking, children learn more by rote than in the UK and are expected to assimilate known facts and respect their teachers. High achievement is emphasised, with a focus on technical subjects such as mathematics and sciences, while sport, art, music and personal development come further down the list of priorities. Exams are frequent and children are given extra classes or repeat years in order to come up to standards. Homework is given from an early age and children are expected to choose a career path fairly early.

Expectations for pupils were laid down by education minister Gilles de Robien in 2005, who made it clear that pupils are expected to attain the following seven skills:

1. Mastery of the French language.
2. Practical knowledge of a living, modern language.
3. Basic elements of maths, science and technology.
4. Familiarity with the common techniques of communication and obtaining information.
5. Humanities.
6. Social and civic responsibility.
7. Autonomy and initiative.

Opinions from British parents differ with regard to the efficacy of the system. The structured approach can prove an advantage for many children, particularly those with learning difficulties such as Asperger's. But some British parents find the French system over-rigid and stifling compared with the UK system, particularly for younger children.

State schooling

Most children in France go to state schools, with only around 15 per cent taking the private option, often for religious reasons. French schools are not required to teach religion, owing to France's separation of church and state, and religious symbols such as crosses and the Muslim headscarf are banned. There are also no morning services, hymns, assemblies, carols or nativity plays.

The majority of people who send their children to private schools do so for religious reasons (most are Catholic) but there may also be other reasons – for instance if the local primary school has closed down, but there is a private option closer than the nearest state-run establishment. There are also private secondary schools and *lycées*, which may offer better grades than the local state schools. Private schools were once seen as the poor relation of the state schools, but this perception is said to be changing.

The high-end boys- or girls-only 'public' school place is not something that is sought after in France and even the private schools are almost all co-ed and non-denominational. Catholic schools usually have contracts with the state and the state pays the staff salaries: fewer than 50,000 pupils attend any other form of private schooling in France.

There is effectively a national curriculum in France, so if you move from place to place, the curriculum in different schools should be roughly the same. Class sizes are relatively large at around 25 pupils per class and there are frequent complaints about this from both pupils and teachers, although the figures have improved from something like 40 in the 1960s. Truancy is rare and frowned upon, with parents liable to serious fines if children truant regularly.

Most primary schools are closed on Wednesday afternoons (employers usually build this into mothers' working hours) and some schools are open on Saturday mornings. The emphasis at school is on academic achievement and there are fewer extra-curricular activities than British parents may be used to. These, however, may be arranged by organisations outside the school – for details contact your *mairie*.

Home schooling is legal in France, but currently only around 500 families do this and the national curriculum must be applied (in French). For details, visit www.lesenfantsdabord.org.

French school or international?

Many British parents are concerned about their children learning French and wonder whether they should send them to an international school rather than a French-speaking one. If you know that you are planning to move back to the UK or to send your children to a British public school within three years, then an international school may prove the better option – the curriculum will be more in keeping with the UK version and reintegrating into the UK system will be more seamless.

If, however, you are planning to stay in France, the kind of school you choose depends on variable factors, such as the character, learning ability and age of your children. It's generally accepted that children under 11 'assimilate' the French language, while those over 11 have to 'learn' it. That said, most children, even above 11, learn French far quicker than their parents, and many French teachers advise that you simply allow your child to drop back one year so that they are covering familiar ground in the curriculum while developing their language skills. Being kept back a year is often seen as a stigma by British parents, but does not have this connotation in France, where repeating a year is more common. Schools are often happy to appoint another child as a mentor, who will help your child with their understanding of lessons, homework, etc.

If you live in a city or large town, you might be able to obtain extra French classes for your children (*classes d'initiation* – CLIN) in order to bring your child up to standard. In fact, attendance might be compulsory if your child's ability in French is considered to be sub-standard.

With regard to character, if your child is outgoing and confident, you might decide to throw them in at the deep end. Quieter, more reserved children might benefit from a year at an international school (if this is a financial option), followed by a move to a French school.

Montessori and Steiner

If you want your child to follow a Montessori education, visit: www.montessoriconnections.com for a list of Montessori schools in France. For a list of Steiner-Waldorf schools, visit: www.steiner-waldorf.org

Special-needs education

Most French children are educated by the Ministry of Education but around 100,000 severely disabled children attend special schools outside of the main education system, run by the Ministry of Health. Since 2005, however, France has made greater efforts to integrate handicapped children into mainstream education.

SESSAD (*Services d'Éducation Spéciale et de Soins À Domicile*) deals with children and teenagers with mental, motor and sensory disabilities, to enable early education and support for the family. Services include counselling and take families through to the end of compulsory education. SESSAD bridges the gap between traditional schooling and the treatments and rehabilitation that take place outside school.

The CLIS system (*Classes d'Intégration Scolaire*) offers special or integrated classes in normal schools for handicapped children who do not need to be in special facilities. Pupils follow the national curriculum. There are four types of CLIS and most schools that offer it offer only one type:

- CLIS 1 for children with mental handicaps.
- CLIS 2 for deaf children and children with hearing difficulties.
- CLIS 3 for blind or visually impaired children.
- CLIS 4 for children with motor disorders and physical disabilities.

For children whose problems are not caught, or do not emerge, before adolescence, there exist SEGPA (*Sections d'Enseignements Généraux et Professionnels Adaptés*) classes. These are aimed at children with psychological, emotional or behavioural problems, and take place at *collège* level on the instigation of either the school or the parents. Students are taken out of normal school and placed in small classes of around 16 pupils for intensive *scolarisation*. Many such children are apprenticed into blue-collar industries but the system aims to ensure that at least they do not fall through the net altogether and leave school unqualified.

UPI (*Unités Pédagogiques d'Intégration*) are units to accommodate mentally handicapped adolescents (generally coming from CLIS 1). The UPI provides adapted school integration and partial participation through teaching and activities, though if pupils' disabilities prove too severe, they are placed in special schools. The system is now being expanded to incorporate deaf and blind children and those with physical handicaps.

Dyslexia

If you have a child with dyslexia, contact the French association for parents of dyslexic children, *APEDYS* at: www.apedys.org for help.

School availability

You are likely to find a nursery or primary school close to wherever you live, but once your child goes to secondary school, you may find yourself delivering him or her long distances each morning. The French expect you to send your child to a school within your catchment area (this will be assigned by your *mairie*), so if you want a particular school, you'll have to move to the right district. However, exceptions can be made – a parent can, for instance, ask for the children to be educated in the town where one parent works, rather than the town where they live. In this case, however, both head teachers of the schools involved have to agree to it (and this may be an issue if, for instance, one school is facing closure due to lack of pupils).

The curriculum

French state schools do not have compulsory religion on the curriculum, and do not usually have sports and games teams – in fact, sports and games may not be taught at all, which is a bugbear in many inner-city schools lacking sports facilities. Many schools do not offer out-of-hours activities of any kind, though primary schools usually have a *garderie* where children can play after school until such time as their parents can come to collect them.

Year by year

Nursery school

Nursery school is optional but French children often attend very young, with many attending from the age of three onwards, as soon as they become too old for crèche. Many French parents take this opportunity because *maternelle* is free of charge, whereas if children remain in crèche or with childminders, they have to pay (though they also receive large tax credits).

Nursery school education begins with socialising and play in *la petite section*, and children don't begin to learn subjects such as maths until they join *la grande section* at the age of five. Many children ease their way into *maternelle*, attending for odd half-days to start with and gradually building up to a full week (except Wednesdays, when *maternelles* are closed). Meals are usually provided on-site, and after school hours a *garderie* nursery might be available for a fee. *Maternelles* are usually attached to the local primary school.

Note that to join nursery school, your children must be toilet-trained (*propre*) and vaccinated against a range of infectious diseases, with the certificates to prove it. See page 230.

Primary school

Compulsory education begins at the age of 6 with primary school and lasts to the age of 11. Right from the start, children have homework and parents are expected to check that their child has done the work assigned, and sign the homework book. In particular, children are expected to learn (and are tested on) the French language. They also learn technical subjects such as maths and sciences, history and geography, as well as liberal arts subjects such as sports, art and music. Altogether they are taught for around 26 hours per week.

Parent/teacher associations (*comités des parents*) exist if you want to get involved with your children's education and this is a good way to integrate into the local community. *Comités des parents* meet with the teacher's association (*comité des maîtres*) and other local luminaries several times a year in the school's council (*conseil d'école*) to thrash out school policy and budgets.

The years break down as follows:

- Ages 6 to 7 attend the CP (*cours preparatoire*). This is the 11th grade.
- Ages 7 to 8 attend CE1 (*cours élémentaire*). This is the 10th grade.
- Ages 8 to 9 attend CE2 (*cours élémentaire*). This is the 9th grade.
- Ages 9 to 10 attend CM1 (*cours moyen*). This is the 8th grade.
- Ages 10 to 11 attend CM2 (*cours moyen*). This is the 7th grade.

From CE1 onwards, children learn one or more foreign languages and most choose English. Given that your child already speaks English, you can ask for them to learn another language in its place, such as German or Spanish.

During the primary school years your child will probably have the opportunity to go on *classes de découverte* (discovery classes). These often take place in a holiday environment such as a skiing area, etc. – children still do their normal lessons, but have field trips on the side.

In the summer holidays, children may also have the chance to attend the *centre aéré*, which is rather like summer camp. Children are taught a wide range of skills and there is strong emphasis on outdoor play. *Centres aéré* charge a small fee, but most working parents find this worthwhile. Around 60 per cent of French children also buy notebooks so they can continue working in the summer holidays!

Secondary school

Secondary school lasts from the age of 11 to the age of 16. Children attend mixed-ability *collèges* from 11 to 15, then have one more year of compulsory education at a *lycée* or vocational *lycée*, or undertake an apprenticeship. Note that many jobs which are considered casual in the UK, such as hairdressing or building, are considered *métiers* in France and require an apprenticeship.

There are fewer *collèges* than primary schools and if you live in a rural area you may have no choice about which one your child goes to, and it may be some distance away. In a city there is generally more choice but also more competition for places. Some *collèges* have a *lycée* attached.

As at primary school, parent/teacher associations give parents an ideal opportunity to get involved with their children's school and education. This is particularly important in *collèges*, when important choices have to be made about your child's future.

The years are divided up as follows:

- Ages 11 to 12: Sixth grade.
- Ages 12 to 13: Fifth grade.
- Ages 13 to 14: Fourth grade.
- Ages 14 to 15: Third grade.

The first two years of *collège* are called the *Cycle d'Observation* and all children follow the same curriculum for most of the week, plus three extra hours tailored to each child's individual needs. The second two years are called the *Cycle d'Orientation*, because children are allowed more choice over their subjects. At this time, they must also study a second foreign language – not surprisingly, German is popular.

At the age of around 14, children decide whether they want to take an academic route or a more vocational route. Those choosing the academic route will sit exams and go to *lycée* and probably take the *baccalauréat*, while those who do not can prepare for an apprenticeship and entry into the workplace. At the very end of their last year at *collège*, students sit the *Brevet des Collèges* exam, which effectively acts as the entrance exam to a *lycée*.

Apprenticeship

Almost no young French person leaves school and goes immediately to a job (rather than a profession or further education) without doing an apprenticeship first. Apprenticeships lead to recognised qualifications and are an ideal solution for those who are not interested in academia.

Apprenticeships last between one and three years and are how France trains the majority of its chefs, hairdressers, carpenters, plumbers, etc. Students receive on-the-job training, for which they are paid a salary and must also attend a training centre for at least 400 hours per year. Effectively, they work about 75 per cent of their time and study the other 25 per cent.

Hiring an apprentice is cheaper for an employer than hiring full-time staff, as the employer does not have to pay the apprentice's social contribution. Nevertheless, it is not an option open to all employers, as the employer himself needs to have a certain level of qualifications in order to be allowed to train. Employers who do hire apprentices are exempt from the apprentice tax that is levied on members of their profession who do not take on apprentices.

Young people under the age of 25 who are not school leavers can also undertake an apprenticeship or other vocational training to improve their employment prospects. Contact ANPE (*Agence Nationale Pour l'Emploi*) at www.anpe.fr for details.

Lycée

Lycées are hard work and competition for places is fierce, so they only suit children who are academically committed. There are also frequent exams, but attendees are treated more like students than pupils, and are expected to manage their own time accordingly. There are fewer *lycées* than *collèges*, and you may have to deliver your children over long distances in order to obtain the curriculum and average grades you want (just like league tables in the UK). Some *lycées* take weekly boarders for this reason.

There are different types of *lycée*:

- The *lycée d'enseignement général et technologique* is the general and technology *lycée*, which prepares pupils to take the *baccalauréat*.

- The *lycée professionnel* is the vocational *lycée*, which is more like a technical college.

There are also international *lycées* which offer the international *baccalauréat*.

The *lycée* years are divided up as follows:

- Ages 16 to 17: *seconde*. Second grade (fifth form)
- Ages 17 to 18: *première*. First grade (lower sixth)
- Ages 18 to 19: *terminale*. Final year (upper sixth)

General and technology lycées

In the second grade, pupils take a wide range of subjects including French, maths, history, geography, sciences, foreign language and sports. They also choose from subjects which are grouped roughly as 'academic' (modern and regional languages, classics, IT, etc.) or 'practical' (lab technology, medicine, applied arts, etc.)

In *première*, pupils decide which type of '*bac*' they wish to take – general, technical or vocational (see below) – and choose their subjects accordingly.

General and technology *lycées* also offer post-*bac* courses for students who already have other qualifications (such as a technology *bac* or *brevet de technicien* (BT) – see vocational *lycée*). Here, students can undertake sixth-form study for the BTS (*brevet de technicien supérieur*), which is a fast track into management in industry.

Vocational lycées

Vocational *lycées* (*lycées professionels*) offer short vocational courses that lead to certificates, rather than the *bac*. The BEP (*brevet d'études professionel*) gives a broad overview for a particular trade or area of business, while the CAP (*certificat d'aptitude professionelle*) is more specialised and geared towards a particular trade. Both offer work experience as part of the course.

If they so wish, students with BEPs or CAPs can then go on to take other qualifications such as the BT (*brevet de technicien*) or a *baccalauréat professionel*.

The 'bac'

The *baccalauréat* acts as the entrance exam to university. There are three types:

- **General bac** – this is an academic qualification and those who take it usually go on to tertiary education at university, the *grandes écoles*, or an institute of technology.
- **Technology bac** – this is science-based but not vocational. Students who take it usually go on to tertiary education in an institute of technology.
- **Vocational bac** (*bac professionel*) – this is vocationally based and students spend 25 per cent of their time training in industry. It is a popular choice with those less enticed by academia and most students go directly into employment rather than into tertiary education.

The *bac* is also graded A, B, C or D, with D being the most difficult. Students who intend to go to university often take As and Bs, while those who take high-end subjects such as medicine or who wish to study for the *grandes écoles* take Cs and Ds.

Students study seven subjects in their *première* year at *lycée* and eight in their *terminale* year. They sit the *bac* in two parts: French language and literature in *première*, then the rest in *terminale*, provided they've passed part one. A mark of 14 out of 20 is considered 'excellent' and enables a student to apply for a special preparatory school for the *grandes écoles*.

Prepa

Any student wishing to attend a *grande école* needs to take the *prepa*, or *classes* preparatoires *aux grandes écoles* (properly known as the CPGE). *Prepa* classes may be held at the *lycée*, or attached to a *grande école* itself. Entry requirements are stringent and require at least 14 out of 20 in the *bac* exams in a relevant subject. Students attend *prepa* for two years and then take the *concours* (examination) for entry to the *grandes écoles*. The failure for this is astoundingly high at about 90 per cent, but retakes are permitted and if the student is not successful and has to attend an ordinary university, the exam can count towards the DEUG exam (*diplôme d'études universitaires générales*) which is taken at the end of the second year of university.

University

There are many universities in France, with an average-size city often boasting several small establishments rather than one large one as in the UK (Paris has 13). However, the majority of ambitious students want to go to the *grandes écoles*, which means the ordinary universities remain underfunded and obliged to accept any student with a *bac*, so standards are often low. Many courses are non-vocational, so there is a high drop-out rate and there is also a high failure rate – around half of all students fail their second-year exams (the DEUG).

Students who pass the DEUG can stay on for a third year and gain their *licence*. However, this has little value in the workplace, and unemployment rates remain high for graduates. Employers are usually looking for graduates of the more stringent four-year degrees such as law or economics, or for graduates with a masters (*maîtrise*) or doctorate (*doctorat*).

In specialist subjects such as medicine or veterinary science, entrance qualifications are much tougher and students are expected to obtain a good C or D level *bac*.

UK A levels are accepted as an entry qualification to a French university, but potential students must speak French well.

French students are not generally given grants, but neither do they pay tuition fees, so their expenses are lower than those for UK students. However, places in halls of residence are few, and other accommodation is usually expensive, which leads many French students to live at home while attending university. In France, parents are obliged to support their student children up to the age of 20 and after this, many students pay their own way through college.

Grandes écoles

There is no equivalent to the *grandes écoles* in the UK. They were founded by Napoleon Bonaparte to furnish the new republic with administrators and engineers, and even today are generally linked to government ministries, with an emphasis on science, engineering and agriculture – activities which will benefit the state. They are extremely well funded and take only the crème de la crème of France's *lycée* output, admitting no foreigners, virtually no women, and almost nobody from the working classes. Many consider the institutions elitist and effectively a closed shop, but places are highly sought after – being a graduate of a *grande école* virtually guarantees that you will be a captain of industry, a government minister or a high-ranking civil servant.

There are now around 250 *grandes écoles* in France, but the most famous include the ENA (*École Nationale d'Administration*), the CNAM (*Conservatoire National des Arts et Métiers*) and the *École Polytechnique*. Entry is not possible without very high grades in the *baccalauréat* and a two-year preparatory course.

CASE STUDY: Education

Mikki and Greg Tink moved to France in 2003 with their daughter Eden. Now eight, she attends school in the next village.

"Eden was in primary school in Berkshire before we left England," says Mikki, "but we had no faith in the teachers there – half of them were younger than the parents."

When the Tinks arrived in France, they visited the primary school in their village – just walking distance away – to ask about arrangements and to their surprise, the teachers asked Eden if she'd like to stay for a few hours. "She said yes," says Mikki, "so we left her there. It was a bit unexpected but we had no qualms as the place felt very safe and clean, and the teachers were really friendly. It's not like in the UK – they still hug and kiss children here if they're upset about something."

"She didn't have a word of French when she started so they put her with a French child who speaks English. Then they assessed her at the end of the first year and suggested that she be kept back a year. She'd only missed that intake by a month anyway, so we were happy to take their advice – the kids in her new class were actually closer to her age."

Eden went to school in her village for two years until it amalgamated with a school just a few kilometres away, but the journey is still only a few minutes drive and the pupils are the same. She is the only British child in her school, though her best friend has a British mother and speaks English well. Nevertheless, the girls speak French between themselves and Eden also speaks French with all of her other friends. "She's well ahead of us," admits Mikki, "but I help her with homework such as maths, while Greg, who speaks French better, helps her with language things."

Mikki feels that Eden receives more individual attention at her French school, where there are 14 pupils in her class, compared with 25 in her former UK school. And Mikki has not found the system rigid as yet, though if she has any reservation, it's about the amount of homework Eden gets, which she feels may be a little too much, considering the school day is already quite long.

The Tinks aren't involved with the PTA, because, says Mikki, "our feeling is that Eden's education is for Eden. We think the teachers are better placed to know how she is doing than we are, so we won't interfere unless there's a problem, and there hasn't been anything yet. We also don't want to push her – we want her to develop at her own pace. She's a creative child, and likes animals, and drawing, and I hope that she'll do something with that in the future."

The Tinks are very well satisfied so far with the French education system and their daughter's progress within it, and as a final word, adds Mikki, one unexpected bonus is the food. "I know it sounds trivial," she says, "but the food is so good it's untrue. They get three courses every day, and it's very healthy and innovative, so I feel that really gets the children off to a good start in life."

Top tips

- The French education system is based on a grades system. Children are expected to repeat a grade if they don't come up to scratch.
- Fewer than 10 per cent of French schoolchildren leave school without any form of qualification.
- French children learn more by rote than British children and there is a heavy emphasis on 'hard' subjects such as maths and sciences.
- Very few children in France go to private schools – most rely on the state system.
- Home schooling is virtually unknown in France.
- Religious education is not a requirement in French schools, owing to the separation of church and state.
- France has a national curriculum.
- Education is compulsory from the age of 6 but many children attend nursery school from the age of 3.
- Primary schools are plentiful, but you may have to travel further to take your children to a secondary school or *lycée* (grammar school).
- Children who are not academically minded are usually able to take an apprenticeship, though many French children go to university.
- The elite universities known as the '*grandes écoles*' are the highest-level educational establishments in France. Virtually all high-ranking members of government or the civil service have attended one.

Glossary

Maternelle – Nursery school

Primaire – Primary/elementary school (6 to 11)

Collège – Secondary school

Lycée – Sixth form

Baccalauréat – The French equivalent of A-levels

Écoles Nationales – Elite universities

Mairie – Mayor's office

Classes d'initiation (CLIN) – Extra tuition classes

Scolarisation – Education

Garderie – After-school childcare

La petite section – The small section, under 5s

La grande section – The big section, for children aged 5 and over

Propre – Toilet-trained

Comité des parents – Parent/teacher association

Comité des maîtres – Teacher's association

Conseil d'école – School council

Cours preparatoire – The 11th grade, for ages 6 to 7

Cours élémentaire – The 10th grade, for ages 7 to 8

Cours élémentaire – The 9th grade, for ages 8 to 9

Cours moyen – The 8th grade, for ages 9 to 10

Cours moyen – The 7th grade, for ages 10 to 11

Classes de découverte – Discovery classes

Centre aéré – Summer activities, similar to summer camp

Métier – A trade or craft

Cycle d'Observation – The name for the first two years of *college*. All children follow the same curriculum for most of the week, plus three extra hours tailored to each child's individual needs

Cycle d'Orientation – The name for the second two years of *college*. Children are allowed more choice over their subjects in this period

Brevet des Collèges – A diploma similar to the GCSE

Lycée d'enseignement général et technologique – Non-vocational sixth form

Lycée professionnel – Vocational sixth form

Seconde (lycée) – Second grade (fifth form), for ages 16 to 17

Première (lycée) – First grade (lower sixth) , for ages 17 to 18

Terminale (lycée) – Final year (upper sixth), for ages 18 to 19

Brevet de technicien (BT) – A technology *baccalauréat*

Brevet de technicien supérieur (BTS) – A advanced technology *baccalauréat*, which is a fast track into management within industry

Brevet d'études professionel (BEP) – A diploma for a particular trade or area of business which gives a broad overview of the subject

Certificat d'aptitude professionelle (CAP) – A specialised diploma geared towards a particular trade

Baccalauréat professionel – Professional, vocational *baccalauréat*

Grandes écoles – Elite education establishments, similar to universities

Classes preparatoires aux grandes écoles (CPGE) – Obligatory classes for any student wishing to attend a *grande école.* Commonly known as *prepa*

Concours – Entrance examination

Diplôme d'études universitaires générales (DEUG) – A general university diploma

Licence – Bachelor's degree

Maîtrise – Masters

Doctorat – Doctorate

19

Work

Working in France is like working in the UK in that the more qualified and experienced you are, the easier it is to find work. However, it is completely different from the UK in the use of the *métier* system, and the fact that, as a Briton, your chances of finding work are directly proportionate to how well you speak the language. Two thirds of Britons who emigrate to France return to the UK within three years, and the major reason is the inability to find regular work.

The long experience the French have of the *métier* system, where apprentices are properly trained and supervised, leads them to expect workers to be qualified in a range of jobs that might be considered casual in the UK, such as waitressing or working as a shop assistant. Such professions are not 'jobs' in France, they are careers. In fact, some areas, such as building and hairdressing, are licensed and you cannot work without official qualifications (artisans such as builders, for instance, are also expected to provide a ten-year bond on their work).

In theory, under EU Directives 89/48/EEC and 92/51/EEC, any British diploma that you have (NVQ, SVQ, etc.) should be recognised in France, but it is sometimes difficult to get the French authorities to accept this. To find out if you have equivalency, contact the UK co-ordinator, Directive 89/48/EEC, Department of Trade and Industry, or visit: www.dfes.gov.uk/europeopen. There you will find contact details for the French end of things, along with full descriptions of the directives and what they mean.

You cannot, incidentally, become a police officer, magistrate or soldier in France unless you have French nationality.

If you are an EU citizen (e.g. British), you are entitled to freedom of movement within the EU and to look for a job like any other citizen. The situation is more difficult, however, if you are not an EU citizen (e.g. American), as reciprocal agreements do not apply. In this case, you'll need a long-stay visa to get employment, and employment to obtain a long-stay visa, so you can find yourself in a catch-22 situation. For details on obtaining a visa, visit: About.com's pages on France (http:gofrance.about.com), which are aimed at a US audience and cover in detail the changing parameters required for French residency.

It is widely accepted that the French favour French nationals when it comes to jobs and this is particularly true when it comes to non-EU nationals. The French national employment agency *Association National Pour l'Emploi* (ANPE) – the equivalent of UK Job Centres – is entitled to propose a French national for any position offered to a non-EU national. It is also more difficult for non-EU citizens to set up or buy a business, and you may not trade before obtaining a *carte commerçante étranger*.

Where is the work?

Work of all kinds is plentiful in cities, particularly casual work, but rural unemployment in France is high, which is precisely why the countryside is depopulated and house prices are cheap.

Many more British ex-pats end up starting their own businesses than they ever thought they would, simply because they can't get any other kind of work (see page 267). Many work in the hotel and leisure industries, run *gîtes*, maintain properties for British holiday home owners, or run meet-and-greet services in areas where there is a British influx. Generally, the key to surviving is realism, flexibility and keeping your overheads low.

Before you go

If you want to have a job lined up in France before you leave the UK, the Government's Jobcentre Plus website at: www.jobcentreplus.gov.uk has many useful links to help you find employment. Just click through to the 'Working or Training in Europe' section, which includes links to the European Employment Services (EURES), an organisation dedicated to facilitating the free movement of workers throughout the EU.

If you are receiving UK unemployment benefit, you can continue to receive it in France while you search for work – contact a UK Jobcentre before you leave and ask for the correct forms.

The Recruitment and Employment Confederation at: www.rec.uk.com also specialises in finding overseas jobs for clients.

Job hunting online

There are now also hundreds of online resources to help you find work in France. To find work in your particular field, type 'working in France' and '*travail en France*' into Google (or other search engine) and start browsing.

The ANPE has a website at: www.anpe.fr with a list of available jobs and recruitment agencies in your area. This is in French only.

English-language forums such as the AngloInfo websites, Living France and Total France often advertise jobs for ex-pat Britons.

The European Employment Service (EURES) covers job vacancies in 31 European countries on the Europa website at: http://ec.europa.eu/eures/home.jsp?lang=en. The agency also has a network of advisers, usually working for the ANPE, who can help British people find work in France – you can search by *département*, or nationwide.

Other places to look for jobs

The ANPE has a network of agencies in addition to its website, where you can search for work throughout France. Most jobs are relatively low level and the majority are temporary.

Designations you may see listed include:

- *Contrat à durée indéterminée* (CDI) – permanent position
- *Contrat à durée déterminée* (CDD) – fixed-term contract
- *Contrat nouvelle embauche* (CNE) – new vacancy
- *Contrat travail saisonnier* – seasonal work

The ANPE also offers other facilities for job-seekers such as CV translation, counselling on job hunting, and free phone calls to prospective employers.

Temporary jobs are also dealt with by temp agencies (*agence de travail temporaire*). Finding temp work is relatively easy provided you're willing to take whatever you can get – factories always need extra staff to fulfil large orders, and there is usually seasonal work available in agriculture, supermarkets and the hospitality arena such as hotel work, fast food outlets, restaurant service, etc. To find an agency, look in the *Pages Jaunes* under *intérim*. The leading French temp agency is probably *Adecco*, though Manpower and other agencies also have a presence. In rural areas you can expect to be paid the minimum wage (commonly known as the *Smic*) and this might apply even in management positions.

If you're looking for permanent work, especially anything office-based, you'll need a recruitment consultancy (*cabinet de recrutement*). However, if you're employed at this level, it's inadvisable to move to France without having a job lined up in the first place. You can also contact APEC (*Agence pour l'Emploi de Cadres*), the French national agency for employment of professionals and executives (www.apec.fr).

Newspapers

All the daily newspapers in France carry job ads, much as those in the UK do. Local papers also advertise jobs. The procedure is the same as in the UK – you usually have to phone or send in a CV, which are usually very brief in France, at only 1-2 sides of A4. If you send a covering letter, it must be in impeccable business French, and handwritten (see the centre pages of dictionaries such as the 'Collins Robert French Dictionary' for details on how to write business letters).

Other sources

You can ask around for casual work in local restaurants, bars, estate agents, etc., depending on what you're looking for. You can also browse the personal notice boards at the local shops and supermarkets. There is also nothing to stop you taking out an advertisement on your own behalf in the local paper or on an ex-pat website, stating that you're looking for work. Professional magazines usually have job adverts in the back, if you are searching for something in a particular field.

Many British people in France do a bit of this, a bit of that to make ends meet or to top up their pension cover, and many become self-employed.

Self-employment

Many Britons opt for self-employment in France, but this option shouldn't be embarked upon lightly. The French system is highly regulated and does not favour the self-employed over the salaried, unlike the UK system.

You also cannot just have an idea and set up a business, or trade on eBay from time to time, or sell antiques out of your barn and only pay taxes when you make a profit, as you can in the UK – the French system does not permit business to be entered into so casually. You must insure yourself, and pay compulsory pension contributions, and in many cases you must have qualifications, particularly for anything involving construction or food handling. You cannot run a business at a loss year after year with a bit of fancy accounting, and it is hard to set up a business without both a detailed business plan and some capital behind you – the idea of using your house as collateral on the business, for instance, would be seen as risible by the average French bank.

Social security contributions are high for the self-employed and you are not entitled to unemployment benefit (though if you become permanently ill or are injured, you can claim invalidity benefit). There are minimum social and set-up charges to pay (in 2007, they were €221 per quarter) and hiring staff can cost you so much money in social security contributions that it becomes unfeasible to grow your business.

Despite what sounds like a doom-laden scenario, France is in fact chock-a-block with small businesses. Realistically, however, many of them are one-man bands or family-owned and the attraction they afford is the freedom to be autonomous rather than the ability to make a killing. Many rural businesses only just scrape by, and a look at any rural high street will show you the ones that didn't make it. Take professional advice before you set up in business in France by visiting your local *Chambre de Commerce* (or *Chambre de Métiers* if you're an artisan).

If you are planning to run a hospitality business in France and haven't yet made your move, it can't be stressed too much that this is an area where it pays to research. You need to buy in an area with a strong tourist market, with interesting or famous local landmarks and attractions, and purchase a property that has a lot to offer visitors – good views, some history, facilities such as a swimming pool, etc. Other amenities such as local restaurants are also important, and you will need a serious budget for marketing your business. In particular, the market for *gîtes* is extremely overcrowded in many regions, especially for those relying on British customers, as many Britons now own houses in France, or know someone who does.

Be aware that bed and breakfast properties are capped at five bedrooms, so if you want to make more money than you can reasonably charge for this, you may have to move up to a hotel designation (with all the attendant regulations regarding second staircases, fire exits, and so on). *Gîtes* are often attractive to ex-pat Britons because you don't need qualifications to run them and there are tax breaks, but they were only ever designed to be top-up income for farmers' wives, not a main source of income. If you start to make too much money from them, or need too much electricity (a necessity if you want to heat the buildings in the off season), you could find yourself being considered as a bona fide business. They are also best-suited to those who have previously worked in the hospitality industry, for instance in hotel management, who have a realistic perception of the issues involved. However, if you have another income stream, enjoy meeting people and are happy to just have *gîtes* as a top-up income, they can prove very worthwhile.

First steps

Roughly speaking, there are three classifications for self-employment in France:

1. The professional classes such as doctors, solicitors and journalists are classed as *profession libérale*. Most people under this classification work alone (or alone other than a secretary). Contact URSSAF (*Union de Recouvrement des Cotisations de Sécurité Sociale et d'Allocations Familiales*) for information on how to proceed. URSSAF will then contact all the other agencies you need for healthcare, pension, etc. on your behalf.

2. Tradesmen come under the heading *commerçant*, which includes shopkeepers, restaurateurs, etc. Contact your *Chambre des Métiers* for further information. The *Chambre* will contact all the other agencies you need for healthcare, pension, etc. on your behalf.

3. If you're an artist, sculptor, builder, etc. you come under the heading of *artisan*. Contact the *Chambre de Commerce* for your area for information on how to register. The *Chambre* will contact all the other agencies you need for healthcare, pension, etc. on your behalf.

If, under any of these classifications, you are planning to hire other people, you're better off setting up a company (see page 267) rather than registering as a *travailleur indépendent*.

For more information on URSSAF and how it works, visit www.urssaf.fr. To find your nearest office, click on your area on the map. The URSSAF in the Poitou-Charentes has set up a handy English-language site at: www.urssaf-englishinfo.eu where you can download information leaflets in PDF format.

General criteria

Qualification criteria for self-employment can be strict, and to set up shop, for instance, as a high street photographer, you might have to show qualifications such as a degree in photography, not just that you like taking pictures in your spare time. Other areas where qualifications are required include building, carpentry, hairdressing, cheesemaking and many occupations that in the UK might be considered casual labour.

If you work alone, you can register as a *travailleur indépendant* (self-employed non-salaried worker) or an *entreprise individuelle* (sole trader) and it's worth taking professional advice on which to choose, depending on who your clients are going to be, how much money you expect to earn, etc. The website of the Chamber of Commerce of Rodez (www.rodez.cci.fr/en/docs/Setting-Up-a-Business-In-Aveyron.pdf) explains in some detail the differences between *entreprises individuelles* (sole traders) and EURLs (one-person private limited companies), and also details SARLs (multiple-person private limited companies) and SAs (public limited companies). See page 267.

You'll need to do a number of things before you can practise as self-employed, including obtain a business registration number (*Siret* number). Ask at your local Chamber of Commerce exactly what is needed as it varies depending on what you want to do. For instance, if you want to open a shop, you'll need to register at the *tribunal de commerce* and obtain a *carte de commerçant*. If you're running a business, you may also be required to attend a short business course that covers areas such as accountancy. (You don't necessarily need to understand anything, only show that you've attended.)

Social charges, including compulsory pension contributions, begin on 1 January, so set up shop as close to this date as possible, or you could end up paying back charges at least for the quarter if not the whole year. It's wise to put aside about 50 per cent of your income to cover tax and social security right from the get-go. Running a business is expensive all over mainland Europe. In particular, social charges are FAR higher in France than in the UK and many Britons find themselves astounded by how much they're expected to pay, even sometimes before they've made any profit (there are minimum charges that have to be paid no matter how much you earn, which pay for things like child benefits). A good accountant will be invaluable to you in this area, just as in the UK, because they know all the allowances that you can claim against tax. It's also worth joining an *Association Agrée* (a kind of trade indemnity association) if you're *profession libérale*, as this gives you an automatic reduction in your taxes (though your social charges remain unaffected).

Working from home

If you use your home as your place of business, you'll have to pay taxes *professionnelles*. These are quite low, however – usually a matter of a few hundred euros – and you can offset them by charging a certain amount of your heating, lighting, etc., as a business expense. Take your accountant's advice on this one.

If your business depends on the Internet, you'll certainly need broadband. France aims to be about 97 per cent covered, but if you're in a rural area, you could find yourself covered only at very low speed or by a wireless network, again low-speed. Ask other local businesses how they find the quality of service in your area, as simply moving 20km up the road can make a huge difference to your speed.

If people visit you on your premises, you'll need public indemnity insurance, as in the UK.

Starting your own business – what's involved?

You can get help to start up a business from your local Chamber of Commerce and also from the *Association pour la Création d'Enterprise* (ACPE), which helps to develop business, especially in underdeveloped areas. At its website – www.apce.com – you can find information on what's involved in starting up in France (in French), and you can order the CD '*Créer ou reprendre un enterprise*'.

Those with experience advise that you don't start a business in France in an area where you have no previous experience, such as the hospitality arena. You should also have some capital behind you. Not only do you need to support yourself until you make a profit, you can't rely on getting a loan – reluctant banks expect lengthy and detailed business plans before they'll grant one, and they won't generally invest in a venture in which you yourself are not making a substantial investment.

One-man bands

If you are planning to work alone, there are two main business designations:

1. *Entreprise individuelle*, similar to UK small trader, and
2. EURL (*Enterprise Unipersonelle à Responsibilité Limitée*), similar to a UK single-director private limited company.

If you turn over less than €27,000 per year for provision of services (such as building work), or €76,300 for sales (for instance if you own a shop), you can opt for the *microenterprise* regime, which enables you to reduce your accounting burden. However, the tax burden is high because your income is calculated as 55 per cent of turnover for provision of services, or 32 per cent of turnover of sales. This can leave you with a shortfall if you have high costs for materials.

Multi-person companies

For companies with more than one person, there are also two main business designations:

1. SARL (*Société à Responsibilité Limitée*) – similar to the English private limited company, for 2-50 associates.
2. SA (*Societé Anonyme*) – similar to the UK public limited company, with a minimum of seven shareholders. This is the only designation that requires minimum issued share capital.

There is also the SCI (*Societé Civile Immobilière*), which some British use to buy property because it enables you to have more freedom to leave the property to whom you wish. However, a proper SCI is a property-holding company, and can be used, for instance, to manage rental property.

There are also other designations of business which are not often used by the British in France, including general partnerships, branch offices and *bureaux de liaison* (non-trading shop windows for overseas companies).

Hiring staff

Staff costs in France have a hidden whammy – social security. As an employer, you must pay your staff's social security contributions at the rate of 45 per cent on top of their salary. This also applies to casual labour, such as a cleaner or child-minder, employed by the *chèque emploi* service system (cash-in-hand payment for this kind of work is illegal).

Anyone permanently or seasonally employed will also normally have to undergo a medical.

If you want to hire an apprentice, you will have to be qualified to teach the relevant skill.

Buying an existing business

There are good reasons for buying an existing business in France, rather than setting up from scratch. To start with, there should (hopefully) be an existing customer base. Also, any existing licences should simply continue, so you should hopefully have less paperwork.

Disadvantages include the possibility of having to take on existing staff or apprentices because of their job contracts, or accidentally buying a business that is failing or has a bad reputation which you then inherit.

You can look for businesses for sale in the professional press (such as the catering press for hotels, bars and restaurants for sale), via estate agents and *notaires* and via the English-language French property press. Businesses are often family-owned and handed down from one generation to another, but it is always possible that you may find one that is closing through illness, lack of heirs or because the children prefer to work in another field. The ACPE also has information on start-ups on its website.

Be very thorough when buying a business that it has a good reputation and the vendor is not selling it simply because it's not viable. Have it valued independently, by two accountants, to make sure it has decent prospects and a fair price.

There are separate costs for the business (*fonds*), and the building that houses it (*murs*). You may prefer to rent the actual buildings rather than buy them but often, with small businesses, the property also houses the family and you effectively live above the shop. Generally, you are expected to buy the business from capital, especially if you need a mortgage on the buildings – banks are unlikely to provide a loan for both.

One other way of buying a business is by franchise. Many of the national supermarket chains, for instance, are franchises. Write to the relevant head office for details.

CASE STUDY: Work

When Rachel Charles came to live in rural France with her chef husband Grègoire in 1998, one of their first priorities was to look for work. Grègoire, who is French, found a job fairly quickly in a hotel 50km away but rural wages tend to be low so they still needed a second income.

Rachel had learned French to a high level at the Institut Français, and to get started she registered at the ANPE (French Job Centre), spoke to friends and neighbours and sent out her CV on spec to companies in larger towns.

"At first, the ANPE was unhelpful," she says, "until they realised I spoke good French. The temp agencies were very good but you have to hassle them to get the first contract." There was plentiful work in the large towns and cities, but she was in a rural area far away from a town of any size. "I got offered a number of jobs that were too far away to be feasible," she says.

Rachel's first job in France came unexpectedly when she was contacted by her old corporation. This entailed her working Monday and Tuesday in Paris, coming home mid-week, then commuting to Brussels on Thursday and Friday. Her social charges were paid by her employer. Although the work was very well paid, the commuting schedule was tiring, and then she found out that she was pregnant.

Rachel didn't quit work until she was near full term, but shortly after the birth, some old contacts came to her with remote translation work that she could do from home. "It was good on the one hand," she says, "because I could do as much or as little as I liked, but it was also frustrating to have to wait a long time for payment." To work as a translator, Rachel registered as *profession libérale, travailleur independent* – a professional self-employed person.

Rachel worked as a translator for some time, and then she acquired a job in a local company working as a translator and then office manager. Once again, this was via contacts. "There were only four of us there," she says, "as opposed to the massive corporate structure I was used to. But not having to endlessly chase virtual meetings in different time zones made for a much less stressful working environment!" Under this arrangement, Rachel was salaried and her social charges were paid by her employer.

The couple's life then took an unexpected turn when a local restaurant came up for sale. Grègoire had always planned to run an *auberge* from their large country property, which he was in the process of renovating, but this was an opportunity too good to miss, so the couple left their jobs, sold their country house and bought the village restaurant with apartment accommodation above.

Since then, Rachel hasn't found running a business in France as expensive or paper-bound as everyone had predicted. "We're glad we have a good accountant, and that we have lots of willing staff available," she says. "We hope to run this restaurant for perhaps another four or five years, then buy another business in another region." Their designation is *commerce* and they run the restaurant as an *entreprise en nom propre*.

Overall, says Rachel, her greatest asset in searching for work in France has undoubtedly been her language skills. "It's essential," she says, "even in this business. About half our customers speak English, but all our suppliers are French, our staff are French, and the other 50 per cent of our customers are French."

Her advice to anyone searching for work in France is simple: learn the language to a level well beyond basic. "If you don't feel confident to go to a job interview in French, don't think about seriously looking for work. You aren't really an asset to a company unless you speak both languages."

Top tips

- The major reason that British ex-pats return from France is inability to find work.
- Many jobs that are considered casual in the UK require qualifications in France.
- Your British qualifications should be recognised in France, but there are exceptions. Check before you move over.
- Many British ex-pats in France become self-employed.
- It is inadvisable to set up a business in France in which you do not already have experience.
- Being self-employed in France means high social and pensions charges but brings freedom along with it.
- There are over a dozen different types of business in France. Take advice on which is the best one for you.
- It is almost impossible to run a business in France without professional accountancy.

Glossary

Métier – A trade or craft

Carte commerçante étranger – Licence to trade for non-nationals

Gîte – Self-catering holiday cottage

Travail en France – Working in France

Département – Geographical area similar to a county. France is divided geographically into 100 *départements*

Contrat à durée indéterminée (CDI) – Permanent position

Contrat à durée déterminée (CDD) – Fixed-term contract

Contrat nouvelle embauche (CNE) – New vacancy

Contrat travail saisonnier – Seasonal work

Agence de travail temporaire – Temp agency

Pages Jaunes – Yellow Pages, business directory

Intérim – Temporary work

Salaire minimum interprofessionnel de croissance (Smic) – Minimum wage

Cabinet de recrutement – Recruitment consultancy

Chambre de Commerce/Chambre de Métiers – Chamber of Commerce/Chamber of Trade

Profession libérale – The professional classes such as doctors, solicitors and journalists

Commerçant – Trade/tradesmen

Travailleur indépendant – Self-employed non-salaried worker

Entreprise individuelle – Sole trader

Enterprise Unipersonelle à Responsibilité Limitée (EURL) – One-person private limited company

Société à Responsibilité Limitée (SARL) – Multiple-person private limited company

Societé Anonyme (SA) – Public limited company

Siret – A company registration number

Tribunal de commerce – The commercial court

Carte de commerçant – Licence to trade

Association Agrée – A form of trade indemnity association

Taxe professionnelles – Local business tax

Microenterprise – A regime enabling the reduction of accounting burden (for companies turning over less than €27,000 per year)

Societé Civile Immobilière (SCI) – A property-holding company, which can be used to manage rental property, etc.

Bureaux de liaison – Non-trading shop windows for overseas companies

Agent immobilier – Estate agent

Notaire – Notary

Fonds – The business itself

Murs – The physical building that houses a business

Auberge – Hostel

Entreprise en nom propre – A kind of sole trader

20

Retirement

Retiring overseas is a dream of many Britons and although the majority still choose Spain, France is the second port of call.

There are many good reasons for this. Many people see the French lifestyle as very attractive, the weather can be excellent if you go south, and if you stay further north you can benefit from the more relaxed lifestyle France affords, while still having easy access to the UK for both yourselves and family.

Retiring to France simply because it's cheaper is not a realistic aim. France is not a third-world country and although the cost of living is said to be some 65 per cent of that of the UK, this is largely skewed by housing costs and mortgage payments: if these are taken out of the equation, France often works out about as expensive as the UK.

The most popular areas for retirement in France are mostly in the south, including the Cote d'Azur, the Languedoc and Provence, but further north, Brittany, Normandy and the Pas-de-Calais are also popular for the easy access they offer back to the UK.

Rules and regulations

There is no barrier to your retiring in France if you are an EU citizen: if you're not, you'll require a visa. Any UK state pension to which you are entitled can be paid into a UK bank account or a French bank account, and it is index-linked to the cost of living.

Some retirees prefer to spend only part of their time in France. If this is the case and you don't spend more than three months in France at any one time, your best bet is probably to simply continue to be paid your pension in sterling, into your normal account. If you're retiring to France permanently, you can make your own choice as to where you want your pension paid, but one thing you will require in France is health cover. To get this, ask the International Pensions Centre (www.thepensionservice.gov.uk/ipc) for form E121. Under France and the UK's reciprocal healthcare agreement, you will then be entitled to the same health cover as a French pensioner once you reach pensionable age (i.e. 100 per cent). Note that the retirement age in France is currently lower than that in the UK and therefore the situation where you are a pensioner but not entitled to full health cover should not arise, but France now has a new government and it is possible that the situation may change in the future.

If you're in the UK and receiving state pension

To find out how to carry on receiving your UK state pension once you're in France, before you leave contact the International Pensions Centre (IPC).

✉ Tyneview Park
Newcastle Upon Tyne
NE98 1BA
United Kingdom

☎ 0845 60 60 265, Monday to Friday 8am to 8pm,
(0845 60 60 285 for those with speech or hearing difficulties)

Phone lines tend to be quieter in the afternoon and towards the end of the week, but staff are extremely helpful.

The IPC has a comprehensive website at: www.thepensionservice.gov.uk/ipc. The pensions situation is changing all the time and visiting the website is a good way to stay up-to-date. Currently, for instance, you're entitled to claim your UK state pension at age 60 for women, 65 for men, but the age for women is set to rise incrementally from 2010, which will change a whole raft of entitlements. The IPC also covers people in receipt of Widows Benefit, Industrial Injuries Disablement Benefit and Incapacity Benefit. You can click through to 'France' for specific details on the country.

If you're retiring abroad, the IPC will need to know the following:

- The date you are leaving the UK.
- Whether the move is permanent or temporary (and a return date, if relevant).
- Your new address.
- New bank details, if required.
- Your nationality.
- Whether you receive a pension from another country.
- Details of any dependants moving with you.

If you're in France when you reach retirement age

If you're living in France when you become of pensionable age, you should be informed of your entitlements by the IPC around four months in advance. If, however, for some reason you are not, you should contact the IPC. Your UK pension can be paid in sterling or euros, into a UK account or a French account, as you wish. If you choose to have it in euros, it will be transferred at a commercial exchange rate, which can prove worthwhile. You can be paid every 4 weeks or every 13 weeks.

Private UK-based pensions

For details of how these are paid, contact your individual pension provider. It's also worth taking the advice of a financial adviser specialising in international tax issues, as there are tax agreements between the UK and France that may affect you. For instance, any tax-free lump sum paid to you from a private pension scheme in the UK is taxable as income in France. If you have substantial means, you might be advised to transfer some money into offshore accounts.

Generally speaking, you can't make payments into a UK pension unless you have a UK income, so if you are under pensionable age, contact your provider to see if they offer a suitable replacement product – again this might be an offshore policy.

Private pension payments, once you reach the required age, might be available in euros, depending on your provider. If they are not, you will need to arrange transfer with a favourable exchange rate (see Chapter 13).

State pension and company schemes in France

If you've worked in France and have paid national insurance contributions, you may be entitled to a certain amount of French state pension, known as the *Caisse de Retraite*. This currently kicks in at the age of 60 for both men and women, but will probably change over time, as France is subject to the same kinds of pressure on the pension system as seen in the UK (the age will probably rise). Employed people often retire earlier, at 55, while the self-employed tend to retire later, at 65.

As in the UK, you receive a pension in proportion to how many years (actually quarters of years – *trimestres*) that you have paid into the system, but you won't get a full French state pension unless you've contributed for 160 *trimestres* – that's 40 years of working life. When you reach retirement age, if you're falling short you can make lump-sum top-ups to improve your future pension provision. If you continue to work after the age of 65, any pensions contributions you make are topped up by the government by 2.5 per cent.

Top-up pensions (complementaire)

State pension contributions are compulsory in France, so if you work, you'll pay into the scheme automatically. However, you can also opt to make extra payments into a *caisse complementaire de retraite*. This can be either a state-run scheme or a company pension – if you're employed, your employer may well offer a scheme, and in fact, you may be required to join it. If you're self-employed, it becomes more complicated, as there are so many designations (see opposite), each of which is different with regard to minimum contributions and so on.

Private pensions in France

Completely private pensions are a very new entity in France, where people have traditionally relied on the state scheme. They were introduced by France's centre-right government in 1997, to shore up a state scheme that was tottering under a mountain of debt (so much so that 'solidarity' payments of a one-off sum for every household in France were charged in 2006 in order to put some funds into the state system).

Private pensions are called *Plans Epargne de Retraite* and the best-known is the *Plan d'Epargne de Retraite Personelle*, which was set up by the government in 2003. You're allowed to pay in 10 per cent of your income, up to the value of €23,500 per year, and if you die, the fund automatically reverts to your spouse or other beneficiary. If you're self-employed, be warned that payments into private pension schemes are very high and the benefits you receive are very low. This is an area where it definitely pays to take financial advice.

Claiming your French state pension

When you reach retirement age, your French pension isn't paid to you automatically as it is in the UK. Four months before you reach retirement age, you should apply for your state pension and also inform your private pension provider, if you have one, of your impending retirement.

To claim your pension, contact your CRAM (*Caisse Régionale d'Assurance Maladie*) to ask for your local retirement information centre (*point d'accueil*). Or, to find a centre, and for other information on how the state system works, visit the website of the CNAV (*Caisse Nationale d'Assurance Vieillesse*) at: www.retraite.cnav.fr. The site includes information on how to retire piecemeal, how to pay top-ups, and how to claim your pension. It is, of course, all in French.

If you are self-employed in France your local CRAM should be able to help you with your claim. Also visit the website *GIP Info Retraite* at: www.espaceretraite.tm.fr for information. This is a specialist site covering the regimes applicable to the self-employed, which are divided into 36 areas, each covered by a different provider. Rules on retirement age, minimum contributions, etc., are different for each category.

Living on a low income

Pensioners in France who do not come up to the minimum standards of living can apply for top-up benefit. This was formerly known as *Minimum Vieillesse* but is now called the *Allocation de Solidarité aux Personnes Âgées*, or APSA. The minimum income is set very low, at around €7,500 per year for a single person or €13,000 for a couple, and the benefit is means-tested. If you think you qualify, contact your local CRAM.

What is retirement like in France?

Overall, living as a pensioner in France is the same, or possibly better than in the UK. You can benefit from excellent weather if you choose the right location, you have free access to the best healthcare system in the world and you can drive a car without a licence, while you get priority seats on public transport and can benefit from cheap rail travel all over France. A French property will not usually cost as much as a UK one, allowing you to free up capital, and if you choose something modern it will be insulated to the hilt and cheap to run. Rural France has many activities for third-agers (and even fourth-agers, those over 80, of whom there are a large number).

So, what might be the disadvantages? The first, once again, comes down to language – suppose you were to find yourself bereaved of your life partner and left alone and ageing in a foreign country? Suppose you were to become infirm and have to move to a *maison de retraite*? If you've lived in France a long time, France may de facto have become your home, but it is very important to be comfortable with the language or, if your life situation deteriorates, a return to the UK might follow in short order.

In particular, many British women, I have found, cannot drive and move to the French countryside completely dependent on a partner. If widowed they can find themselves in a very difficult situation. For these sorts of reasons, it pays to think ahead when retiring to France and have sensible contingency plans.

CASE STUDY: Retirement

Alan Dart, 72, and his wife Maureen retired to France in 2001.

"We lived near Old Sarum airfield near Salisbury," says Alan, "and it was really idyllic when we moved there in 1987. But gradually we were pushed out by development. First it was a business park, then a rifle range, then finally the council put in a 10ft fence that blocked our view and we decided it was time to leave."

The Darts chose France because they'd heard it was still very rural and they looked first in the south-west, in the Bordeaux region. But in the end they chose the north, in order to be closer to family, as both their mothers were still alive and they had children and grandchildren in the UK. France, they say, is "like England used to be" and they do not expect they will ever return to the UK.

In the UK, both of the couple were retired, drawing state pensions, and – in Alan's case – a small private pension. But it was not really enough to live on and Maureen had two part-time jobs on top. "We felt we needed the money," she says. In France, in contrast, they essentially live off Alan's pension, and put Maureen's aside for a rainy day.

"We'd saved a bit towards the French house, and after we sold off the English one, we had a little nest egg to fall back on, even after we bought the French property," says Maureen. Their French house is a stone-built cottage with a small garden, down a private driveway and completely surrounded by fields.

When they knew they were leaving for France, they phoned the Department of Work and Pensions in Newcastle, whom they found very helpful. They sent along the correct forms, and the procedure was quite straightforward. All their pensions are paid in sterling, into UK bank and building society accounts and on a day-to-day basis the couple use credit cards for buying the weekly shopping. They also have current and savings accounts in France, and top these up every so often using UK cheques rather than bank transfer, which they admit is probably not the most efficient way of doing it.

They don't regret their move to France for one instant. "Everything is better here," says Maureen. "There is almost no crime – I mean, we don't have our heads in the sand, but what I mean is, we don't worry about crime here. Older people are also more respected here, and the culture is more family-oriented. There are lots of clubs for pensioners, and a real community spirit."

Alan concurs: "The French live naturally," he says, "and there isn't the apprehension that there is in the UK – you can achieve your aims and you don't constantly feel that the goalposts are being shifted. There's no keeping up with the Joneses – the French take care of each other. The government also feels like it's for the people, not just for money."

Overall, the couple find life in France cheaper than the UK because they feel that luxuries are more expensive but that staples cost less. They also have a *potager*, and receive regular gifts of surplus fruit and vegetables from their neighbours. They are members of *Familes Rurales*, which organises meals and get-togethers, and Maureen is also a member of a local sewing club, an art class and a horticultural society. Alan is less gregarious and spends much of his time renovating the house, but is a member of the local classic car club, and other car clubs associated with his pride and joy – a vintage Jowett Jupiter.

Growing older, and possibly infirm, in France, is not something they spend much time worrying about, but they agree they would rather age in France than in the UK. "For instance, the healthcare system is fab," says Maureen. "Not that I've used it as I never seem to ail here." And if the worst should happen and one of them predeceases the other, they are certain the other would remain in France. "This is our home now," says Alan, "it's where our roots are."

Top tips

- You can retire to France and your UK state pension can be paid into either a UK bank account or a French bank account – contact the International Pensions Centre for details.
- Your UK state pension will be index-linked if you retire within the EU (this is not the case if you retire to other countries such as Canada or Australia).
- If you are a French-resident, you are entitled to 100 per cent health cover once you reach pensionable age.
- Lump-sum, tax-free payouts from British pensions schemes are taxed as income in France. Take professional advice.
- If you have a private pension scheme, it may or may not be payable in euros, depending on your provider.
- The French pension is calculated by the number of quarters of years you have worked in France.
- Be realistic about how important language skills are for British pensioners living in France.

Glossary

Caisse de Retraite – Pension fund

Trimestre – A trimester (three months, a quarter of a year)

Caisse complementaire de retraite – Top-up pension fund

Plans Epargne de Retraite – Private pension

Point d'accueil – Information centre

Allocation de Solidarité aux Personnes Âgées (APSA) – Top-up pension benefit for elderly on low incomes

Maison de retraite – Retirement home

Afterword

So, you've reached the end of this book. Hopefully, if you were unsure about France, it gives you a clearer idea of some of the things a British person might expect to encounter in their new country, which is separated from Britain by a distance far greater than the English Channel. The rest is now up to you.

Over the years, my husband Steve and I have seen many Britons come and go, so it's worthwhile outlining, once again, the ways in which you can make your French move successful.

Be flexible. Don't have a rigid idea of what life in France will be like, or hold beliefs that the British way of doing something is 'right' and the French way is 'wrong'. Learn to enjoy the difference, even the strangeness of things, even when this might pose challenges. Life in France is an adventure, not an escape – you are at the start of something that will throw up a lot of surprises.

If you are of working age, come to France with a good idea of what you will do for a living. If you intend to continue in the same line of work, make sure that this is legal – that your qualifications will be accepted. The primary reason for Britons leaving France is that they cannot find enough work to support a family.

Do not underestimate how depopulated the French countryside can be. If you are happy with the idea of moving to deepest Wales or Scotland, you will probably be fine *en plein campagne*. If not, choose somewhere within 20 minutes of a large conurbation, where you are likely to meet more people and have access to facilities such as bars, restaurants and cinemas. Most Britons are far more urban than they realise.

Your assimilation into French life (though not necessarily your happiness in France) will be proportionate to how well you learn the language. If you wish to remain on good terms with your neighbours, to deal with authority, to cope when you're sick, and simply feel at ease in your new surroundings, you need to learn enough French to achieve this.

Be prepared for homesickness. For people who are very close to their family, it can be enormously stressful to move away from them, and the truth is they will not visit you as often as you think. The first year is the hardest, as are visits where you see that the family children are growing up without you. If your family (and friends) are important to you, take measures such as setting up an email account and perhaps even a webcam, or budgeting for regular trips back to the UK.

We have lived here for over a decade now and life here has been different from what we imagined – and mostly better, to the extent that we visit the UK only with extreme reluctance and have quite happily become strangers in our own land. But life in France – like life anywhere else – is essentially what you make of it. Be trusting but not gullible, assertive but not arrogant, and above all be flexible, and relocating to France could be the best move you ever made.

Resources

French public holidays

Fixed dates

- 1 January — New Year's Day (*Jour de l'An*)
- 1 May — Labour Day (*Fête du Travail*)
- 8 May — VE Day – WWII Victory Day (*Fête de la Victoire* 1945)
- 14 July — Bastille Day (*Fête nationale*)
- 15 August — Assumption of the Blessed Virgin Mary (*Assomption*)
- 1 November — All Saints' Day (*Toussaint*)
- 11 November — Armistice Day (*Armistice* 1918)
- 25 December — Christmas Day (*Noël*)

Moveable dates

	2008	2009
• Easter (*Pâques*)	23 March	12 April
• Easter Monday (*Lundi de Pâques*)	24 March	13 April
• Ascension Day (*Ascension catholique*)	1 May	21 May
• Whit Sunday (*Pentecôte*)	11 May	31 May
• Whit Monday (*Lundi de Pentecôte*)	12 May	1 June

Useful resources

Websites, newspapers and magazines

AngloInfo

💻 www.angloinfo.com

Living France

💻 www.livingfrance.com

Total France

💻 www.totalfrance.com

WebVivant

💻 www.webvivant.com

The BBC's international radio station

💻 www.bbc.co.uk/worldservice

Pages Jaunes (Yellow Pages)

💻 www.pagesjaunes.fr

France magazine

☎ +44 (0)1242 216080
Fax +44 (0)1242 216084
@ subscriptions@francemag.com
💻 www.francemag.com

French News

☎ +33 (0)5 53 06 84 40
Fax +33 (0)5 53 06 84 41
@ subs@french-news.com
💻 www.french-news.com

French Property News

☎ +44 (0)20 8543 3113

Fax +44 (0)20 8540 4815

@ info@french-property-news.com

💻 www.french-property-news.com

Living France

☎ +44 (0)1242 216050

@ subscriptions@livingfrance.com

💻 www.livingfrance.com

Paris Match, weekly newsmagazine

💻 www.parismatch.com

Le Nouvel Observateur, weekly newsmagazine

💻 www.nouvelobs.com

Le Figaro, conservative newspaper

💻 www.lefigaro.fr

Le Monde, liberal newspaper

💻 www.lemonde.fr

Liberation, left-wing newspaper

💻 www.liberation.fr

La Tribune, financial newspaper

💻 www.latribune.fr

Ouest France, regional newspaper

💻 www.ouest-france.fr

Home and garden

Électricité de France (EDF)

www.edf.com

POWEO

www.poweo.com

Vivendi (mains water)

www.veoliaenvironnement.com

Gaz De France (GDF)

www.gazdefrance.com

ADEME (Agence de l'Environnement et de la Maîtrise de l'Energie)

Environment agency, advises on local providers and on ways to cut energy consumption

www.ademe.fr

Consuel (Comité National pour la Securité des Usagers de l'Electricité)

www.consuel.com

Stoves Online

For ideas on types of wood and their heat output

www.stovesonline.co.uk

General information on windpower in France

www.suivi-eolien.com

Current Internet service providers (ISPs) providers

www.lesproviders.com

www.budgetelecom.com

Alice (formerly Tiscali)

💻 www.aliceadsl.fr

Altitude Télécom

💻 www.altitudetelecom.fr

Cégétel

💻 www.cegetel.fr

Neuf Télécom

💻 www.neuf.fr

Orange

💻 www.orange.fr

France Télécom

💻 www.francetelecom.com

List of ISPs who offer reduced prices or more services if they can connect to you independent of the national provider

💻 www.degrouptest.com

Purchase a French telephone adapter

💻 www.bigdishsatellite.com

Mobile phone services

France Télécom (trading as Orange)

💻 www.orange.fr

SFR (has links to Cégétel)

💻 www.sfr.fr

Bouygues

💻 www.bouygues.fr

Jacques Briant (mail order plant catalogue)

www.jacques-briant.fr

Les Chemins de la Rose (handy links)

www.cheminsdelarose.fr

RHS Plantfinder

www.rhs.org.uk

Max Havelaar (encouraging the uptake of free trade in France)

www.maxhavelaarfrance.org

Le marché citoyen (details of fair trade suppliers)

www.lemarchecitoyen.net

Learning the language

About.com

http://french.about.com

Alliance Française

www.alliance-fr.org

Anysubject (tuition)

www.anysubject.com

BBC Languages – French

www.bbc.co.uk/languages/french

Eurotalk

www.eurotalk.co.uk

Floodlight (adult education in London)

www.floodlight.co.uk

Institut Français

www.institut-francais.org.uk

Linguaphone

www.linguaphone.co.uk

National Extension College

www.nec.ac.uk

Open University

www.open.ac.uk

Personal Tutors (agency)

www.personal-tutors.co.uk

Rosetta Stone (online courses)

www.rosettastone.co.uk

Thomson Directory

www.thomsonlocal.com/Language-Schools

University of London

www.londonexternal.ac.uk

Yellow Pages

www.yell.com

Travel

Air France

www.airfrance.co.uk

BMIBaby

www.bmibaby.com

EasyJet

www.easyjet.com

Flybe

www.flybe.com

Ryanair

www.ryanair.com

All budget international carriers going to France

www.attitudetravel.com

Eurostar

www.eurostar.com

Eurotunnel

www.eurotunnel.com

Eurolines (coach service)

www.eurolines.com

Brittany Ferries

www.brittany-ferries.com

Condor Ferries

www.condorferries.co.uk

Direct Ferries

www.directferries.co.uk

LD Lines

www.ldlines.com

Norfolkline

www.norfolkline.com

P&O

www.poferries.com

SeaFrance

www.seafrance.com

SpeedFerries

www.speedferries.com

Transmanche Ferries

www.transmancheferries.com

John Parker International

www.johnparkerinternational.com

The AA

www.theaa.com

Euro NCAP

www.euroncap.com

French road signs

www.drivingabroad.co.uk

Speed cameras

www.securite-routiere.gouv.fr

Régie Autonome des Transports Parisiens (RATP)

Public transport route planner

www.ratp.fr

iSubwayMaps (Downloadable underground maps)

www.isubwaymaps.com

Voyages SNCF (buy train tickets online)

www.voyages-sncf.com

Work and retirement

Association pour la Création d'Enterprise (ACPE)

💻 www.apce.com

Association National Pour l'Emploi (ANPE)

💻 www.anpe.fr

Agence pour l'Emploi de Cadres (APEC)

💻 www.apec.fr

European Employment Services (EURES)

💻 http://europa.eu.int/eures

Jobcentre Plus

💻 www.jobcentreplus.gov.uk

Quorum Training

💻 www.quorumtraining.co.uk

The Recruitment and Employment Confederation

💻 www.rec.uk.com

La Sécu (social security system)

💻 www.service-public.fr

Union de Recouvrement des Cotisations de Sécurité Sociale et d'Allocations Familiales (URSSAF)

💻 www.urssaf.fr

✉ International Pension Centre (IPC)
Tyneview Park
Newcastle Upon Tyne
NE98 1BA

☎ 0191 218 7777 Monday to Friday 8am to 8pm

💻 www.thepensionservice.gov.uk/ipc

Caisse Nationale d'Assurance Vieillesse (CNAV)

💻 www.retraite.cnav.fr

Caisse Régionale d'Assurance Maladie (CRAM)

💻 www.cramif.fr

Department for Work and Pensions

💻 www.thepensionservice.gov.uk

Department of Trade and Industry

✉ Kingsgate House,
66-74 Victoria Street,
London
SW1E 6SW,

☎ +44 (0)20 7215 4405,
Fax +44 (0)20 7215 4489
💻 www.dti.gov.uk/european

Europe Open for Professions

💻 www.dfes.gov.uk/europeopen

GIP Info Retraite

💻 www.espaceretraite.tm.fr

Further reading

Bescherelle Complete Guide to Conjugating 12,000 Verbs

Collins Pocket French Verb Tables

Collins-Robert French Dictionary

French Menu Reader by Maggie Plunkett

Glossary of Medical, Health and Pharmacy Terms by A.S. Lindsey

Le Petit Robert: Dictionnaire de la Langue Française

Haynes – 'Driving Abroad'

Consulates, embassies and ministries

European Union

www.europa.eu

EmbassyWorld

www.embassyworld.com

Ambassade de Grande-Bretagne (The British Embassy)

35, rue du Faubourg St Honoré
75383 Paris Cedex 08, France

+33 (0)1 44 51 31 00
Fax +33 (0)1 44 51 32 34
www.amb-grandebretagne.fr

French Embassy in the UK

58 Knightsbridge
London
SW1X 7JT

+44 (0)207 073 1000
www.ambafrance-uk.org

Department for Environment, Food and Rural Affairs (DEFRA)

Nobel House
17 Smith Square
London
SW1P 3JR

+44 (0) 207 238 6951
Fax +44 (0) 207 238 2188
@ quarantine@ahvg.maff.gsi.gov.uk
www.defra.gov.uk

French Chamber of Commerce in Great Britain

✉ 21 Dartmouth Street
Westminster
London
SW1H 9BP

☎ + 44 (0)20 7304 4040
Fax + 44 (0)20 7304 4034
💻 www.ccfgb.co.uk

The French Ministry of Agriculture

✉ Ministère de l'agriculture et de la Pêche
Bureau de l'identification et du contrôle des mouvements des animaux
251 rue de Vaugirard
75 015 PARIS

☎ +33 (0)1 49 55 84 72
Fax +33 (0)1 49 55 81 97
💻 www.agriculture.gouv.fr

British consulates in France

Bordeaux

Consulat general

✉ 353, boulevard du Président Wilson, 33073 Bordeaux
☎ +33 (0)5.57.22.21.10
Fax +33 (0)5.56.08.33.12

Lille

Consulat general

✉ 11, square Dutilleul – 59800 Lille
☎ +33 (0)3 20 12 82 72
Fax +33 (0)3 20 54 88 16

Lyon

Consulat general

✉ 24, rue Childebert – 69002 Lyon
☎ +33 (0)4 72 77 81 70
Fax +33 (0)4 72 77 81 79

Marseille

Consulat general

✉ 24, avenue du Prado – 13006 Marseille
☎ +33 (0)4 91 15 72 10
Fax +33 (0)4 91 37 47 06

Paris

Section Consulaire

✉ 16, rue d'Anjou – 75008 Paris
☎ +33 (0)1 44 51 31 00
Fax +33 (0)1 44 51 31 27

In an emergency

Service d'Aide Médicale Urgente (SAMU)

www.samu-de-france.fr/en

SOS Médecins (specialist emergency doctors)

www.sosmedecins-france.fr/en

- ☎ In an emergency, dial 112
- ☎ If the emergency is life-threatening, dial 15
- ☎ If the emergency is not life-threatening, or you're not sure, dial 18
- ☎ If you need the *gendarmes*, dial 17

944.084 Man
Mansfield-Devine, Patricia
Living in France :